Total Tripping

Europe

CARL LAHSER

Order this book online at www.trafford.com
or email orders@trafford.com

Most Trafford titles are also available at major online book retailers.

Printed in the United States of America.

ISBN: 978-1-4907-4458-2 (sc)
ISBN: 978-1-4907-4459-9 (e)

Trafford rev. 08/23/2014

 www.trafford.com

North America & international
toll-free: 1 888 232 4444 (USA & Canada)
fax: 812 355 4082

Contents

Contents

Summary in Europe 1962

In December, 1961, I was an E-5 in Uncle Sugar's Canoe Club (the U.S. Navy) assigned to VAW-33 and based at Quonset Point Naval Air Station, Rhode Island. I had been assigned to bases in California, and Florida and 18 months at Argentia, Newfoundland, as an aviation electronic tech and had accumulated about a thousand hours aircrew time flying as an ECM operator. In general, I had enjoyed my assignments but not Rhode Island.

In January, 1962, I volunteered for the first deployment that came along. This was a couple months on the aircraft carrier, USS Forrestal (CVA-59), to Guantanamo, Cuba, tracking Cuban mobile missile sites. This tour had been interesting, and the weather beat January and February in RI. On the way back we made a liberty call in Haiti and were part of the task force to pick up the first astronaut, Col John Glenn, in a space capsule called Friendship 7. We would have picked him up of he had landed on the blastoff or first orbit of his three orbit flight.

I was back in Quonset Pt a couple weeks when they asked for volunteers for a six month Mediterranean cruise. I said "Don't throw me in the briar patch, Chief. When do we leave?" I had joined the Navy to see the world. This cruise would end about the time my enlistment was up and my college career would begin.

Four four-person aircrews and three AD-5Q electronic warfare aircraft and ten maintenance personnel and equipment soon headed for Norfolk, Virginia, to board the aircraft carrier USS Independence (CVA-62). The day before we left we had a CIA briefing on what to look for and reporting procedures. We sailed on the morning tide headed for Gibraltar and doddled along for five days so that our escort of destroyers could keep up without burning all their fuel. Sunrise found us nearing Asinara (donkey) Bay in Sardinia for a change of command.

We twelve enlisted were billeted in a small compartment two bunks high with a personal storage compartment under the mattress. The compartment was right under the flight deck and three frames in front of the bow. (On the Forrestal we had been located under the mess deck below the hanger deck and beside the ordnance department. The ordnance people had a sign on their door- "Peace through Total

Destruction". The ordnance elevator came up to the hanger deck in the middle of the dining area and we used to laugh at the armed guards escorting nukes advising us we saw nothing.)

Over the first three weeks we flew along the coast of Egypt, Libya, Tunisia, Algeria, Morocco, Malta, Crete, Turkey, Greece, Italy, France, and Spain and mapped the radars we would be dealing with. It was quite a geography lesson. We stayed outside of everyone's territorial waters except for Libya that claimed 50 miles and even sent a couple fighters as a bluff.

Our first port call was Cannes, France, in May. We anchored a mile off shore and had two alert fighters with nukes sitting on the catapults. All the liberty parties and guests went by one of the ship's launches.

This was during the week of the Cannes Film Festival. So far as I know none of us enlisted was given tickets to the activities nor could afford one if we had wanted to go. Also, enlisted were required to wear our white uniforms while officers were required to wear civilian clothes.

One evening while heading back to fleet landing some drunk sailor jumped out in front of several sailors and shouted "Savate" while kicking in all directions. (Savate is a style of French kick fighting.) He got knocked on his butt by this and several other groups of whitehats.

One evening a shipmate and I were walking along the harbor looking at the fancy yachts when an American woman struck up a conversation. She introduced herself as an author who had written "Fear of Flying" that had nothing to do with aviation. She invited us to a party that evening. We would have gone but we had to be back on the ship about the time her party was to begin. She was the first author I had ever met, and she persuaded me to keep writing.

Our group got together for a trip to Grasse to see fields of roses grown to make rose water for perfume. We could see the houses of the very rich hidden in the trees along the cliff line. Just like in the movies.

Another day two of us took a trip to Monaco. We walked along the route of the Monte-Carlo Gran Prix road race. We went to the Prince Albert museum and aquarium and, then, to the beach. It was interesting to see girls come to the beach all dressed up then wrap up in a towel and emerge in a tiny bikini. We met a couple girls with a full-size poodle and spent the afternoon tossing a ball so the dog would let us talk. We had to leave to get back to the ship before anything serious began.

We were anchored off of Cannes on Bastille Day, July 14. Cannes out did itself on a fireworks display that was coordinated along about two miles of waterfront. All shore leave had been cancelled but we had a front row seat to the show.

We had a farewell beach party where everyone was allowed two beers. One Lieutenant had his share and several that were donated to him. By the time we headed back to the ship he could hardly walk. We packed him in one of the large trash cans that had held the beer and ice and lugged him back to the ship undetected.

My unit was transferred off the carrier to fly for NATO out of Capo de Chino Air Base near Naples. We stayed in downtown in Naples in the Hotel Mediterraneo for a couple weeks. Then we moved to Athens living on Glifádha Beach and flying out of Hellenikon Air Base. Our assignment was to test all the US and NATO European radar sites from Spain to Turkey. In early August, we went back on board the carrier and returned to Norfolk with a short stop at Gibraltar.

One flight path out of Naples was north to Rome, Firenze, and Bologna then east along the Po River Valley to the Adriatic then south crossing over the tiny country of San Moreno then west of to Rome to Monte Casino and back to Naples. Another route was east to Bari, Italy, over Taranto on the heel of the Italian boot then across the Gulf of Taranto to Syracuse and Catania in Sicily. Then we took the scenic route and flew over Mt Etna and through the Straits of Messina to Stromboli and across the Tyrrhenian Sea to Naples. Whoever planned these flights did not miss too many tourist sites. From the air I could see why the battle for Monte Casino took so long. Also, we had to make a detour to miss the power line strung across the Strait of Messina. Both volcanoes, Mt Etna and Stromboli, were glowing red and kicking out a little lava.

In Italy the average day was up at 6 for the bus to the base. Four hours flying then back to the hotel. In the evenings it was party time. Almost everything cultural was closed for the day. One week there was a national election so in our civilian clothes we visited several political rallies because they handed out wine and sausages. We yelled for whichever of the 16 candidates was holding the rally and left early. Other nights there was booze and singing in someone's room or an evening at the USO.

There were several outstanding things about Naples. One was the public pistoreas or free standing urinals along the streets similar to phone booths.

There were holes along the alleys that dated back to the 17th century that also collected rain water and kitchen and laundry wastewater that were also used as urinals.

Another was the wolf packs of kids that tried to sell stuff, buy cigarettes or mug sailors. Their favorite thing to sell was a necklace with the ancient sign of the brothel in Pompeii – the flying cock-and balls.

We seldom flew on weekends, so one weekend I visited Pompeii and climbed down into Vesuvius. The Pompeii excavation was only about half as large as today. Another weekend I visited the Amalfi Coast to see Sorrento and Positano. It was interesting to see the use of terraces for fruit and vegetable culture. The fishing boats were beached for the weekend just like in the paintings.

One Sunday a couple of us went to the zoo. An old man began talking to us in English. He had been a prisoner of war and interned in Bryan, Texas. This was news to me, since I had not known that there were any internment camps in the US. He had learned to cook and had opened an American restaurant in Naples when he came home. We talked for about an hour strolling and looking at the animals. He invited our whole group over for supper one evening.

Another Sunday several of us went to the opera. It was presented out of doors in an ancient amphitheatre and was standing room only. I forget the opera but every time someone sang an interesting passage or hit a high note, the crowd went wild. Instant replay – they backed up the production and sang it over again. Sometimes twice.

We moved back to the ship for a couple of days of war games. We must have won because the ship pulled into Genoa for liberty. This is the alleged hometown of Christopher Columbus. Genoa is called the city of palaces for the number of 17th century Doge palaces in an area called the *caruggia*. The streets were narrow and grungy. Many of the palaces had been converted into museums or hotels. We were free only in the evenings, so I missed the museums and most of the historical sites.

I took a week of leave to visit Switzerland. The bus went west from Genoa along the coast to San Remo, Monaco, Nice, and Cannes then inland to Aix-en-Provence, France, just north of Marseille. In Aix I intended to visit a newspaper friend from back home in San Antonio while in Aix, but she was away on assignment.

A train took me through the mountains to Grenoble. I had a couple of hour's layover and looked at the churches and narrow streets and at where the Olympics would be one day. Hard to imagine this little town could hold twenty thousand visitors.

The next train was an overnight run to Genève, Switzerland. I found a tourist hotel near the lake with no view and running water with a bucket under the sink. A walk took me through down town, across the lake on a bridge where Rodin's "*Thinker*" sat contemplating *le Jet,* the tall water jet in the middle of the lake. I turned back at the rose garden. The jet and the rose garden were lit and Mozart played in the garden in the evening.

I toured Genève next day and went to Chamonix and took the tram up Mt Blanc. I remember it being very cool and there being window boxes of geraniums. There were a couple crows on the mountain top black against the snow.

Back in town I caught an overnight train to Lausanne. The trains were crowded with standing room only. The train arrived about dawn, and I spent a couple of hours wandering around this old town. I caught the late afternoon train to Bern. The next morning I toured Bern and caught an afternoon train to Milan and on to Genoa to rejoin the ship. I have some pictures from the trip but if you want to know what I saw find an old travel guide from the 1950's and 60's. There have been many changes in the past 50 some years.

We flew a mission to Madrid and Barcelona with a couple hours of sightseeing overnight. The ship went south and around Italy to stop for the day at Corfu, Greece. There was a day in port. Some of us enjoyed mezethes (meze) and a bottle of ouzo under an historic oak tree near the old fort. We pulled anchor in the evening as the U.S. Navy put on a show of force - passing the aircraft carrier through the narrow (mile wide) passage between Corfu and Albania.

As the ship headed south to play more war games, my group took off for Athens for another adventure. We landed about sundown and were met by our ground crew personnel. They had been waiting a couple days for our arrival. Tough duty. They had brought our bags and supplies and had found a hotel for us on Glifádha Beach. (About a mile off the beach was anchored the bright yellow converted Naval cruiser *Caroline* with Jackie Onasis.)

The maid slipped in each morning and left tea and rolls. My roommates wanted the extra sleep, so I took the tea and rolls out on the balcony to watch the sky brighten over the *Caroline* and the fishing boats returning. Evenings, after a good Greek meal, were spent at a local bar or at the USO.

One Sunday morning I took a taxi to downtown Athens. The main square with the palace and the parliament and the Hotel Grande Bretagne with its revolutionary bullet holes. Talking to some old expatriates about WWII. Hadrian's Arch. The Temple of Olympian Zeus.

Another Sunday the hotel packed us a lunch for a trip to the Acropolis. Climb the Propylea. Walk inside the Parthenon and Erechtheion. No one but us on the hill top.

The country around Athens generally looked like south Texas. From Spain to Greece the coastal plain was largely flat or low rolling hills. Vegetation was xeric dry stubble, thorny shrubs and low trees. The ancient coniferous forest had been cut a couple thousand years ago to make ships of war to invade Troy and other sea battles. Erosion had washed away the soil and the forest had been replaced by olive and grape culture.

One flight path was to the south to Crete and Rhodes, east to the southern coast of Turkey and return. The Greek islands were beautiful from the air.

Another route was direct to Izmir, Turkey (old Smyrna), then northeast across mountains and conifer forests checking hilltop radar sites up to the Black Sea. There we turned west across the Sea of Marmara south of Istanbul and the Bosporus to the Dardanelles. We continued across Anatolia to Thessalonica, Greece. While popping along over the Anatolian hills we came across a big flock of sheep that took off in all directions with the shepherd shaking his fist at us. Near Thessalonica one if our planes had engine trouble, and we turned straight south to Athens.

After we fixed the plane, we packed up to rejoin the ship to return to Norfolk. We sailed for Sardinia and the change of command then headed to Gibraltar and an eight hour stop. Several of us went up to see the Rock and the Barbary apes and stopped for a little sightseeing and cider in this snug little British enclave. Five days later we were back in Norfolk. We flew the planes off and landed at Quonset Point a week before my enlistment was up.

After four years active duty with the US Navy I had pretty much satisfied my intent of seeing the world. California. Hawaii. Florida. Washington, DC., Newfoundland. Iceland. Scotland. Spain. France. Italy. Greece. Turkey. The African coast from Egypt to Morocco. Mostly from the air but with a lot of good liberty. It was time to return to the real world and hit college.

Carl Lahser
4 July 2014

Let's Go to Italy

By

Carl Lahser

1. Return to Sardinia

Once upon a time, a magical floating island found refuge in the Mar di Sardegna the timeless Island of Sardinia in the Mediterranean Sea. Five thousand men gazed out on the placid water, the rugged coastline, and the ancient castles shrouded in mist. Other men had lived on this coast for ten thousand years fishing, mining copper and silver and trading in saffron and lace. Then, out of the morning sun, came a flight of dragons.

How about that for a mythical style introduction to a mythical adventure? Actually these scenes were in May of 1962 on board the aircraft carrier USS Independence, CVA 62 and we were there to take command of the US Naval Fleet in the Mediterranean. We had passed the Straits of Gibraltar the night before and had run 24 hours to make anchorage.

We had glided in quietly until vibrations and a muffled roar of reversing props followed by a clunking rattle of anchor chains marked anchors being set in the Sea of Sardinia. The anchorage was off the town of Bosa founded by the Phoenicians over 3000 years ago. Capo Cacia lay to the north with the 12th century town of Alghero

I was on the starboard catwalk watching the anchor detail going about their various duties. A Navy cruiser and a couple destroyers or destroyer escorts were already at anchor. The Admiral's gig was slowly circling waiting for the anchor detail to be finished. Another couple destroyers and a submarine or two in our battle group were still at sea making sure nothing slipped up on us.

Out of a hazy washed-out blue sky, just over the sun, came a welcoming fly-over from the carrier we were replacing. They came in on the deck and made mock attacks. A-1 Skyraiders. A-6 Skyhawks. The carrier would retrieve its aircraft and anchor in the Golfo del Asinara north beyond Capo Cacia. That was my welcome to the Mediterranean and Europe, in 1962.

In May 2005, my wife and I were going to spend three weeks in Italy. We had planned for a week on Sardinia and added a week on each end to visit Rome, Pisa, and Florence. A time-share exchange was reserved on Sardinia. Airline, hotel and rental car reservations were made a year in advance. Hotel, car, and ferry reservations were made on the internet.

For homework I rounded up my 35mm slides of the Med and several reference books. Travel books included Fodor's 1996 *Exploring Italy,* and the 2003 *Italy 2003,* Fromer's *Italy 2003,* the 1991 Colored Guide-Book *Tuscany,* the 1990 Cadogan Guides *Tuscany and Umbria,* the 1990/91 New Practical Guide *Florence,* Karen Brown's 1993 *Italian Country Inns & Itineraries,* and the 1998 *Eyewitness Travel Guides Sardinia.*

I looked at the medical area intelligence reports concerning Italy in the Monthly Disease Occurrence (Worldwide) and looked at the Disease Vector Ecology Profile (DVEP) prepared by the Defense Pest Management Information Center. I also looked at websites for the Communicable Disease Center (**http://www.topix.net/us/cdc**) and the World Health Organization (**http://www.who.int/en/**) for health hazards.

There were also numerous websites for weather, antiques, birding, etc. I checked the US State Department for terrorist threats and any political hazards (**http://travel.state.gov/**) and Internet weather sites: **http://www. discover-sardinia.com/weather/forecast for Olbia.cfm** and **http:// www.wunderground.com/global/IY.html**.

Medical supplies included Neosporin, Pepto tablets, Imodium, aspirin, Tylenol, sunscreen, several flashlights, tweezers and a needle, alcohol wipes, all our daily medications, and a spare sets of glasses and sunglasses.

Since I keep a journal of sorts, I now take a microtape recorder, a digital and a film camera, a laptop PC, two pairs binoculars, a few reference books including *Collins Pocket Guide - Birds of Britain and Europe* and *Mediterranean Wild Flowers* by Blamey and Grey-Wilson. I thought I managed to keep this to a minimum but forgot an electrical adaptor kit that would accept polarized plugs. I did not take watercolors or acrylic paints and did not have time to do much painting anyway. I did shoot about 800 digital and film shots.

As it got closer to leaving I went over Italian lessons and bought a digital translator hoping these won't be a waste of time and money. The rudimentary Italian worked fine but I may return the translator since it did not have many useful phrases.

The week before leaving was spent in deciding what and what not to take. The goal was one each suitcase plus a carryon each. We wound up with an extra bag, which became a nuisance.

2. Roman Holiday

Monday. Carol was ready before the taxi arrived for a change. We were at the check in counter almost two hours early as recommended. Because of our international destination the first class check in counter could not be used.

Our Delta tickets were called enhanced business class instead of first class. We had spent frequent flyer miles for the upgrade. We had business class to Atlanta with an upgrade to Rome. Seats to Rome were larger and further apart. They laid back for sleeping but were not all that comfortable. Food selection was from a menu with two choices and a choice of wines. Service was with cloth napkins, silver (the knife was plastic) and china. There were several audio channels and several movies plus the channel which showed where you were, speed, altitude, etc.

Tuesday. Weather was a thick cloud deck beneath us with several contrails in the distance. We were feet dry over Portugal but could not see Portugal or most of Spain. The route over the Med crossed Sardinia near Alghera and hit Italy north of the Rome airport. We landed from the north about 0800 on Tuesday morning.

The airfield was alive with wildflowers. Several Hooded Crows (Corvus commix sardonius) and a flock of small finches were feeding on the infield.

We left the plane and passed through immigration and customs easily. We had the choice of a 30 Euro (€) train ride with the bags plus a 10 € taxi to the hotel, a taxi for about 100 € or a shuttle bus for 65 €. We took the shuttle and were checking in at the hotel by 10 AM. The official € was $1.45 but charges were from $1.60-1.80/€. During our three week stay the rate was as low as $1.17. The hotels were paid in advance in dollars.

Major roadside vegetation on the way to Rome consisted of yellow gorse (Ulex europaeus) and white myrtle shrubs (Myrtis communis) and false acacia (Robinia pseudacacia) trees that I first thought were locusts. The route was mostly pasture and hay with trees along the ridges and in the bottoms. Numerous bright red Common Poppies (Papaver rhoeas) lined the right-of-way.

We got sort of a tour of the city since we were the third and last to be delivered to our hotel - the old city wall of Rome; the Coloseum; the Roman forum; Circus Maximus.

This log contains observations and generalities. I'm not going to go into detail of the things seen if details are already readily available elsewhere.

Our hotel, the Grand Hotel Fleming, was relatively new. The room was on the fourth floor and had a bath and a balcony. The bath was crowded with a bidet, toilet, large pedestal sink, and a tub that was about two feet wide and 30 inches deep. The shower was on a hose. I forgot the electrical adaptors kit and could not plug in the razor or computer and the hotel did not have one to loan. There was a fire suppression sprinkler head but I saw no smoke detector. Continental and American breakfasts were included.

Lunch on this day was at a *restorante* recommended by the hotel. It was a couple blocks away and served mostly pasta. Carol had dime-size ravioli with a Coke Lite and I had pasta with clams in the shell with a mediocre Italian beer.

Back at the hotel we arranged for three tours through Vastours. One covered the Trevi fountain, Pantheon, Piazza Navona, St. Peter's basilica, lunch, the Roman forum, the Coloseum, the Capitol and St. Paul's cathedral. Another tour covered the Vatican museums and Sistine Chapel, lunch, St. Mary Major, St. John's in Lateran, the Holy Stairs, the old Apian Way, and the Catacombs. A third tour was to Naples and Pompeii.

For the afternoon and evening we took a taxi to Piazza Navona. The plaza was two blocks long and one block wide with three fountains. I was surrounded by a church and several office buildings, several antique shops, and a lot of sidewalk restaurants. The plaza was scattered with artists, vendors of purses, sunglasses, etc, and an assortment of mimes and musicians. Artists ranged from oils and watercolors to ink sketches. Subjects ranged from collages to copies of classics to landscapes and street scenes. Several were very good. We bought an unframed oil painting that we neatly rolled for transit. Many of the vendors selling purses and sunglasses were Africans from various countries. Pakistanis walked around selling bubble guns and other small items.

I had wondered how they could move the huge piece of marble that made up the central fountain. Looking closely the marble was in horizontal pieces about 18" thick. Even these pieces would be heavy but at least be manageable. I guess they stacked them and then carved the figures and then moved the pieces to the plaza for final installation.

We split a pizza and a 3€ liter of water. The Italians don't believe in cutting their pizza or drinking tap water. I added a local beer. All the artists packed up by 8 PM so we did too and took a cab home.

Piazza Navona

Piazza Navona

Wednesday morning dawned overcast with a little ground fog. From the balcony Rome was quite and pastel. A landscape of tile roofs and a zillion antennas in the morning sun. A blackbird or European robin (<u>Turdis</u> <u>merula</u>) was singing. A hooded crow (<u>Corvus</u> <u>corone</u>) cruised by. House Sparrows (<u>Passer</u> <u>domesticus</u>) and spotless starlings (Sturnus unicolor) were twittering about. Temperature was 18°C (in the lower 60s).

Roman Roofs

After breakfast we waited to be picked up for our tour. They called the hotel to tell us to take a taxi to their office at their expense.

Our first tour was to the Vatican museum and the Sistine Chapel and then to Vatican square.

We arrived at the Vatican museum and joined a block-long line of tourist and school kids that only took about 20 minutes. We passed through the gate and entered the independent country of the Vatican.

A metal detector checked everyone before entering the museum proper. Ticketing was next followed by a ride up an escalator under what they identified as the "worlds tallest dome" (?).

Vatican Museum

The museum was the former Vatican Palace built in 1377 covering 13 acres. The first gallery was the Stanza di Rafaela or rooms of Raphael. Pope Julius hired Raphael to paint of biblical and historical scenes beginning in 1503. One room, the Signature Room where there hung the only picture with the signature of Raphael.

The path led through the Chapels of Nicholas V and Urban VII, then to the hall of statues, the hall of maps, and several self-contained museums including the Vatican Library, the Museum of Pagan Antiques, the Ethnological Museum, and the Historical Museum. These were followed by a visit to the Sistine Chapel.

Many of the works had been recently cleaned. The newly restored Sistine Chapel was outstanding with faux drapes on the lower wall then paintings of the life of Jesus and Moses on the upper walls then the ceiling with its representation of the Old Testament and the unbelievable ceiling.

It is remarkable that Raphael and Michael Angelo both painted friends and enemies into their frescoes the way Dante had written his friends and enemies into the Devine Comedy.

Panic time. At the Vatican bookstore I discovered my card case with two credit cards, my driver's license and military ID card were missing. I think I left it at the tour office where the tour people had handed me my credit card and the slip to sign for the trip and announced the bus. Since I am not into multitasking I may have left the card case on the desk at the Vastour office.

Vastour people claimed not to have seen it. Our guide suggested that it could have been pick-pocketed by one of the Capitol of Catholic Christianity's less than honest customers.

Later we visited a police station to report the loss. After waiting an hour for an over weight officer he said he did not speak English and besides it was quitting time. Come back tomorrow. Since the credit card companies did not require a police report we gave this up as a lost cause.

We left the museum and went to Vatican square. Looked just like it did on TV with a few less people than when the new Pope was chosen. Some of the Italians were unhappy with a non-Italian Pope calling him Papa Boche the French slur for the Germans.

Vatican Square

Lunch was included in the tour but was mediocre at best. Antipasto was limp grilled zucchini and fava beans. This was followed by pasta with white sauce. The meat course was veal. There was a carafe of wine and a liter of mineral water. Desert was a flaky pastry.

We cancelled the afternoon tour to return to the hotel and try to cancel the credit cards and traded that tour for a night tour of Rome that was a flying tour of many sights from the bus. It was a tour in Italian, German, Spanish and English, the kind that if you quickly look over your shoulder you might see what you just passed. We made a stop at the Fontana di Trevi and tossed pennies into the fountain to assure a return to Rome and abandoned the tour at the Plaza Navona and got a cab home.

Fontana di Trevi

Thursday. Several 1-800 calls finally got the credit cards cancelled. The MasterCard representative was reluctant to replace the card but his supervisor agreed to FedEx (for $35) a replacement card to the hotel by Friday. Visa said that San Antonio Credit Union where we had the card since 1982 had blocked our card and refused to replace it. On returning home we climbed the SACU chain of command chomping all the way. Finally an officer said they did send emergency replacement cards and the clerk had not been properly trained. He also said they required that anyone leaving town notify them and the credit card company that you were leaving town or they would block the card. He apologized for any inconvenience of stranding us in a foreign country but it was for our protection. He would see that his customers were notified of this requirement. They sent an apology and two movie passes.

As plan B we called our son to send money through Western Union. Picking up the funds proved another goat rope and required another call home since the recipient name did not exactly match the name on the passport and we did not have the confirmation number.

The Western Union offices were at the central train station. The terminal was a functional, nice looking structure with three levels of shops with lots of shopping opportunities. There were 30 covered platforms for tracks or "*bins*". Outside were several out buildings with newspapers, etc. Every corner and anywhere out of sight smelled like an outhouse. Not a bad place to pass through but not a pleasant place for a walk or lunch.

We visited the US Embassy and that was a waste of time. They said if I went to a police station and called them they would provide an interpreter. Since the passports were not involved they have no obligation to do anything. They could provide an affidavit to use to collect the money from Western Union for only $35 in a day or two because they were shorthanded with training. To top things off the only toilet available to non-embassy employees was closed.

We had cancelled the morning tour and took the afternoon tour of the Roman Forum and the Coliseum. It began near the pyramid that Cleopatra wanted built for her burial and the old Roman wall. We drove past the Capitol with the Palatine Hill behind it. The walk began near the monument to Victor Emanuel, past Michael Angelo's New Museum, and then into the Piazza di Campodoglio and Capitol Hill and finally into the Forum itsaef. The Arch of Settimio Severo. The Basilica Aemilia. Many

13

other remains of buildings and temples. The Coliseum. Past the Arch of Constantine. The tour description did not mention all the steps in the Forum or the uneven slate slabs, cobblestones streets and few handholds. This was not a tour for handicapped. There was a relatively long ride to St Paul's Cathedral.

I saw some tall Alexander's along with other wildflowers. There was a blackbird along with swifts darting through the cool damp air.

St. Paul's Cathedral was unique in having 80 one-piece granite columns. There was a lot of gold trim, a malachite alter and a copy of a Raphael painting in mosaic. The gift shop had mosaic and pictures. Large 20X30 in were several thousand €. Smaller ones were a few hundred and 2 in squares were about 80€. The mosaics were neat art all made by the Vatican mosaic shops. We drove back to the area near the pyramid and were transported home.

Coliseum

Roman Forum

St Paul's Cathedral

We tried a *restorante* across from the hotel. I had squid and a local wine. Pretty good.

Friday. Tour transportation was ready at the hotel by 0645. We were on the bus and off to Naples by 0730. The mountains began half hour south of Rome. The highway was well designed and in good repair. Thick wildflowers lined the highway – red poppies, white Myrtle, yellow Gorse, a field of red clover. Vineyards and peach orchards were scattered across the hills.

Old houses were scattered through the hills with poodle pines and olive groves. Power lines and their right-of-ways marked up the hills.

We made a pit stop at a restaurant just off the turnpike that specialized in tours. Ten busses were parked there by the time we left. Landscaping was somewhat tropical with Canary Island palms, false bamboo, gardenias, pyracantha, pines, spruce, creeping juniper, and seasonal pansies. There was an adult locust eating pyracantha leaves.

The road passes the town and monastery of Montecassino. The monastary sits high on a hill overlooking the village of the same name. This was the site of a long battle to dislodge a strong German emplacement. It finally resulted in a heavy bombing that destroyed the monetary. It was rebuilt for the fourth time in the 1960s. Last time I saw Monte Cassino was flying over it in 1962.

Monte Cassino

The roads were lined with False Acacia trees and spiny Gorse. Grape arbors were of several kinds. Concrete or wooden posts with wire strung between them, a V-shaped frame of two wooden stakes or a single stake. Grapes also covered some of the fences. Gardens contained orange and lemon trees as well as assorted vegetables. Several fields were colored red or yellow with clover and Brassica. The sky had become overcast with possible showers.

Further down the road we passed through Caserta. This was where fine porcelain had been manufactured in previous centuries and the site of the huge former royal palace.

We got into the edges of Naples in the industrial district and found numerous shade houses growing vegetables and flowers for the market. These were frames covered with plastic sheeting installed over rows of plants. There were also typical greenhouses.

In Naples we drove past the old French capitol, the Palace, the opera house, etc, then into new Naples with several big parks, lots of hotels, past the old fleet landing and past Castile de Ovo and the new harbor. There was a rest stop and then the drive back the same way and on towards Pompeii.

My first time in Naples was in 1962 after a long flight. We were told specifically not to bring anything along since our ship would be at anchor in the Bay of Naples by the time we landed. Neva hoppen. We were shuttled from Capo do Chino airport to the Hotel Mediterraneo and lived in our scroungey orange flight suits for three days of flying, shopping, sightseeing, and lots of beer. The only exception was the flight commander who had civvies with him and ignored us whenever we were around. We were about two blocks from the USO and ate several meals there. One evening we took a horse cab back to the hotel and I drove. We lived in the hotel for a month flying for NATO before going to Athens for a month. This was in the midst of the elections with sixteen political parties having rallies all over town so we shared in their salami and wine and hollered for their candidate then went to the next rally.

Naples was still had high crime and high unemployment. I asked if there were still "pistoreas" and urinals up the alleys in Naples. Pistoreas had been screened sidewalk urinals where men could do their business while talking to people on the street. The old male guide said there were still a few and the new young female guide said she had never heard of them.

On the way to Pompeii we passed more shade houses raising vegetables and flowers. The volcanic soil around Naples was rich but the weather got cool in the winter.

There was a stop at a cameo factory. I had visited it in 1962 and had bought a cameo for my mother. Carol bought a pair of coral earrings. They had cameos and other items running from cheap up to the thousands of euros. In 1962 I visited Vesuvius volcano and gone down into the crater. I had also taken a trip down the Amalfi coast to Positano and Sorrento.

We passed into Pompeii and parked at a restaurant for lunch, five courses with antipasto, pasto, primero, secondo and desert. I had fish and Carol had veal. I split a bottle of a Pompeii wine, Lacrema di Christo (the "Tears of Christ") with another couple. It was a little too dry for me.

We entered the west gate into Pompeii. The area excavated was twice the size I had seen in 1962 and some of the displays were different. They now rotate the display houses to allow for maintenance and efforts to stabilize the frescoes. One change was the home of the bachelors where the frescoes that were highly controversial in the prudish 1960s were on display without charging extra and women were allowed to see them. Also some of the casts of the victims were on display. These death casts had been made by filling the fused-ash molds of people and animals with plaster. Some new digs were underway such as a dining room where spaces were found under the floor for cool storage of wine, etc.

Details of Pompeii are available in books and History Channel videos.

The overcast turned to rain but it was a short warm shower. By the time we left the weather had cleared.

We exited the site to catch the bus. There was about 20 minutes to shop and snack before we left. I tried one of the local oranges – very good Valencia. One thing I noticed was the lack of kids hustling tourists with objects like "flying cock and balls" charms representing the sign of the bawdy houses of old Pompeii and begging cigarettes and money. I don't know if the infamous Naples wolf packs of kids were still around. They were the hazard to the safety of a solitary sailor.

We flew back to the crowded rest stop then back to Rome and were at the hotel about 2100.

The credit card arrived as promised.

Saturday. Early was morning quiet. Clouds were gone and the sky was black with stars. The bottom of the big dipper was directly overhead.

There was a problem with the GPS - no satellites. The walkie-talkies worked fine.

We visited a neighborhood supermarket. They had about the same as a 7-11. I was looking for an adaptor so I could plug in the computer, razor, hair dryer, and clippers. We tried a medium-size department store and a larger grocery supermarket and a retail electronics shop each of which sent me somewhere else. I passed an electrical supply house that had just what I wanted and cheap.

I passed a patch of Mallow-leaf Stork's-bill (Erodium malacoides) and Hedge Bedstraw (Galium mollugo) in a vacant lot.

We went back to the Piazza Nuova for the afternoon. This piazza has been the social center of Rome forever. Artists and vendors of all kinds were out. We found another painting and walked a couple blocks to the Pantheon that was under renovation. We had lunch at an outside pizzeria and went back to the hotel to wait for the limo.

I walked around the local Plaza Fleming and photographed some anti–Bush graffiti.

Italy was big on the siesta from 1300 to 1600. A grocery had just opened so I bought a bottle of water, a couple apples and half-dozen loquats that were as large as large eggs and weighed about 70 gm each. I saved the seeds. Maybe Mr. Moy can grow some.

There were a few English sparrows and pigeons. A white butterfly with black spots on the upper wing (cabbage butterfly?) was flying around a potted flowering lemon tree.

Rome and Italy in general looks like crazy driving. They drive aggressively but at speeds of 20-30KPH. Cars, busses, scooters, motorcycles all get along and pedestrians still have the right-of-way.

I looked at Rome and Naples with a different perspective from 1962. Italy has a historic conscience that is rare in the US. They have sacrificed a lot of comfort and efficiency to retain historical context. Although the various wars over the past 200 years with massive destruction gave opportunities to tear down and rebuild and upgrade the infrastructure the old structures and streets were mostly retained and rebuilt partly because there was no captor or occupying force or money. Many other places under US or Russian domination were bulldozed, redefined and built from scratch like Berlin or Agana, Guam. It is difficult to build in an area where the soil cannot be touched without uncovering historical artifacts. Of course, progress is expensive and the tourists love the primitive and historical and different and are a major source of income.

The driver picked us up in a new Honda Maxima with leather seats at 1730 for the 30 km drive. Land along the highway was scattered farms and wooded hilltops. Sheep and some cattle were grazing. We entered Civitavecchia and drove down the Viale Garibaldi passing a number of other ferries and some tour boats and a respectable fleet of trawlers tied up along the dock.

Civitavecchia has been the port on the Tyrrhenian Sea that serviced Rome, Sardinia, Corsica, and several other Italian ports. Civitavecchia and neighboring Corneto were part of an ancient fortified port facility (the ancient Centumcellae) dating back to the Emperor Trajan. It was built on the ruins of an important Etruscan outpost called Tatquinii with Etruscan tombs and archeological sites. Christian catacombs date to the third century AD. A large stone fort and custom house and several grain elevators sat along one of the docks. We were at the ferry terminal at Civitavecchia about 1830.

We checked in and Carol decided to try the local McDonald franchise instead of the terminal snack bar. Burgers had tomato and cheese but no lettuce and the fries were crisp.

I checked out the men's toilet. There were no urinals and the crapper had no seat. Most remarkable was that the toilet was set on a grating. I guess this was efficient in keeping the place clean. I don't remember but one public toilet in Italy that had a seat. The most unique was in the train station in Pisa with a half-euro entrance fee. The stalls were lit with purplish UV light to keep them sanitary.

I took a walk along the dock watching gulls and swallows. Besides McDonalds there was a Chinese takeout and several shops including a tattoo parlor and surf/dive shop. There were seats and a view of the harbor and a kiddie carnival for the kids. We were on board about 2000.

The cabin was two bunks and a bath. Since the tourist season had not begun yet they had extra rooms so we were allowed to put our five bags in the adjoining cabin for the trip to Sardinia.

The ferry had a dining room, a snack bar and a bar/lounge. We sailed at 2100 into the setting sun for the 125 mile run to Golfo Aranci.

Sunday morning I was up and showered and on deck by 0530 to see the sunrise. Morning temperature was about 15 degrees C and smelled of the sea. The hills were green as we passed Cape Figari and approached the harbor. Yellow-legs and Common Gulls (<u>Larus</u> <u>michahellis</u> and <u>L</u>. <u>canus</u>) were checking out our wake. White houses with red tile roofs speckled the hills. What looked like a jagged mountain range stood purple in the morning mist. Actually the mountains were no more the 400m or 1300 feet.

We docked at 0700 in Golfo Aranci. We disembarked onto a bare asphalt parking area of a couple acres. Other than a couple cars we were the only passengers. The tourist season would not start until mid June so museums would not be open, tours were unavailable and tourist facilities were still being readied.

There was a bar and newsstand with a phone about half a mile away where I called a cab.

The 40€ ride to the airport gave the first view of the ecology. This is maquis country with myrtle, thorny gorse and numerous wildflowers.

It was 20 km to the Olbia airport where we were to pick up the rental car. The airport was modern and well managed with lots of commercial and private flights. Next time I will know better and fly or land in the port of Olbia. Also, Hertz did not say they had an office at Cannigione where we were staying. This would have saved a hundred euros in taxi fares and allowed for a smaller car. I had reserved a little Ford but since I could not drive with my license stolen and the car was not available and the luggage would not fit in a compact. We wound up with a Mercedes diesel with six in the floor for only three times the price for Carol to learn to drive.

We were on our way and arrived at our condo about 1030. The road was almost a continuous switchback. It was two-lane blacktop with numerous steep cuts and steep grades. Much of the road had concrete curbs but no shoulders. Lots of wildflowers were in bloom but most were mowed by the end of the week.

No one had used the unit the previous week so they did not make us wait until 1500 to move in. The condo consisted of a living room, a kitchenette, one large and two small bedrooms, two baths and a front and rear patio.

We moved in and did the inventory then went out for lunch. The office recommended the Anchor. We ate there three times during our stay and it was outstanding. This first time I tried fried Dory and a local red wine. Apparently Sardinians drank red wine with seafood. Carol got veal cutlet and Coke lite. We got an order of fresh focaccio and ordered *Seadas* for desert with a local white desert wine. *Seadas* are cheese and lemon peel fried fritters served with local bitter honey. Bill was 48€.

Back at the ranch I went to the beach and walked a couple miles. The path to the beach was half a mile through maquis of Holm Oak (Quercus ilex) and Mastic (Pistacia lentiscus) shrubs. Several ponds with cattails (Typha latifolia) and giant reed (Arundo donax) supported a frog and toad population of Painted Frog (*Discoglossus pictus*), Common Toad (*Bufo bufo spinosus*), and Green Toad (*Bufo viridis*). There was also a tidal marsh with Sea Rush (Juncus maritimus) and Sharp Rush (Juncus acutus) with Coots (Fulica atra) and Moorhens (Gallinula chloropus), a Little Egret (Egretta garzetta garzetta), and an occasional Yellow-legged Gull.

At the beach the water was clear but cold and the shells were mostly broken. A list is included with my other lists. The sand on this beach was granite with a few pebbles of white limestone. A pair of Dunlins (Calidris alpina alpina) was spooked and flew into the maquis. Sea rockets (Cakile maritma) and Sea Bindweed (Calystegia soldanella) a beach morning glory grew in the sand. Small black army ants had a roadway cleared to the mound. No mosquitoes but a few midges and crane flies.

I walked home along the top of the beach with lots of wildflowers.

We went to the condo snack bar for supper. I had a seafood salad and sampled both the red and white wines. Carol had spaghetti and meatballs (special order since this mixture was not a common Italian dish) and Coke lite. Apparently pasta mixed with tomato sauce and meat was an American invention about 1830 and never caught on in Italy. We each had a dish of ice cream for desert. Came to 28€ or about $35.

The sky was dark and clear and the bottom of the Big Dipper was straight overhead. At least three species of frogs or toads were calling.

Monday morning we were up early to see the sunrise and went for a walk on the beach. The wildflowers were opening as soon as they were brushed with sunlight. There was a white butterfly with black spots on the forewing and a small blue butterfly that just sat there instead of being jumpy like the Blues. The beach was cool and totally empty.

We stopped at the snack bar for breakfast then drove north along the water and past the lighthouse to Palau. On the way was another beach so I stopped for a look. Schools of small fish crowed against the shore. I found several small delicate abalone shells and some limpets. A tidal pond across the road had a Little Egret wading around feeding.

We drove into town. After several wrong turns and passing the ferry landing twice we found the waterfront with several restaurants. I had squid and a local Sardinian beer, *Ichnusa*. There are some advantages to not driving.

Once more around town and we found the right road to Santa Teresa Gallura and its lighthouse. There were several small communities that did not appear on the map.

We were back home about 1700 just as the grocery store was opening. We bought makings for a green salad and ham and cheese sandwiches, along with several liters of bottled water, cold cereal, milk and fruit. I stopped at the snack bar for beer and an ice cream cone.

23

Tuesday morning came up overcast. We got BBC on the TV and they said a front was coming in over Corsica and northern Sardinia. Sure enough.

Looking over the condo it was built for low cost and easy maintenance. Concrete block, paint and tile. The only two plugs that would take my adaptor were in the bathrooms. I charged up the razor but I was not enthused about sitting on the toilet to use the computer.

In the morning cool blackbirds were hopping on the lawn. A Cetti's Warbler (Cettia cetti cetti) was calling and picking up stuff for a nest. Common Swifts (Apus apus apus) and Barn Swallows (Hirundo rustica rustica) were slicing up the gray sky feeding on invisible insects. European Turtle Doves (Streptopelia decaocto decaocto) were calling in the maquis.

Flowers (Centaurea pullata) were growing in the dirt insulation on the roofs down hill from our condo units.

We headed off to Sassari. Entering Olbia we took the branch to the right that led to downtown and wandered around a half hour trying to find our way to the highway. It was about 100 km of good two-lane blacktop bypassing most of the little towns. We took a couple detours to look at the countryside. One stop was Berchidda at a Museum of Wine Making that was closed. Lots of vineyards and sheep. We tried to find a couple of the ancient nuraighi sites but the directions were bad. We finally arrived in Sassari and made a big loop through town without seeing a parking place or place to eat.

We went on down to the 12th century city of Alghero built by the Doria family of Genoa. We found the walled old town sector and a parking place on the waterfront near all the yatchs. We entered through one of the old gates and stopped for lunch. I had prawns and red wine while carol had a green salad and a pizza with mozzarella. We wandered along most of the old narrow cobblestone streets passing the Duomo and old buildings. Several shops sold coral jewelry. Two shops sold seashells from the Philippines for inflated prices. At siesta time most shops closed. We headed back about 1600 and were home in about two hours.

We stopped at the condo office and visited the snack shop for pizza and then visited a shop selling local craft items with examples of cork ware, weaving, pottery and other local art. Carol dropped off two sets of clothing for laundry that would be ready Friday.

Wednesday morning we scheduled a trip the islands off the north coast. I walked over to the office through wildflowers.

I watched a Cetti's Warbler flying: a couple wing beats popped him up a couple feet then he glided dropping a couple feet.

At the office was a dead locust that may have been blown in from Africa.

We drove about 2km to the dock and boarded the tour boat. The boat made about a five minute run to the dock at Cannigione for more passengers then another a ten minute run to Baia Sardinia for more passengers. On every rock sat one or more Cormorants (<u>Phalacrocorax</u> <u>carbo</u> <u>sinensis</u>). There were also some Yellow-legged Gulls.

The weather was overcast and cool. We passed Caprera Island where Garibaldi had lived and passed the waterfront at Palau and St Stefans Island before landing for 45 minutes at the port of la Maddalena on Maddalena Island. This was a nice little town of about 4000 mostly fishermen and merchants.

We were served a spaghetti lunch on the way to Santa Maria Island. We finally stopped on the Island of Spargi. I walked the beach and found no new shells. There were several new plants, Greek Spiny Spurge (Euphorbia acanthothanos), two kinds of ants, the Common Wall Lizard and several piles of rabbit droppings. One person did some snorkeling. We chugged back home and were in the condo by 1700.

Thursday morning was partly cloudy and cool. We had been present for the peak of the flowers and now the edge was off. After breakfast we went to see a travel agent to book a hotel room near the airport for the return flight. He charge 25€ for his services. Every body tries to get in your pocket. Carol picked up her laundry for 28€ or almost $40.

We took a ride over to the Costa Smeralda. This included Baia Sardinia, Porto Cervo, Capriccioli, Portisco and Porto Rotondo. We drove into each village and through the civic center then out around the harbor with the fancy yachts then out to see the homes and condos. We were back home about 1600.

I looked at the vegetation in the lawn. The weeds were familiar cosmopolitan invasives like Dichondra and Creeping Charlie. I noticed that the wildflowers along the trail to the office had been cut.

Friday we took a ride to Nuoro, which had 4 museums advertised. It was a nice 100 km drive. We stopped for a flock of sheep being driven down the highway. One of the men was controlling traffic on one lane. Not many wildflowers but there were several Alexander's, some large geraniums and purple as well as red poppies.

The town was much easier to find than Sassari but was just as crowded. None of the museums were open, which made little difference since there was no parking. Wonder how crowded it was during the actual tourist season? There was a real live parking lot where we stopped for a few minutes while looking for information on the museums. One of the local city employees said the museum was only three kilometers away and we could walk there in an hour. It was 1230 and siesta began at 1300. We got lost up on the edge of the hill with tight steep turns so I got to drive for a few minutes.

On the road back there were no places to eat. We drove through several small towns and between the small and the siesta there was nothing. Even the gas stations closed. Back at Olbia we found a mall near the airport and had lunch.

We went to Porto Cervo to return a shirt that was too small and arrived just as siesta was over. Nothing in the shop including extra and extra extra large fit across the shoulders since I am neither young nor Italian.

We went to the Anchor for supper. I had fried squid and Carol had veal. I tried another red wine. For dessert I had *Sedas* and Carol had a hot chocolate pie. We reserved *Porceddu* (a suckling pig) for Saturday night

We watched TV for a while. Both CNN and BBC repeat themselves every half hour. Watching these stations give a better picture of the world. The US is not the center of the universe. Politics and finance happen in other parts of the world. Most of the world was unhappy with Bush and the Bolton nomination. Most people who travel bring back trinkets instead of new ideas or viewpoints.

Saturday morning came up overcast and it had rained overnight. We went over to the office and told them we would be leaving early Sunday morning. I walked back along the trail to the condo and met a British couple photographing wildflowers. They had seen a small Grass Snake (*Natrix natrix*) and a small turtle (Emys orbicularis) along the trail to the beach.

We cleaned up and packed up then took a ride back to Porto Cervo and returned in mid-afternoon. I went down to the beach and found several new plants. I was back about time to go to supper.

The *Porceddu* was ready about 1930. The pig as served weighted maybe ten pounds which was really too much for us two. I had a couple beers and we had the hot chocolate pies for dessert. This was similar to the *luncheon* or barbequed whole pig in the Philippines and Hawaii that are buried and cooked over night. The piglet was roasted on a spit about 2-3 hours and served with roasted potatoes.

Sunday morning we left about 0730, dropped the key off and headed for the airport. We stopped the fill the car 28 liters at 1.4€ at $1.40/€. We dropped the bags at the airport and Carol turned in the car while I took everything inside.

The terminal was large and modern and the airport was busy with commercial and private traffic. Nice. Genoa. Zurich. Rome. Venice. I was told there were no flights to Venice.

We read and walked around until about 1800 and took a taxi to Golfo Aranci for the ferry. As we crossed the bridge over the channel at Olbia a celebration for the patron saint was taking place.

When we arrived at the ferry landing the ferry from Genoa was unloading. It left for Cagliari and our ferry docked. Although we were the only passengers to embark there were numerous students heading back to school that had boarded at Cagliari. We stuffed everything in the room and went to supper.

Monday morning I was up to see the sunrise and the docking. We had breakfast as we docked at Civitavecchia. We let the students go first and we were the last off.

In the terminal one of the local policemen called a cab for us to take us 5 blocks to the train station. Trains to Pisa ran every hour so we only had a few minutes to wait.

Getting five bags on the train was good exercise – up and down two flights of steps and under the tracks to track or "*bin*" 2 and then getting the bags onto the and off the train. There were no seats and baggage storage was not available so I had the pleasure of standing in the landing with the bags. There were signs saying reserved seats but I saw none. Reminds me of standing or squatting in the aisle all night getting to Switzerland 40 years ago with students – girls with unshaved legs and combat boots and long-haired guys that had not bathed since forever. I had bought tickets for a compartment that was not available.

The ride was through Tuscany with rolling hills with woodlands, grain fields, vineyards, olive groves, orchards, and cattle grazing and occasionally along the coast. There were many old houses and a lot of new homes. Cities were a mix of old brick and new glass. Lots of graffiti. Not what I had pictured.

Just outside of Livorno several men were spraying herbicide on the roadbed and right-of-way. I saw a magpie in a grain field.

As a whole a drive or train ride through Missouri would have been as exciting and a lot less expensive. Farmers were doing farm work. Major difference I saw was the brand of tractors and the architecture details. Towns looked like any town along a railroad track in midday. Including stops at Grosseto and Livorno we arrived at Pisa a little over two hours later.

We crossed the Arno River. The area between Livorno and Pisa was marshlands and a number of streams in the valley of the Arno.

We arrived about 1100 and got the bags off and into the terminal. The Hotel Touring was about two blocks away but Carol insisted on taking a cab for 8€. I think we got took since we drove considerably more than two blocks.

We got checked in and went to a restaurant the hotel recommended. There was an overtone that we were intruding on the Italian lunch hour. Of course seating us in a back room by ourselves and giving real slow service was probably an honor rather than just normal.

After lunch we walked four blocks along the Corso Italia to the *Pont di Mezzi* crossing the Arno and return. We stopped in many shops looking at clothes, shoes, and jewelry noting and prices. Seemed like the all the clothes and shoes were 100+€.

Tuesday morning we were up and hit the hotel breakfast - rolls, jam and weak orange juice. We walked back along the same street to the Arno, crossed the river, then four blocks along a street that changed names every block to the *Piazza dei Miracoli* with the *Duomo* and the leaning tower. The front of the church *San Michele in Borgo* had a dozen Africans selling scarves, purses and sunglasses.

We took a couple side trips for a flea market and to see the *Piazza dei Cavalieri*. The flea market contained a dozen large tables piled with cheap clothing and was surrounded by shops selling Indian jewelry and meat and vegetables.

Fuzz from sycamore trees was flying on the breeze but no trees were in sight. Looked like someone had shaken a huge rug.

The *Piazza dei Cavalieri* was the site of the Roman forum. It was designed by Giorgio Vasari for Cosimo dei Medici around 1560. The most striking building was the *Scuola Naomale Superiore*, Italy's top university, with its facade of graffiti patterns and a statue of *Cosimo I dei Medici*. It was designed as the headquarters of the Order of the Knights of St. Stephan. Next-door was the church of *Santo Stefano dei Cavalieri*. Across the plaza was *Palazzo dell'Orologio* built around the *Torre dei Gualandi* and a large administrative building.

A couple blocks further we came to the *Campo dei Miracoli* officially called the *Piazza del Duomo*. We entered the *Museo del'Opera del Duomo* where we bought tickets for the museum and the *Composanto* or cemetery. Although the Leaning Tower or *Campanile* was open a ticket was 20€. There was a long line since the number of people in the tower was limited and regulated.

The museum, built in the 11th centaury, was officially known as the Palace of the Cathedral Canons and the cathedral treasury. It housed a collection of models of the buildings, artifacts from previous construction projects, statues, paintings, frescoes, etc. It had several good vantage points for pictures.

We walked around the leaning tower and passed the cathedral to the cemetery and entered through a door that must have been 20 feet tall. This walled cloister forms the north wall if the Piazza. It was begun in 1277 to house a famous relic, soil from the Holy Land. There is a collection of Early Christian and Roman funerary art and sarcophagi art and is the burial place for church and local notables with mosaic portraits set in the floor. There are a number of giant frescoes. The walls surround a landscaped inner courtyard with the Dal Pozzo Chapel.

In a light drizzle we walked around the cathedral begun in 1064 and the circular Baptistery begun in the 12th century and passed the former hospital that currently housed the Museo delle Sinopie with the artists outlines of frescoes under the frescoes and passed the home of Galileo and the natural history museum.

We stopped at a sidewalk restaurant with a view of the leaning tower for lunch. I had pasta with clams and a red wine and Carol had pasta and a Coke Lite. The clams were in the shells instead of extracted like in bottled spaghetti sauce. The small clams or broken shells were hard to chew.

It stopped raining and we went window-shopping towards the botanical garden. Carol found a hairdresser while I went to the garden that turned out to be closed for the day. Pisa had very little urban greenery like trees and even the planters by some of the shops contained dead or wilted plants. There were few birds- a few sparrows and pigeons- and I heard a couple of blackbirds at dawn singing in the rain.

I had about an hour so I looked around the university area and admired the graffiti on the walls. "Stop Bush. Stop War." "Mussolini Rules." "Pisa for the Pisans." Complaints about the mayor and governor in Italian and English.

When the hair job was finished we window-shopped some more back to the river then across the bridge and to the hotel. Good-looking fashions for angular young skinny people. What ever happened to the rounded curves of Gina and Sophia a few years in the past? Many of the young females wore jeans low and had tattoos on their belly or lower back. Everyone was wearing ragged jeans that cost 150€. In northern Italy there were more blonds and brown hair and the people were taller than in southern Italy.

Supper was an experience. We found the restaurants did not open until 1900 and good ones were crowded. We finally picked one and were seated before being told there would be no service for eleven minutes. I had tripe Florentine and a white wine. Carol had a veal cutlet.

After supper we walked to the train station to pick up tickets to Florence. The trains ran about every two hours so we picked one at 1100.

Wednesday morning we packed up after breakfast and walked over to the train station toting our bags. Here began a half-day comedy of errors.

Shuffling five big bags was a nuisance if nothing else. I asked in Italian at the ticket counter if we could check the bags (like on an airplane or a passenger train in the US) and was told in English where the checkroom was. You might already get the hint of a basic misunderstanding. I showed the guy the ticket and told him we wanted to check the bags to Florence. He said, "OK. Bags checked." I thought it looked like baggage storage but we did it anyway at a cost of 10€. When we arrived in Florence we went to the checkroom and found I had been right - the bags were still in Pisa. We went to the hotel, checked in and had lunch and returned to Pisa for the bags.

The Tuscany countryside was largely farmed with grain, vineyards and orchards. Infrastructure of railroads, power and water distribution and mixed housing and light industry looked much like the NE US. Some of the small towns were in a building frenzy with new architecture. Some of the trip was along the Arno R. A small white egret and several yellow-legged gulls and a sparrow hawk cruised the river.

The train to Florence was cleaner and more modern than the one we had taken to Pisa. No compartments. Plastic seats.

The train station in Florence was better than the Pisa station. The tracks end in the terminal so no walking across tracks or up and down stairs.

The hotel I had reserved was a 17th century palace that had been renovated as a hotel probably in the 1950s. It is the site where the Mona Lisa was discovered many years ago. It had no elevator so we told the clerk we needed a handicapped room since Carol had both hips replaced. They gave us a room on the first floor, which in Europe is one floor up the stairs. Breakfast was just down the hall.

I took a walk while Carol rested. I was looking for a laundromat and barbershop. The man at the desk gave me directions to pass the Chapel of San Lorenzo about a block and there they were. I got a haircut. I asked for a flat top and got a crew cut. I got the hours of operation of the laundry and returned to the hotel.

Supper was at a small place next to the hotel. Carol had pizza and I got lasagna.

Thursday morning it was barely light when the low roar of suitcase wheels began on the sidewalk from people hurrying to or from the train station.

After breakfast of rolls and tea we left to see the city. We walked about three blocks to the Piazza San Giovanni with the Battistero (Baptistery) with the famous bronze doors by Pisano and Ghiberti and the Campanile (the Duomo bell tower) and the Piazza del Duomo then around the Duomo (Santa Maria del Fiore) to the Duomo museum.

We visited the bookstore while waiting fifteen minute for the museum to open. The museum contained works from the Duomo and other facilities by masters including Michelangelo, Donatello, and della Robbia. Touring the museum took about an hour and a half. Then we walked about four blocks to the Piazza della Signora (city council).

We stopped for ice cream. I can't believe 20€ for two sundaes. The streets back to the hotel were narrow and, as the sun dropped, dusky. Little shops with office supplies, wine, shoes and you-name-it. Some had well decorated windows while others the windows probably matched the quality of merchandise. I found one antique shop with mostly religious stuff and two art galleries.

We walked over to the train station and bought tickets for Rome and the airport for 1100 Sunday morning. Cost was 77€.

For Friday I had booked a bus tour of town but we found the busses were on strike for half the day. Come back tomorrow. Apparently these strikes were largely symbolic, well coordinated, and advertised in advance.

We took a taxi to the Ponte Vecchio and walked across shopping on the way. The bridge has several stories of shops and no traffic. There were over a hundred shops of goldsmiths and jewelers. We crossed the bridge several times and it cost me about a hundred euros each way.

We returned to the Piazza della Signora for lunch along narrow cobblestone streets with car and motorcycle traffic, parked vehicles and little or no sidewalk. On the way there was a pair of carbinari on horseback complete with swords escorting a small marching group with uniforms, flags and feathered hats. These were veterans from various wars heading somewhere for a ceremony like Veterans Day.

We toured the Palazzo Vecchio. Four floors tall with rooms with 16 foot vaulted and decorated ceilings. The main hall was done in frescoes by Vasari and statues. It had a vaulted ceiling that must have been 30-40 feet high.

There was a brass band playing and as we were leaving groups of veterans marched into a big room. By the time we got outside the Piazza was full of tourist attracted by the band and numerous police and military groups.

We left and walked back to the Ponte Vecchio and a couple blocks to the Piazza Pita with its six museums that were closed for siesta. One museum, the Galleria Palatina, contained 11 Titians, 14 Raphaels and works by Andrea del Sarto, Perugino, Caravaggio, Velasquez, Rubens and Van Dyck.

Since everything was closed we went to the formal Gardino di Boboli with numerous trails and formal steps leading to a formal rose garden and crystal museum. There were few flowers except the occasional weed.

We got back to the hotel and crashed for a couple hours then were out looking again including a shop that sold Morano glass.

I looked at real estate listings. Rent ran around 1000€/month. To buy a house prices began about 80,000€ to 1.5 million€ ($2.2M)for a house 300 square meters depending on location, view, garage or not, etc. Don't know what the wages are but this looks like an expensive place to live. I know unemployment in Naples was about 40%.

Saturday morning we packed up and put the luggage in storage for the day. We checked out and finally found the double-decker red bus like in London. We took both routes. One route went northeast through number plazas, past the stadium and up the hill to San Marco and return. The morning air was crisp and cool on the open upper deck of the bus. The driver was not photography and sightseeing friendly speeding along. The narration was provided by earphones on a multi-channel recorded program. The streets were two lane divided with trees down the middle. We went through Fiesole with lots of big villas. Plane trees. Poodle pines. Lime trees.

We changed to the other loop that went from the Piazza della Signora, through the residential section of town, across the river through the high-end real estate to the Piazzale Michelangiolo and the Iris Garden, to the Piazza del Pitti and back to the Piazza della Signora. We stopped at the Michelangelo statues. The site overlooks Florence and the Arno. We had a coke and found that the Iris garden was closed until 1500. We caught the next bus and got off at the Pitti Palace to walk across the Ponte Vecchio one more time to Piazza della Signora. Lunch was a couple pizzas in the plaza.

A city bus had a sign that said it ran on *gas naturale*. We had a propane bottle under the kitchen stove in Sardinia.

We went back and checked in at the new hotel, an international chain. Central air. Good mattress. Just like an $80 motel at home but this ran 225€ ($340).

About 1600 we took the bus back to the Iris Garden. It covered about 20 acres on a hillside overlooking the Arno River Valley. Paths crisscross the hillside defining iris gardens that contain over 20 plants. The garden is only open in May when the Irises are in bloom. This is the home of the Societa Italiana dell Iris that began in 1954. They maintain historic plant lines and do hybridizing and propagation of new varieties. Outstanding.

Dinner was a Tuscany fiest at the hotel.

Sunday morning We went down for a really good breakfast with fruit and juice and fried eggs and sausage. Thee price was going to look good on my frequent flyer account.

I got the bags down and checked out about 1000 when a parade began. Band and soldiers and canons and jeeps and a good crowd.

We got everything arranged and headed down the sidewalk and beat the train by a couple minutes. There was an hour train ride to Rome and a transfer to the airport train. Lots of construction was visible and numerous houses and apartments were being built. We got into the hills north of Rome and dove through a dozen tunnels. There were still a number of olive groves and vineyards. Grain fields were accompanied by grain elevators. Electrical transmission lines, roads and rails carved up the countryside. There were a few picturesque small villages with old churches and new villas. We passed several tree farms with Plane trees and oaks. I guess these were for landscape specimen trees.

Near Rome the land flattened into a wide valley with grain and hay fields and numerous greenhouse installations. Closer to Rome were rolling hills with villas on the hilltops and grain fields and vineyards and creeks with lots of trees.

At the Rome station we must have walked a mile or more from the arrival point to the airport train.

We arrived at the airport about 1530 and caught a van to the hotel for 10€. The Mach 2 hotel was a $30 beach motel for 150€. Halls and lobby were under construction. There was a deposit on the TV remote. I looked out at the view of the parking lot and the kitchen dumpster. But it has AC and TV. No electrical plugs except in the bath.

It was Sunday and nothing was open so we took a taxi back to the airport for supper.

Supper was steamed sandwiches and Cokes. Italian style you pick what you want and pay for it before it is prepared.

We decided to find another bag since a couple bags were probably over weight. We found a small duffle bag with wheels.

It rained for the evening and over night the temperature dropped to about 16. This is a flat delta near the beach.

Monday morning we had an early flight and were scheduled on the 0730 shuttle. The hotel restaurant opened at 0700.

The enhanced business check in had two people ahead of us but it took almost 30 minutes. Security check took about 10 minutes to check in then we went to the VP lounge that went with out upgraded tickets.

We sat for 45 minutes with free drinks and newspapers and CNN on TV. Excellent toilets built to US standards. I remember one toilet in Rome with five sinks and one working commode with no seat. The only toilets with seats were in the Florence where they charged a half-euro and the stalls were sanitized with UV light. Strange what fluorescences does in a toilet.

We boarded and away we went. We were at 10.000 feet before it got down to freezing. A few minutes later we passed over Elba then north of Corsica with snow-covered peaks.

The stewardess took our lunch order. Antipasto of salami and artichokes, then a pasta course and a main course of shrimp with fruit for desert.

We hit land near Nice, France, at 30,000 and –56°F. We passed over Grenoble then NE of Paris to Dunkirk. The route was north of Greenwich and London, north of Manchester and Liverpool and across the Irish Sea and Ireland. The North Atlantic was relatively calm with no clouds and no large ice floes visible. We came in over southern Labrador and the Gulf of St Lawrence. Newfoundland was visible to the south. We soon passed north of Prince Edward Isle and on in to Cleveland. After a short break we were on the way to San Antonio and home.

I'm glad to be back home. Three weeks on the road gets long. The trip was more expensive than I planned for. It was interesting to see how Italy had changed in 43 years but I am in no hurry to go again. Maybe China or Australia next time.

Bibliography

Travel books

Aedito, Fabizio (1998). *Eyewitness Travel Guides Sardinia*. DK Publishing, Inc.

Brown, Clare (1993). *Karen Brown's Italian Country Inns & Itineraries*. The Globe Pequot Press.

Donati, Germano (1991). *Tuscany Colored Guide-Book*. Plurigraf.

Facaros, Dana and M. Pauls (1990). *Cadogan Guide to Tuscany and Umbria*. The Globe Pequot Press

Jepson, Tim (1996). *Fodor's Exploring Italy*. Fodor's Travel Publications, Inc.

Lombardi, Matthew (2003). *Fodor's Italy 2003*. Fodor's Travel *Publications, Inc.*

Porter, Darwin and Danforth Prince (2003). *Fromer's Italy 2003*. Wiley.

Serra, Vittorio (1990). *A Day in Florence New Practical Guide*. Bonechi Edizioni il Turismo.

Natural History

Blamey, Marjorie and C. Grey-Wilson (1993). *Mediterranean Wild Flowers*. Harper Collins.

Heinzel, Hermann, R. Fitter, J. Parslow (1995). Collin's Pocket Guide to Birds of Britain & Europe. Harper Collins.

City Guides

Pompeii and Naples. Bonechi Edizioni "Il Torismo".

Vatican City. Sdizioni Musei Vaticani. 1997.

Pisa and Piazza dei Miracoli. Bonechi Edizioni "Il Torismo". 2004

A Day in Florence. Bonechi. 1991.

Florence – The Cathedral. Madragora. 2002

Societa Italiana dell Iris. The Iris Garden in Florence. Cassa de Risparmio de Firenze.

Art and History of Florence. Bonechi

Itinerary

Italy trip	Trans	Hotel	Telephone	Tours
2-May	**Delta 708 at 1126A SAT to ATL 244P**			
	Delta 70 at 520P ATL to Rome 520P-855A			
3-May	**arrv Rome 0855**	**Grand Hotel Fleming**		
4-May		P. Monteleone di Spoleto 20	Rome	city
5-May		Rome 00191		
6-Jan				
7-May	**Ferry to G. Aranci (Olbia) Sardinia lv2100**			
8-May	Arr 0700 Rental car – Hertz	**Portolaconia Residence**		
9-May	Rental car – Hertz	Villaggio Tanca Manna		
10-May	Rental car – Hertz	Cannigione		
11-May	Rental car – Hertz	07021 Arzachena (SS)		
12-May	Rental car – Hertz	IT 0789-8511		
13-May	Rental car – Hertz			
14-May	Rental car – Hertz			
15-May	**Ferry to Civitavecchia Lv 2100**			
16-May	**Arr 0700 Train to Pisa**	**Hotel Touring Pisa**	1 (0) 39 (050) 46374	city
17-May		Via Puccini 24, Pisa 56125		city
18-May	**Train to Florence**	**Hotel La Gioconda**	1 (0) 39 (055) 211023	city
19-May		Via Panzani 2, Florence 50123		
20-May				
21-May				
22-May	**Train to Airport Hotel**	Mach 2		
23-May	**Delta 33 at 1055A Rome to Cincinnati**			
	Delta 430 at 430P Cincinnati to SAT 628P			

Birds of Italy

F = Florence
N = Naples
P = Pisa
R = Rome

Pelicanidae: Pelicans
    Dalmation Pelican – <u>Pelecanus philippensis</u>   Isla Magdalena

Phalacrocoracidae: Cormorants
    Cormorant – <u>Phalacrocorax carbo sinensis</u>   S and islands

Ardeidae: Herons, Egrets, and Bitterns
    Great White Egret – <u>Egretta alba</u>   Rome airport, Arno
    Little Egret – <u>E. garzetta</u>   S

Anatinae: Ducks
    Pochard – <u>Aythya ferina</u>   S

Rallidae: Rails and Crakes
    Coot – <u>Fulica atra</u>   S
    Moorhen – <u>Gallinula chloropus</u>   S

Scolopacidae: Waders
    Dunlin – <u>Calidris alpina</u>   S

Laridae: Gulls
    Audouin's Gull – <u>Larus Audouinii</u>   S
    Common Gull or Mew – <u>L. canus canus</u>   S
    Yellow-legged Gull – <u>L. michahellis</u>   R, S, F
Sterninae: Terns
    Caspian Tern – <u>Sterna caspia</u>   S

Apodidae: Swifts
  Swift – <u>Apus</u> <u>apus</u>   R, S, F

Hirundiniae: Swallows
  Barn Swallow – <u>Hirundo</u> <u>rustica</u> <u>rustica</u>   S, F

Motacillidae: Pipits and Wagtails
  Yellow Wagtail – <u>Motacilla</u> <u>flava</u>   F

Corvidae: Crows
  Hooded Crow - <u>Corvus</u> <u>commix</u> <u>sardonius</u>   R, S
  Jay – <u>Garrulus</u> <u>glandarius</u>   S
  Magpie – <u>Pica</u> <u>pica</u>   Livorno

Hirundinidae: Swallows and Martins
  Swallow – <u>Hirundo</u> <u>rustica</u>   S, F

Turdidae: Thrushes, Chats and Allies
  Blackbird – <u>Turdus</u> <u>merula</u>   N, R, S, P, F

Sylviidae: Warblers
  Cetti's Warbler – <u>Cettia</u> <u>cetti</u> <u>cetti</u>   S

Troglodytidae: Wrens
  Winter Wren - <u>Troglodytes</u> <u>troglodytes</u>   S

Sturnidae: Starlings
  Starling - <u>Sturnus</u> <u>vulgaris</u>   R, F

Passeridae: Sparrows
  House Sparrow - <u>Passer</u> <u>domesticus</u>   R, S, F

Herptiles of Sardinia

Common Wall Lizard (*Podarcis muralis*) - *breviceps* and *nigriventris?*
Grass Snake (*Natrix natrix*) - *sicula* and *lanzai?*
Emys orbicularis?

Heard
Painted Frog (*Discoglossus pictus*)
Common Toad (*Bufo bufo spinosus*)
Green Toad (*Bufo viridis*)

Invertebrates

Insects

Locust	N, S
Blue Butterfly	S
White Butterfly black upper wing spots	R, S
Crane flies	S

Sea Urchin	S
Stone Crab	S
Sponge	S

Land Snail

Masularia niviensis – Nice Helix	S

Seashells

Haliotidae

Haliotis terberculata – Lemellose Omer	S

Patellidae

Patella caerulea – Rayed Mediterranean Limpet	S
Patella ferruginea – Ribbed Mediterranean Limpet	S

Vermetidae

Vermicularia arenaria – Worm-shell	S

Cerithidae

Cerithium vulgatum – European Cerith	S

Naticidae

Euspira poliana – Poli's Necklace Shell	S
Neverita josephinia – Josephine's Moon	S
Payraudeautia intricata – European Gray Moon	S

Muricidae

Hexaplex trunculus – Trunculus Murex	S

Columbellidae

Columbella rustica – Rustic Dove-shell	S

Nassariidae

Nassarius cuvierii – One-banded Nassa	S

Nassarius mutabilis – mutable nassa   S
Bullidae
   Bulla striata – Atlantic Bubble   S
Arcidae
   Arca noae – Noah's Ark   S
   Barbatia barbata – European Bearded Ark   S
Mytilidae
   Mytilis galloprovincialis – Mediterranean Blue Mussel   S
Spondylidae
   Spondylus gaederopus – European Thorny Oyster   S
Limidae
   Lima inflata – Inflated Lima   S
Chamidae
   Pseudochama gryphina – Graphin Jewel Box   S
Cardiiae
   Acanthocardia tuberculata – Tuberculate Cockle   S
Veneridae
   Dosinia exoleta – Mature Doscinia   S
   Venerupis aurea – European Aurora Venus   S

Plants of Italy

Numbers from *Mediterranean Wildflowers*

32	Cytinus hypocistis	Cytinus	S
38	Ulmus canescens	Mediterranean Elm	S, F
74	Rumex angiocarpus	Dock	S
77	Rumex cyprius	Dock	S
106	Amaranthus retroflexus	Pigweed	R, N, S
110	Bougainvillea glabra	Bougainvilla	R, S
121	Lampranthus roseus	Lampranthus	S
147	Spurgularia media	Lesser Sand-Spurrey	S
243	Ranunculus muricatus	Buttercup	S
277	Paeonia coriacea	Peony	S
283	Papaver rhoeas	Common Poppy	R, N, S, F
284	Papaver dubium	Long-headed Poppy	S
293	Glaucium flavum	Yellow Horned-Poppy	S
313	Malcolmia littorea	Sand Stock	S
316	Malcolmia maritima	Virginia Stock	S
336	Lobularia maritime	Sweet Alison	R
352	Lepidium latifolium	Dittander	S
363	Cakile maritima	Sea Rocket	S
364	Crambe hispanica	Spanish Seakale	S
389	Sedum rubens	Reddish Stonecrop	S
400	Platanus orientalis	Plane Tree	R
402	Pittosporum tobira	Pittisporum	R, N
421	Prunus dulois	Almond	R, N, S
423	Prunus persica	Peach	R, F

438	Acacia retinoides	Acacia	S
440	Acacia pycnantha	Golden Wattle	S
428	Rubus sanctus	Bramble	S
452	Calycotome infesta	Thorny Broom	R, N, S
456	Cytisus scoparius		S
475	Ulex europaeus	Gorse	R, S
488	Robinia pseudacacia	False Acaia	R, N, S
534	Vicia narbonensis	Vicia	S
602	Medicago intertexta		S
605	Medicago marina	Sea Medic	S
652	Trifolium fragiferum	Strawberry Clover	R, S
656	Trifolium campestres	Hop Trefoil	S
752	Erodium malacoides	Mallow-leaf Stork's-bill	R, S
794	Euphorbia acanthothamnos	Greek Spiny Spurge	S, Spargi Is.
798	Euphorbia pinea	Spurge	S
1024	Tamarix tetragyna	Tamarix	S
1052	Mytis communis	Common Myrtle	R, N, S
1053	Callistemon citrinus	Bottlebrush	N, S
1060	Eucalyptus globules	Blue Gum	R, S
1087	Smymium olusatrum	Alexanders	R, S
1109	Peucedanum anisum	Dill	S
1169	Daucus maricatus		S
1176	Arbutus unedo	Strawberry Tree	S
1198	Anagallis arvensis	Scarlet Pimpernel	R, S
1240	Jasmine grandiflorum	Jasmine	S
1244	Ligustrum lucidum	Chinese Privet	R, S
1256	Nerium oleander	Oleander	R, S
1294	Galium mollugo	Hedge Bedstraw	S

1315	Calystegia soldanella	Sea Bindweed	S
1334	Convolvulus arvensis	Bindweed	S
1417	Lantana camara	Lantana	S
1418	Verbena officinalis	Verain	S
1425	Ajuga chamaepithys	Ground Pine	S
1545	Salvia amplexicaulis	Sage	F
1528	Lavandula stoechas	French Laverder	S
1664	Orobanche minor	Commom Broomrape	Spargi
1696	Plantago coronopus commuta		
	Buck's Horn Plantain	S	
1701	Plantago elaia	Ribwort Plantain	S
1760	Campanule trachelium	Nettle-leaf Bellflower	S
1800	Achillea santolina	Goldilocks Aster	S
1857	Anthemis maritimus	Chamomile	S
1887	Matricaria recutite	Scented Mayweed	S
1897	Coleostephes myconis		S
1952	Cirsium argentatus	Thistle	S
1958	Cirsium vulgare	Spear Thistle	S
1961	Cirsium creticum	Thistle	S
2006	Centaurea pullata		S
2091	Asphodellus albus	White Asphodel	S
2222	Smilax aspera	Common Smilax	S
2224	Allium roseum	Rosy Garlic	S
2245	Allium nigrum	S	
2252	Phomium tenax	New Zealand Lilly	S
2265	Leucojum trichophyllum	Three-leaved Snowflake	S

2305	Gynandriris sisyeinchium	Barbary Nut	S
2458	Cynosurus echinatus	Rough Dog's-tail	S
2462	Melica ciliata	Hairy Melick	S
24??	Orchis sp		S
2473	Lagurus ovatus	Hare's Tail	S
2504	Juncus acutus	Sharp rush	S

Dichondra sp.		S
Myosaurus sp.		S
Typha latifolia	Cattail	S, F

Naples 1962

In the summer of 1962 I was in Naples for about six weeks. We were flying for NATO evaluating member radar sites around the Mediterranean.

One Sunday afternoon several of us decided to go see some of Naples we had not visited before. We heard opera being sung in a park and decided to check it out. It was a restored Roman amphitheatre and they were staging *La Traviata* by Giuseppe Fortunino Francesco Verdi. We stood at the rear since all the seats were filled on this sunny afternoon. Most interesting. Everyone was in street clothes including the cast. At every high note everyone cheered. At the completion of *Libiamo ne'lieti calici* (Drinking Song) everyone stood and cheered until the opera was rewound and the passage was done over twice more before they were allowed to finish the opera.

Later we wandered through the park and found a zoo. It was a bright clear Mediterranean afternoon and we were in civvies. Somewhere around the lion den a couple of our party met girls and disappeared. We were looking at the camels when a middle aged Italian man asked, in American English with only a hint of Italian, if we were Americans. We admitted that we were and that we were in the US Navy. I asked where he had learned English. He said he had joined the Italian Army in 1940 and had been sent to North Africa. He said he was already disillusioned about Hitler and the war and only hoped he would survive to return home to Naples.

We found a table at a sidewalk coffee shop. He ordered a round of espresso and we sat in the shade sipping while he told his story. In western Egypt his unit had been cut off and surrounded by American soldiers. He was taken captive. He was deloused and given a clean uniform, and since he had been a regular GI and not been wounded, he was sent to the American invasion headquarters for interrogation. Because he knew nothing of value he was included in a group of his fellow Italian prisoners and shipped to a prison camp in Bryan, Texas. He had been apprenticed to his uncle in a small restaurant and was assigned to the kitchen. To him the food on the troop ship and train to Texas was wonderful.

He rapidly learned Texas-style English. There was an incentive. Many of the prisoners who spoke English were loaned out to farmers and businesses to replace men who had enlisted or been drafted into the war. It wasn't long before he had landed a position in a small restaurant. The restaurant gradually shifted it menu from burgers to pizza and spaghetti based on his cooking.

Near the end of the war as American troops returned home there were several incidents where Italian prisoners were beat up because of their relations with local girls. The prisoners were locked up until they were sent home to Italy a couple months later.

Our hero returned to Naples and, with the help of his family, opened an American restaurant catering to the occupation troops and, later, to tourists. American food. Burgers and fries. Shakes. Chicken fried steak. Many of his supplies were imported directly from friends back in Bryan.

He practiced his English at every opportunity and invited us to visit his place. We had every intention of taking him up but did not have time because we were transferred to Athens for a month before returning to the States. A chicken fried steak sure sounded good.

Carl Lahser
20Mar12

Cross Section through a Rainbow

Athens, Corfu, and Rhodes

April 1997

Carl Lahser

I

We arrived home from Greece via New York and St. Louis about noon on Monday. It's two A.M. in the morning Tuesday, and I can't get to sleep. Jet lag from eight time zones has my body thinking that its about ten in the morning. Might as well do something useful like write a report of the trip. Why not?

*****

A Starting Place

As our 29ᵗʰ anniversary approached in 1996 we began to plan something special for number thirty. Adventure doesn't come easily so we began looking for a place for two weeks at one place or two places relatively close together where we could trade two timeshare condominium periods and get back-to-back weeks in the spring of 1997.

I like beaches and had never been to Africa but nothing was available in the whole Pacific area or in Africa. We decided not to look at Canada or Mexico just yet so we looked at Europe. We decided to concentrate in the warmer Mediterranean region. Nothing that fit our requirements was available in Spain, Italy, or Portugal but we found back-to-back weeks in Greece - a week on Homer's Corfu followed by a week on Rhodes with a day or two in Athens.

This sounded good to me. In the summer of 1962, I had flown out of the US Air Base at Athens as a young Navy aircrewman. It would be interesting to see how things had changed. It had been tough duty - living on Glifádha Beach on the Apollo Coast, visiting the royal palace in Athens, seeing the *Evzone* guards, climbing the Acropolis, and walking through the Parthenon. I had also visited Corfu, taking *Oúzo* and *mezédhes* under a big oak tree, and had flown over many islands of the Aegean. The books of Lawrence Durrell had been read in the 60's and their fire still smoldered. This would be an opportunity to look at present day Greece from different perspectives in education and philosophy and contrast the realities of the present with the memories of the past.

Reflecting on my all-too-short stay in Greece I had two poems from 1962. One poem describes Glyfáda Beach. The other poem describes a portcall in Corfu now called Kérkyra. Considering the political changes in recent years, it would be interesting to see how Athens and Corfu had changed in thirty-five years and to compare present day Greece with accounts from sixty and 150 years ago.

Corfu Afternoon

In the shade of a large oak tree
near the customs house
the Venetian-style new fort looming overhead
we listened to Greek music at a *mesedhopolía*
feasted on a *pikilía* of *mezédhes* -
feta cheese, dried squid, roasted lamb,
and sampled licorice-flavored *oúzo* to excess.

We were anchored off the commercial Port.
The Pindus mountains and Albania,
an ancient and Cold War adversary,
lay just two kilometers across the strait.
carl July 62

*****

GLIFA'DHA BEACH

Four thousand years of
    beachcombers,
    philosophers,
    soldiers,
    poets and kings
trod this beach.

Their eyes have feasted on
    hills covered with oak and olive trees
    good anchorage in the Saronic Gulf
    fair country girls
as they approached Athi'nai from the south.
Forty civilizations spilled their blood and seed
on this beach and on these hills.

I came as a warrior
but my summer was spent in peace
    in a small family hotel
    on the shore looking southwest
    across the Gulf.

Up each day to catch the morning,
awakened by the soft knock of the maid
    who left croissants and jam,
    and tea on a terrace.
Alone in the pastel dawn
    I watched the sky soften
    and the fog lift

Seeing the yellow and white Caroline
    anchored a mile off shore,
    I wondered if Jackie Onasis
    was joining me for tea,
    waiting for the sun,
    listening to the gentle slap
    of wavelets at the changing of the tide.

I watched as fishing boats returned silently
    lamps trimmed,
    oars and nets shipped.
Baskets of squid and cuttlefish
    were the reward
    of those who correctly answered
    the nymph's question,
"How is it with Alexander?"
"He lives and reigns still."

My war went well
as I dressed for the day's flight.
Like Icarus of old
    we strapped on wings
    and chased the wind east
    to Keá and A'ndros
    to Sa'mos and Ephesus
    north to Ankara
    over forested mountains
    to the Black Sea beaches.

We raced the sun west
 across the Bosporus
 down the fields and pastures
 of the Ergene Valley
 to Xanthi and Dráma.

Banking left, we drifted southward
 to Thessalonniki
 across the Gulf of Thermaikos,
 across the bottomless blue Aegean
 under a cold clear blue sky,
 over rocky islands and narrow beaches
 to Athi'nai.

Warm nights
 oúzo and retsina,
 slabs of white feta cheese
 raw squid,
 fried fish cakes with garlic sauce
 beneath spreading oaks,
Bif stek and stuffed grape leaves
in tavernas
where no Greek was spoken
and drachmas got dollars in change.

Overcast nights were like
 a large room with carpeted walls.

Warm breezes filled with the smell
 of acacias
 and the sea
 as lights of the Caroline
 disappeared into the dropping mist.

I waited on the beach
for the dawn
when we would fly again.

Carl July 62

*****

As homework, I reviewed my 35 year old 35mm slides of Greece and read several travel guides including Baedeker's **Greek Islands**, Fodor's **Greece**, **The Real Guide to Greece** published by Prentice Hall Travel, and **Mainland Greece** by Victor Walker. I listened to the Berlitz Greek language tape several times and relearned a few terms and common phrases. I reviewed reading Greek and read parts of Homer's **Odyssey** and the epic poem, the **Argonautica**, about Jason and the Argonauts whose author, Apollonius Rhodius, had lived on Rhodes for years.

I tried to find books on the wildflowers, seashells and birds of Greece with little luck. I eventually found Peterson's **A Field Guide to the Birds of Britain and Europe** and the **Collin's Pocket Guide to the Birds of Britain and Europe** plus a couple of big coffee table books of European birds. For plants, I discovered **Mediterranean Wildflowers, a Complete Guide to the Plants of the Mediterranean Area**. I looked at **Sea Shells of Western Europe** by Bouchet, Danrigal and Huyghens, the **Compendium of Landshells** by Tucker Abbot and the **Compendium of Seashells** by Abbot and Dance. Tom Rice's shell catalog offered distribution information.

For modern historical insight, I read Hans Christian Andersen's **A Poet's Bazaar**, recounting a trip to Athens in 1841 and Laurance Durrell's books, **Prospero's Cell** and **Reflections on a Marine Venus,** on Corfu (Corcyra) and Rhodes respectively.

*****

Checking with the Air Force Office of Special Investigations (AFOSI) I got their latest anti-terrorism briefing and found the terrorist threat for Greece to be moderate.

I checked the medical area intelligence reports for Greece, Turkey, and Albania in the **Monthly Disease Occurrence (World- wide)**, reviewed the **Disease Vector Ecology Profiles (DVEP)** prepared by the Defense Pest Management Information Center, and called the Communicable Disease Center (CDC) Malaria Hotline. Everything looked like it should with the exception of hepatitis A for which we got an Imunoglobulin shot.

*****

Reservations had been made in September and had gone through numerous minor changes prior to tickets arriving in March. The only significant change was that TWA no longer flew to Athens.

*****

II

It's 3 AM and I'm still wide awake. Maybe a little more typing will put me to sleep.

Off and Running

I got back from a business trip to Albuquerque about midnight on Wednesday, the second of April. I unpacked, washed clothes, and packed up again for the trip to Greece. We were up at 0400 Friday morning ready to go, but the taxi that was supposed to pick us up at 0430 called at 0435 that they would be a half hour late. Our son drove us to the airport a little after 0500 for a 0710 flight. There had been a number of changes since the tickets were issued so it took almost an hour to rebook everything. This was completed by 0615. But don't bet on this being the end of ticketing problems.

Cool mist accompanied us off the runway. Dense clouds hid the ground all the way to St. Louis where we changed planes. Takeoff from St Louis was delayed half an hour for a Muslim man who refused to be seated until his three Muslim women were properly seated. He would not allow them to be seated next to men.

Over Indianapolis the cloud cover broke. I could see a trailer park with the trailerhouses arranged in circles like big silver flowers waiting for the next high wind. Snow still covered the fence lines and streams of Pennsylvania and New Jersey.

We landed at JFK about 1330 and had a four hour layover. A half mile trek through oval precast concrete corridors as big as a 747 took us from gate 23 to 37. Carol dozed while I watched people and airport operations. I even got to see a supersonic Concorde land.

*****

Loading began about six in the evening, and we leapt into the dusk heading north and east for Gander, Newfoundland. We would be east of Paris for sunrise, then to Rome for a change of planes.

After sunset the Hale-Bopp comet was visible in the northwest.

*****

Saturday morning. I woke south of Geneva to the sight of snow covered peaks and fog-bound valleys of the Alps twenty thousand feet below.

*****

Alps from 30,000 feet

The Alps from the Air

Those narrow twisting roads
through steep, green valleys
around snow capped peaks
of mile-high mountains
present a different aspect
when seen by Phineas Fogg.
Days of driving
in thin, crisp air scented with evergreens
took only minutes in sterile shirt-sleeve comfort.

*****

We continued over rugged mountains east of Turin towards Genoa. (The Genoese had raided Corfu twice in the 15th century.) Early morning bluegreen water of the Mediterranean contrasted with the snow covered Maritime Alps, the tan beaches of the Italian Riviera, and red tile roofs of San Remo and Monaco. There appeared to have been recent rainfall with brownish eddies drifting parallel to the coast.

*****

Italian coast

Monaco Memory

The little beach
below the Prince Albert Museum
spawned a magic maid
with long black hair
who tossed stones into the water
so her full-size poodle would let us talk.
She disappeared
over cold sweet vermouth.

*****

As we passed over the northeast corner of the Ligurian Sea towards Pisa and Livorno, a hint of Corsica appeared faintly on the horizon under thin clouds. The outside temperature at 30,000 feet was about -55°F, and the numerous aircraft contrails showed no jet stream and little wind. Contrails were caused when the heated jet exhaust provided condensation nuclei and water vapor to form long, thin man-made clouds.

The Italian coast slid under us, and we continued southward down the coast of Tuscany above a solid cloud blanket. The approach into Rome took us out over the Tyrrhenian Sea. We turned east and north over green fields, red tile roofs and roads lined with Lombardy poplars into DiVinci International Airport west of Rome. A Great White Egret (*Egretta alba*) crossed under us just prior to touchdown at 0930 Rome time.

*****

As we landed, we passed numerous airfield obstructions. Occupied houses were not more than two hundred yards from the runway. A lone propane cannon sat near the touchdown point to scare birds. Active construction projects were prominent along the runways and taxiways. The airfield turf appeared to be Bahiagrass and a profusion of pink and yellow flowers.

After taxiing for almost twenty minutes, we off-loaded onto busses for the ride to the terminal. There we were separated from the passengers stopping in Rome. A half mile alpine tour up and down stairs took us to the international departure lounge. Since TWA no longer served Athens, we transferred to Alitalia Airline for the remainder of the trip.

This international gate area, about the size of a football field, was clean and well lighted. The seats were an uncomfortable and virtually indestructible plastic covered metal mesh. We had lunch and watched the weather on CNN [A cold front was approaching Greece and the expected temperature range for Rome was 6°-19°C (43° - 65° F)]. We took turns watching the bags and browsed the duty free stores, read or dozed until boarding time.

*****

About 1330, we boarded a 12X60 foot portable lounge for the trip to our A-321 Airbus. We had aisle seats in the smoking section, but it was only a little over an hour's flight to Athens flying over Foggia and Brindisi. We out ran the cold front over central Italy.

After landing at Hellenikon Airport, we were taken by portable lounge to the terminal to pick up our luggage and go through Greek customs. We had to transfer everything to the domestic terminal at the other end of the airport.

*****

We checked in at Olympic Airlines for a flight to Kérkyra otherwise known as Corfu or Durrell's Corcyra. This terminal was strictly utilitarian with well worn plastic seats. It seemed that everyone smoked and there were no no-smoking areas.

Restrooms were down stairs and cost a hundred drachma (40 cents) contribution to the female maintenance staff whom the male customers ignored. At least the restrooms were clean.

Carol bought a bag of pistachios for 300 drachmas. We finished them before the plane arrived. There were no waste cans so the shells went on the floor with the rest of the shells and cigarette butts.

The Boeing 737-400 arrived half an hour late due to weather. Since there were no jetways, we were bussed out to the plane and stood in a cold, gray mist blowing out of the Hymettas Hills while we waited to board.

*****

A hundred and fifty-six years before, in April of 1841, Hans Christian Andersen had remarked, "Heavy rain clouds hung across the mountains of Hymettos: the weather was gray and cold." Remarkable.

*****

Takeoff was down the old Hellenikon Air Base runways I had flown off of thirty-five years before. Greek Air Force planes were parked near some of the old hangars. I saw a F-4 Phantom, a T-37A, six C-47s, and parts of several old T-33 Shooting Stars all painted desert camouflage.

*****

The route to Corfu was south out of Athens, then west passing just south of Piraeus (Atki Posidonos). A snowy Mount Parnassos, at 2457m, stood out among the snow covered mountains to the north. We crossed the Gulf of Saronica as hundreds of sailboats replaced the Greek and Persian fleets. During the flight briefing the flight attendents had announced that we were not to take pictures over Athens. Security?

We passed over the island of Salamis near the site of the Greek victory over the Persian fleet in 480 B.C.. Landfall was over Corinth of Bible fame. Our track took us along the northern shore of the Peleponesos and down the length of the Gulf of Corinth. The snow covered mountains wispered out loud that it was still winter in April. Mountains of central Greece rose over 2,000 meters (about 6,000 feet).

Small fishing villages hung tightly to the narrow beaches. Náfpaktos, known to the Venetians as Leptanos, was the site of a large Venetian castle. There was a decisive naval battle in 1571 when a Christian coalition fleet, under the command of John of Austria, won a decisive victory over the Ottoman Turks. In this battle, the Spanish author and patriot, Cervantes, lost an arm to a cannonball.

Further to the west stood snow covered Mount Zygos. The city of Messolóngi hugged the Gulf. This was where the British poet, Lord Byron, died of swamp fever (probably malaria). Byron had contributed much of his personal fortune to the Greek War of Independence. In January, 1824, he was made commander of the 5000 resistance troops in Messolóngi. He caught a fever and died on April 19, 1824. Byron is considered a national hero with a street named after him -Vironos- in many Greek cities. In 1826, after a year long siege by the Turks, the 9,000 people in Messolóngi tried to break out and retreat to Mount Zygos. They were betrayed and ambushed by Albanian mercenaries. The enraged French, English and Russians sent a combined fleet to negotiate with the Turks. On the night of October 20, 1897, this fleet of 27 warships met 89 Turkish and Egyptian warships of Ibrahim Pasha in Ormós Navarínou (Navarion Bay) near Pílos to discuss a cease fire. During the night, shooting erupted and the Turks lost, 53 ships to none. Greek independence was assured.

*****

Byron's Contribution

Lord Byron came to look at Greece
but stayed to lead and died
An inflamed European fleet at Navarion Bay
sunk a superior fleet, the Pahsa's pride
Then Greece, inspired, its freedom won
the art world's loss
bought freedom not denied

*****

Intensive farming was evident on the delta of the Ahéloos River which drained the Pindus mountains. Here we turned north up the Ionian Sea to Kefalloniá, the first of the Heptanese or Seven Ionian Islands, with mile-high mountains and subtropical valleys. We crossed the island of Lefkádha (Lefkas) with Cape Lefkádas where the poet Sappho threw herself into the sea from the Leucadian Rock over the love of Phaon. Itháki (generally accepted as Homer's Ithaca) crawled beneath our plane. We finally crossed Paxi before landing on Corfu at the southern end of the Adriatic about dark.

*****

Durrell discussed the origin of the island's name in *Prospero's Cell*. The current etymology for Corfu is from a Byzantine corruption of *Polis ton Koryphon, a* term meaning "twin peaks", describing the old fort and the original settlement. It might also have come from the Greek, korpos, meaning "gulf". Durrell's term for Corfu was Corcyra. This, and the current demotic term, Kérkyra, appear to relate to the island's shape, possibly, kerkos, meaning "a tail" or, kerkobros, for "fish" or, kerkis, for "thigh bone".

*****

As we left the shuttle bus from the plane, I noticed an armored car on the ramp in front of the terminal. Several soldiers with machine guns were on duty, but there was no obvious of tension.

It was about nine P.M. local time when we got the luggage. This was about 32 hours on my body clock since we left the house, and I was feeling it.

We caught a taxi to our condo on Goúvia Bay. The trip took us through a maze of narrow streets, and the only landmark I remember was the spire of the Church of St. Spyridon with its red top and collection of antennas.

*****

After we checked in, I took the bags to the room. It was cold so I turned on the electric heat, and we went to eat. Lunch was at the condo's taverna - a Greek salad, soup, a *pikilía* (which is a plate of assorted *mezédhes)*, and bottled water. I had a glass of Ouzo and was ready to crash for the night.

*****

III

I'm still wide awake at 4 AM, and my body thinks it is mid afternoon. Its just three more hours till I get ready to go to work. Might as well stay up and get some more notes typed while they're still fresh.

*****

Sunday morning. I was up just as the sun was rising into a silver and platinum sky of high cirrus clouds from behind the headland of the bay. Silhouettes of tall, stiletto-thin cypress trees shot above the olive trees and arbutus still in shadow. The Old Fort on Cape Sidero at Corfu Town and a passing merchant ship were embedded in the blue haze that divided the real sky from the sky reflected on the flat surface of the bay. Above Corfu Town peeked the distant snow-covered Píndus mountains, on the mainland about 20 km east. Prominent peaks included the 5440 ft peak near Paramithiá where lived the Oracle of Zeus mentioned by Homer and Herodotus, and a nameless 5,925 ft peak up north near the Albanian border. (Also near Paramithiá is the Áheron River, one of the proposed entrances to Hades.)

The view through the window was like a postcard scene. Tempted, I went out to enjoy the sunrise and look at the beach but immediately returned for a sweater. The temperature was in the low 40's F.

Gouvia Bay to East

Condo Complex

The beach was of flat, rounded stones and silty sand that had been partially covered with trucked in sand. This was the case on many of the tourist beaches, like painting the roses red.

I walked out on a spit of land which turned out to be a spoil bank from dredging a drainage channel. It was in the spoil that I noticed the first shells including Truncate Donax (*Donax trunculus),* terebras, two Venus clams (*Venerupis decussata* and *V. aurea*) and a couple of land snails. Glasswort (*Salicornia europaea*) and a bush that looked like wolfberry, locally called the Tea Tree (*Lycium schweinfurthii*), grew near the salty shore. The tide had just turned and was coming in and the water was very cold and clear. Numerous Snakelock Anemones (*Anemonia sulcata*) of the family *Cribrinidae* were attached to rocks just below the low tide line.

The rising sun back-lit the trees across the bay giving the scene two dimensions like a Greek shadow play without Karaghiosis and friends.

The intensifying light slowly lit tan strips of beach, the white houses nestled in the trees, and the white church on the point.

A Venetian armory had been located nearby. In June of 1716, during the seventh and last of the Venetian-Turkish wars, about 30,000 Turkish soldiers came ashore, many of them landing on the beaches of Goúvia Bay. It is hard to imagine Turkish warriors wading ashore on this cool and quiet April morning. They were met by John Schulemberg, with 8,000 Venetian mercenaries and local volunteers. The Turks, having lost some 15,000 troops, withdrew on August 11, 1716. This was right after a vicious storm had hit, and it was rumored that Saint Spyridon had appeared threatening the Turks with a flaming sword. The colors of the sunrise and sunsets and the fast hitting storms out of the Adriatic make this easy to believe. A local celebration is held on this day to commemorate the victory.

Days of Conquest

For three thousand years
more time has been spent on war
than peace and a sea of tears
has been wept
for the dead of a dozen cultures,
the bloody message clear -
FREEDOM
will always live in Kérkyra

*****

Looking at the flat surface reflecting the sky it was easy to see Goúvina Bay as the home for Imperial Airlines flying boats prior to WWII. Must have been beauttiful.

*****

About ten, we went to the office to check the bus schedule, tours, groceries and a map. We found we were almost alone in the complex since the season did not officially begin until 1 May. There were no tours, the condo's minimart would not be open for another week and the bus ran every two hours on Sunday. We decided to rent a car, a little Fiat Panda convertible stick shift, for $200 US a week including insurance.

Aside from quickly relearning how to drive a stick shift, the first trip into Corfu Town was an adventure in itself.

The road varied from one to three lanes of sorts, with or without shoulders and with intermittent construction. The most scenic portion was the two km along the shore from Kontokali to Alykes. I stopped to absorb the view of the succession of the Píndus Mountains on the Greek mainland and snow covered Píndus peaks above the dark blue Ionian Sea. The road swung east passing the port before diving into the narrow one-way streets of the old town.

*****

We finally found Dimokratías St., the main road along the bay, about noon. I parked near the entrance to the Paleó Froúrio (Old Fort) on the Esplanade. We walked across the Esplanade for lunch under a clear blue sky with what must have been half the island's population.

Downtown

The Esplanade had a soccer field which was being used by a man tossing a Frisbee to his dog. There was also a bandstand and several statues. Landscaping was a hodgepodge of plants, as appeared to be the custom in Greece. Chinese privet, Pittisporum, date palms, figs, olive trees, Aloe, the pink blossoms of Judas Trees that looked like Redbuds, almonds and Plane Trees were mixed with some formal plantings of annual flowers.

The olive and Plane trees of the park had been "polled" or cut back to the trunk to induce numerous new branches. Pollarding maintains a relatively healthy tree of uniform size and shape for formal settings or where space is limited or to provide firewood.

*****

About two P.M., some shops began to close for siesta. We headed for the archeology museum that stayed open until three. The museum was in an old Venetian home and was one of the few air conditioned buildings on the island. Showcases displayed artifacts dating back 4000 years including coins and small metal or glass items. Several funerary works in marble traced Greek, Roman and Venetian occupation. A prize piece was the Gorgon pediment from the Doric Temple of Artemis (590-580 B.C.) with the Gorgon flanked by a pair of leopanthers. Another prize was an Archaic lion found near the tomb of Menekrates.

The route north out of town wound around finally passing the port and the Neó Froúrio (New Fort) that I remembered from 35 years before.

*****

We drove out past the condo intending on going up the beach road towards Pyrgi but missed the turn. We missed a lot of turns during the week for several reasons. All the signs were in Greek, only some had English subtitles, and many of the signs were missing. Many of the roads looked like trails of only a lane and a half or less wide. It was often difficult to tell the main roads from the "secondary" roads. Some of the roads were not on the map or had been upgraded from trails to roads. Speed limits and distances were in kilometers. The map size was the same, but the scale was different - on the same size map of Texas the 70 mile length of the island would equal almost a thousand miles and the 8 miles from our condo to downtown Corfu looked about the same as the 200 miles from San Antonio to Houston. Anyway, we were just out for a ride.

*****

We drove through hills covered with Valonia Oak (*Quercus aegilops*), arbutus (*Arbutus unedo*), Italian Cypress trees (*Cupressus sempervirens*), and dotted with Judas Trees (*Cercis siliquastrum*) and pink almonds (*Prunus dulcis*) in full bloom. Highway 15 climbed over the rolling Megas Kremm Hills and passed through the town of Ágios Markos which was founded by Cretans in 1669. Serpentine highways 23 and 26 led us through Sokraki, Zigos and Sqourádes.

On highway 29, we stopped at a taverna on the southwest edge of Mount Pantokratos for a cold drink. The view from the terrace towards the south included the central half of the island. From about 3000 ft altitude, we could see from Pirgi to Corfu and the Achillion to the east, the length of the Livadi Ropa (Ropa Valley) and the Ionian Sea on the west.

A little further north, over the divide, we could see Rodo and most of the other towns on the north coast. The rocky coast and the snow covered mountains of Albania were clearly visible. Shadows of the northern most Greek Heptanese Islands - Othonoi, Erikousa and Samotharki - were visible twenty miles to the northwest in haze in the Strait of Otranto.

*****

A trail, alias highway 33, took us west to Nimfes. We turned south on highways 32, 27, and 25 to Kastellani continuing on 25 west to Lakones and the beach at Paleokastrítsa. The narrow, winding roads led through groves of olive trees on terraced hillsides.

The Overlook

Phaceans, Spartans, and Byzantine Turks
to this very vantage point trod
to watch for Vandals, Venetians
and others from the north.
Priests, in the Holy name of God,
built monasteries and temples and chapels
and tramped these stony hills unshod.
All paused to briefly contemplate
the soft Mediterranean view
and were awed

*****

The olive trees, gnarled and twisted, looked more like a bunch of small trees braided together by a blind novice. Olive magazines, the sheds where the presses and other processing equipment were stored, looked like abandoned homes for trolls. Many of the black plastic fabric cloths used to capture the olives were still on the ground. A few of the nets had been rolled and were sitting in the crotch of the tree. Olive season was nearing its end.

The olive harvest season ran from October through May and there were still some olives falling. Olive processing, fruit picking and wine making were formerly major sources of income. These occupations now extend the working season for many people in the tourist industry through the winter.

Olive Tree

Several small blue and white Greek Orthodox chapels on hillsides contrasted with the pink blossums of the Judas Trees and gray-green olives and arbutus.

*****

We passed through Lakones and, from about 600 feet, we could see Liapadon Bay and the village of Paleokastrítsa. Near vertical cliffs dropped into the sea and were accented by small, white beaches. With a light chop stirring the surface, the sea now imperfectly reflected the light blue of the sky.

We stopped several times to take pictures of the changing view below - condos; hotels; the yacht club; a suspicious cat eyeing me from a rusting tin rooftop. Again, the pink of Judas Trees blazed out of the greygreen olives and dark green cedars.

Lipadou Bay

Almond Trees and Buildings

Greek Cat

After a few thousand shifting of gears, we were again at sea level. The beaches that had appeared white from above were composed of rounded granite and marble stones - white, pink, yellow and mottled - and partially covered by truck loads of tan granitic sand. I walked about half a mile of the beach and found some drilled Coquina, two small species of clams and four species of land snails. Every available space was occupied by housing, condos or tavernas. Quite a few people were on the beach since this was a beautiful sunny Sunday afternoon.

*****

Durrell proposed that the island of Fanos (now called Othónoi), about twenty miles northwest of Corfu, was the Homeric island where Ulysses met Calypso and that Paleokastritsa might be the home of the Phaecians where Ulysses met Nausicaa. But then, he also posed the possibility that Kanoni and Kassiopi could be the Phaceian capitol. Historians back Kanoni.

*****

The trip back over highway 25 was through the rolling hills of the Ropa Valley. The roadsides and many hillsides were covered with wildflowers. The most common flowers were the yellow *Brassica fruticulosa*, white composites and bushy magenta Cretan Mallow (*Lavertera cretica*).

*****

About dark, we decided to go out for supper. If navigating in the daylight was bad, the night driving was worse. The 180 degree climbing turns without being able to see where the turns stopped turning were great fun. We finally found that the New Wave Greek Taverna we were looking for was no longer taverning. Supper was at the Taverna Gloopa somewhere near Kastania, a Greek salad and roasted lamb. We managed to bypass most of Corfu Town and were back to the room by 2300.

*****

IV

It's 5 AM and I'm still not sleepy. I can type another hour then its time to go to work for the first day in three weeks. Maybe I'll sleep tonight.

*****

Monday morning, I was up to see the sunrise, all gold and peach, with purple clouds reflecting off the smooth half of the bay. The temperature was about forty so I went back to a warm bed for another hour.

We left about 0900 for Corfu to look at the old town. Parking on the Esplanade cost a hundred drachmas (about 40 cents) an hour on business days. The shops were just opening so we had breakfast and took some pictures of the narrow Venetian marble streets with parked motor scooters and laundry strung across the streets. Wrought iron railing and wooden shutters were common.

Pigeons dominated some of the squares. Flocks of pigeons were fed by adults, scattered by kids, and chased by hungry dogs expecting to share the pigeon's lunch.

Some of the buildings needed a paint job, but many were being repaired and painted in anticipation of the opening of tourist season. The rugged old buildings may be picturesque, but to me they show a gross lack of infrastructure maintenance.

*****

Aghios Spyridonas Church

Central Square

We shopped and looked until noon. There were numerous T-shirt shops and high-end botiques. Jewelry shops and leather goods were the most common shops. Jewelry was the good stuff, well designed solid gold or silver.

After lunch, we decided to go find Achillion, the Italian Renaissance villa built in 1890 for the Empress Elisabeth of Austria. We missed a turn again and were half across the island before we realized it, so we continued on to Pelekas and the beach at Glyfáda.

The road wound through the hills and olive groves at the south end of the Ropa Valley. Wildflowers were rampant. Blackberries (*Rubus sanctus*) were just leafing out. Ferns were unfurling. Passion Flower (*Passiflora caerulea*) was beginning to climb. The clover (*Trifolium speciosum*) had a purple-blue flower. Course White Horehound (*Marrubium vulgare*) grew three feet tall. Two Plantains (*Plantago seraria* and *P. squarosa*) and several white composites were accented by half inch blue Euphorbia (*Euphorbia characias*). Peach colored mallows and wild roses (*Rosa sempervirens*) grew along the road.

I mistook a private road into a farm for the highway. This was fortunate since there were birds flitting around the reeds near a drainage ditch. These were identified as a Reed Warbler (*Acrocephalus scirpaceus*) and a Ringed Ouzel (*Turdus torquetas*).

We passed through Pelekas and down the switchbacks to Glyfáda. This beach was deep tan granite sand stretching far to the south. Loess walls twenty feet tall backed the beach. The tide was out leaving a three foot step to the forebeach.

Glyfada Beach

The water was cold with low waves. No shells were present except in the high tide drift - Ribbed Mediterranean Limpet (*Patella ferruginca)*, Whitish Gibbula (*Gibbula albida*), a wormshell (*Vermicularia arenaria*) and some barnacle spat. The taverna was not yet open for the season. Plants on the beach included Arundo (*Arundo donax*), Erodium, and several small composites. Landscape plants at the taverna included European Holly (*Ilex aquifolium*), Geraniums, iceplant (*Mesembryanthemum crystacrystallinum*), the two-needle Austrian Pine (*Pinus nigra*), wisteria, and oranges. Blue-leafed Wattle (*Acacia cyanophyla*), a yellow flowered Acicia, grew along the road.

*****

We passed again through Pelekas. It was too late for lunch and too early for supper. Near the village of Ágios Nickolas there was what appeared to be a roadkilled snake. I stopped and moved it off the road for inspection. I was surprised to find external ear openings, eyelids and no visible teeth. This was a glass lizard (<u>Ophisaurus</u> <u>sp</u>.) in the family, *Anguidae*. It was a male about three feet long with the vent 14 inches from the snout. Diagnostic lateral folds extended from behind the head to the vent. It was dark brown on top and tan below.

Down one of the narrow roads we passed an old woman in black pushing a wheelbarrow full of hay. A little further on was a wisteria vine that covered a cedar tree a good thirty feet tall. Really magnificent. I stopped to take pictures of the wisteria. As the old woman approached, she asked, in Greek, where I was from. I told her I was from Texas, and she replied that Greek weather was cold, not hot like Texas weather.

*****

Wisteria

85

We picked a taverna near the port for supper. Carol had a slipper lobster. I had steamed fish in Corfu sauce and a grilled snapper washed down with a half liter of retsina. The slipper lobster was tougher and not as sweet as the Atlantic Homerid or tropicalPanulurid lobsters.

*****

Off to Market

V

Wednesday morning at 3 A.M.. I slept two hours longer than last night. I may finish this by the time I catch up with my jet lag.

*****

Tuesday morning, we left about 0900 to go around the north end of the island. The office was not open yet and we were running short of drachmas. "Not to worry - there will be plenty of cambios to change money", I thought. But the season was not yet upon them, and we did not find one open all day. The bright side of this was that car and scooter rentals were not open either, and the tourists were not out.

This time we stayed to the right and found Highway 14 to go up the coast. We passed Dassia. At Ipsos, we stopped at four closed cambios before giving up. A stream discharged into the bay in the middle of town. The mouth of the stream was full of red mullet.

Continuing north to Pirgi, we took a short detour to Agios Markos to see the Church of the Pantokrator and the Byzantine Church of Aghios Merkourios. Access to the Church of the Pantokrator, about 100 feet up the cliffside, was up several flights of stone steps lined with cascading geraniums and grape vines. About half way up the hill was the church's terraced garden with potatoes, artichokes, tomatoes, grapes, figs and surrounded by olive trees. Growing out of the walls were two species of Gallium (*Gallium mollugo* and *G. heldreichii*) and several ferns. Cracks in the steps supported grape hyacinth (*Muscaari neglectum*), mallows, Tuberous Crane's-bill (*Geranium tuberosum*) and Long-beaked Storksbill (*Erodium gruinum*).

A black capped Coal Tit (*Parus ater*) with his conspicuous white nape, sat on budding grape vines.

Neither church was open to the public, so we returned to the coast road. We passed through Pirgi, Barbati, and Nissaki and, then, went about six hundred feet down a steep twisting trail, lined with Fodder Vetch, to the beach at Kendroma. This beautiful little community had rooms for rent, a picnic area and camp ground, a small "supermarket" and three closed tavernas.

Church of Aghios Markos

Everyone was busy painting everything in sight. I found no shells amongst the rocks on the beach. A white butterfly and another that looked like a Fritillary crossed the road on the way back up to the highway.

*****

Back at the top, we stopped at several overlooks including that of Kalami with a view of Durrell's "white house" mentioned in his book, *Prospero's Cell*.

It was about a mile across the strait to Albania and, although the weather was calm where we were, we could see waves smashing on the rocky point nearest Corfu. Several ships were passing through this narrow passage. An acquaintance had told me of his cruise to the Greek Islands in December when their luggage had been tossed around their cabin and waves were breaking over the ship while traversing this channel.

Kalami Bay and Durrell's House

We stopped for lunch at Kassíopi where the Emperor Nero once sang at the altar of Jupiter. It was after the typical lunch time and everything was on siesta. There was no one in sight but a painter and his five sidewalk superintendents painting one of the discos. They were carefully pointing out every spot the painter missed. We found a taverna with crisp fried anchovies and chips for me and the local cat. Carol had bifstek with rice.

*****

This northeast shoulder of the island along Apraos Bay receives the north wind and a number of streams draining off Mount Pantokrator. There was less vegetation and no villages for the 10 km to Agios Spiridon on Spiridonas Point. The brackish Andinioti Lagoon stretched a little over two miles between Point Spiridonas and point Agios Ekaterinis. The lagoon was bordered by reed beds. About half the lagoon was open water. Gulls and a few Great White Herons were present, particularly near the big fish trap. This lagoon and Lake Korrison to the south had been hunting preserves for whoever the ruling class was at the time.

The snow-covered 6,926-foot Mount Qendrevicac, in Albania, was clearly visible. The surrounding land area was sparsely vegetated with few small trees and some Judas Trees and Tamarisk (*Tamerix tetragyna*) were in bloom. A colorful European Stone-chat (*Saxicola torquata rubicola*) was perched in an orphan olive tree.

The road turned towards the southwest through several small farming communities with olives, apricots, peaches, grapes and some truck crops such as artichokes and potatoes. The beach was not visible from the road. Two big resort developments stretched between the road to the beach. What were once the small fishing villages of Acharavi and Roda was now one continuous tourist center with apartments, tavernas, discos and rental centers for cars and scooters. I walked a half mile of the sanded rocky beach at Roda in a cold wind with waves breaking over the mandraki and found neither shells nor trash.

Olive Trees and Wild Cabbage

Another 5 km through groves of old olives trees and new middle class homes took us to Sidari. This town had a well developed tourist industry.

*****

The road began to climb Mount Rekini. The road turned serpentine with steep hills and 180 degree turns. There was almost no traffic until we neared Ágios Athanasios. Here, we came upon a line of cars following a funeral. The hearse drove at walking speed and about a hundred people followed it down the road and into the cemetery. Even with this delay, we were home in about an hour.

****

According to the guidebooks, the sunset seen from Kaiser Wilhelm's estate, known as the Kings Throne, was not to be missed. On the map, it looked like driving from San Antonio to Laredo but was actually about 15 miles, if you don't count the up and down distance. We left an hour before sunset and drove through the olive groves, the ups and the downs and around the rounds to Pelekas. A sign pointed the way, but we could have just followed about fifty young people at a snail's pace for about a mile up the narrow road to the top of the hill.

Sunset from the Kings Throne

Half the lower floor of this large two story villa, the former ball room, was a restaurant with a large open patio. The view from the parking area to the east displayed the entire Ropa Valley and the Pindus mountains on the mainland and north to Mount Pantokrator. From the patio, the Ionian Sea stretched to the horizon to the south and west.

The Kaiser had built an observatory of sorts about fifteen feet high with a bench and telescope. This was located at the end of the parking lot about a hundred yards north of the house. It was in disrepair, and a big olive tree had grown up and blocked the view.

The wind was blowing and cold, so we drank hot chocolate and waited for the sunset out of the cold in the dining room. I went out to the watch the sunset use up its pallet of reds and blues and shot several pictures of the golden sun in an orange sky as it sunk into a deep purple sea and pulled the colored clouds behind it. The crowd dispersed into the night as couples and small groups flowed down the road to town. We drove back to Goúvia in the dark.

*****

VI

I'm bright-eyed and bushy-tailed at a little after four A.M., and its still a long ways to sunrise.

Wednesday came in a little hazy. On the way to breakfast, we stopped at a leather shop. I bought several leather belts, and Carol bought a leather purse. At least one of the belts was knockoff because Levi Strauss was located in Kalifornia.

I asked the owner if he could make a leather bag like the well-worn canvas book bag I had picked up in Canada. "Certainly. Come back tonight." When we returned about dark the bag had been finished. He had made several others and already sold one. He said he would call it the "Carl" model.

*****

We drove to town and parked near the old fort. Carol settled in a sidewalk cafe to read while I went through the fort.

When the Roman empire had been divided into two parts in A.D. 337, Kérkira was included in the eastern part which became the Byzantine Empire. Raids by the Vandals, Goths and Saracens over the next 300 years devastated the island. The Goth raid in 562 A.D., lead by Totila, resulted in the construction of a fort on two peaks of Point Kápo-Sidero. This became the nucleus for the *Polis ton Koryphon* or City of the Peaks, the present town of Corfu. The city continued to grow the outside the walls as the *xopoli* or *borgo* sections which are now the Esplanade and the old section of downtown Corfu.

*****

The entrance to the Old Fort had once been a drawbridge. It was now a two lane bridge 60 meters (200 feet) long across the *Contrafossa* or moat. The moat was about 30 feet wide and 30 feet below the bridge to water level. Boats are berthed in the moat, and storage sheds are built against the landward side. The Contrafossa was built by the Venetians in the early 15th century and effectively cut the fort off from the mainland.

Further modernization and the fortification of the two high points led to the fort being called two peaks or *korfi*.

Corfu from the fort

Old Fort from South

After the Turkish siege in 1537, the two citadels were connected and the moat widened. The *Esplanade* or *Spianada* was constructed by demolishing everything outside the wall within cannon range to allow a clear field of fire in all directions. The siege of 1571 led to the construction of more walls and a new fort (*Fortezza Nuova* in Italian) completed in 1576. Buildings inside the fortifications were built 3-5 stories high because of space constraints.

Across the bridge, the road passed through the original city gate currently occupied by administrative offices. To the right was a piazza that was once the site of the commander's house. The piazza now contains a summer theater and the Doric style Church of Ághios Géorgios built by the British in 1840. On the lower level of walls overlooking the harbor are traces of the old firing positions with a clear field of fire of Garitsas Bay and the mainland to the south and west.

Marble steps, polished by a million footfalls, lead to a second wall that surrounds most of the promontory. The tiled road lead past a well with the halloed lion of Venice. It lead up through a tunnel under the second wall, past a prison and storage area, then past where the palace of the Governor General had stood. He had a picturesque vista overlooking the little harbor at Mandraki. The view covers west and north from the Esplanade to the commercial port and the New Fort. There were rumors of tunnels leading outwards from the fort.

The road continued around and up through the cypress and sweet gum trees, serenaded by sound of whistling wings of Collared Doves, to the third level and protective wall. This wall contained the Land Tower and the Sea Tower on the two peaks with the British barracks block sitting between them. The Land Tower contained a lighthouse and antenna farm and a view of a quarter of the island.

*****

I left the fort and crossed the Esplanade to find Carol and a soda. We walked a block to the Museum of Asian Art in the former British governor's home. A statue of the British Lord High Commissioner, Sir Fredrick Adam, dressed as a Roman, stood looking out over the Esplanade. The Museum had some Asian art on display but the structure itself was the attraction. The throne room and the ball room was a display of the height of British Imperialism.

*****

A cab driver was found who could give us a short tour of Kanóni. We had tried to find it on our own but got lost in the not-user-friendly one-way streets. Driving south on Dímokratias, we passed near the monument to King Menecrates dating to about 600 B.C.. Over the past 2,500 years, the bay had filled in and the shoreline was now a thousand feet to the east.

The wall of the ancient city of Paleopolis crossed the isthmus with a gate spanning the present Alkinoou Street. The wall extended from north of the ancient agora or market place and the harbor of Alkinoos on the east that were mentioned by Thucydides in his history of the Peleponesian Wars. The harbor's narrow mouth had been protected by two guard towers. The eastern tower was found during the construction of the Church of Aghios Athanasios built in the 18th century in the village of Anemomylos. Alkinoos Harbor had completely silted in and was located under Anemomylos.

The wall ran atop the ridge south of the present Chrys. Smyrnis street and the route to the airport westward then south past the Temple of Artemis to Hyllaic Harbor on Chalikiopolous Lagoon. The city dates from about 700 B.C. and is possibly the Phaeacian capitol and Nausica's island mentioned by Homer.

*****

We slowly passed by the archeology site of the Temple of Zeus and into an area of new condos and apartments to Kanoni. The cliffline overlooks two islets that form the trademark of Corfu. The nearer and smaller of the two is Vlacherna connected to the mainland by a causeway. It is occupied by the Convent and Church of Vlacherna. The other islet is called Pontikonissi or Mouse Island. This, also, has a church, an 11th or 12th century Church of Christ the Pantokrator.

A narrow causeway for foot or bicycle traffic crosses the harbor mouth from Kanoni to Perama. A large permanent fish trap just south of the end of the single runway takes advantage of the changing tides. The airfield, built on fill, runs the length of Chalikiopoulous Bay.

Returning, we passed the Analipsis and turned into the grounds of the villa of Mon Repos. Mon Repos was built in 1831 as the summer residence of the king and had later became state property. Nearby were the spring and Temple of Kardaki. The temple was found while investigating an interruption of the spring flow caused when part of the buried temple collapsed.

On the way back to the car, we swung through Anemomylos to see the 12th century Church of SS Jason and Sosipater and the ruins of the Basilica of Paleopolis or Aghia Kerkyra. The Basilica was built in the 5th century A.D. by the Bishop of Corfu after removing some pagan shrines on the site. It was destroyed in the sixth century, replaced by a smaller church. It was destroyed again in the 11th century, replaced in the 12th century, renovated in 1537 and finally destroyed by the bombing raids of WWII.

*****

We returned to the condo about 5 P.M., Carol went in to crash while I drove about a mile south and stopped at the Corfu Shell Museum. The large new facility, run by Sagias Napoleon, was not yet open for business. It will feature not only fine specimen shells, but many other marine artifacts. Sagias and his family were unpacking and painting in anticipation of the tourist season. He had worked in Australia for several years and had recently returned to open a shell museum and shop.

Back at the condo, I walked about a half mile to a local minimarket. There was no such thing as ziplock bags. I bought some bananas, apples and oranges and another quart of irradiated milk and walked back passing the local bakery and meat market, which were closed, and a hardware store that also sold fishing supplies.

For supper, we hit one of the local tavernas. It was less than satisfactory with frozen food and dehydrated soup. I tried a shot of the local brandy called Kumquat. It tasted like tangerine peel and was very good.

****

Fish trap and airport

Mouse Island

Vlacharna Convent

VII

It's now 0500 and I'm still wide awake. Writing about all that running around makes me wonder where the energy came from.

*****

Thursday morning. I was up with the sun and watched the swallows feed with dashes and dips among the condo units.

About 9 A.M., we left to drive to Kavos on the south end of the island. Bypassing downtown, we found Kanalia and turned south on highway 5 to the turnoff east to Perama. (The turn was easy to find heading south but the sign was missing if you were coming from the south.)

There were several scenic views from Perama of the Kanoni, the islands of Vlacherna and Pontikonissi and the Ionian Sea towards the Greek mainland. The road turned south and descended to sea level along an area known as the Cote d'Azur of Corfu but with rocky beaches. Numerous hotels were located along the road and bus loads of German tourists were checking in. We passed part of the Kaiser's bridge. It had been built by Kaiser Wilhelm II to cross the road from his estate to the beach. The bridge had been dismantled to allow truck traffic passage.

*****

The next town was Benitses. It was described as a small fishing village. Tourist fever had attacked and it was full of discos and fastfood.

Down the beach road were the villages of Tzaki Strongilis and Aghios Ioannis Peristeron and the towns of Episkopiana and Moraitika. We crossed the Messogi River and, at the town of Messogi, made another wrong turn.

It turned out to be a beautiful, narrow, and practically deserted road leading to the little communities of Spillo and Aghios Dimitrios, the village of Chlomos, and then down a continuously twisting road to the town of Linia.

Twisted olive trees. Old men walking to town. Men and women riding sidesaddle on donkeys. Greenbriar and ferns. Magpies (*Pica pica*) and Fly Catchers. Fantastic vistas of Limni (Lake) Korission and Aghios Georgios.

Aghios Georgios was a well developed tourist center so we turned off at the road to the village of Santa Barbara and its beach. There were few shells on the tan granite sand. Loess banks behind the beach extended up about thirty feet and had been carved like 3-D graffiti.

*****

Carol began to itch from a reaction to sulfa drug she had started just before we left on vacation. I drove to Argyrades and stopped at two public clinics to find they were not open for the season yet. We stopped at a pharmacy to get some Benedril and headed back to Corfu via Messogi and the beach road. The other two alternative roads skipped along the tops of two ranges of hills. We were at the condo by two to find that their doctor was not on island until the next week and that thee doctors downtown were closed from two until six.

We found the doctor's office shortly before six. He was by himself. He spoke good English having gone to school in England. After concurring that a sulfa drug allergy was the problem, he recommended a shot to get the relief started to be followed by the Benadryl we had bought. He gave me the prescription which I took around the corner to a pharmacy. They gave me a syringe and the medicine which I took back to the doctor for administration. All this cost $26 US for the doctor and $8 for the medicine.

*****

We were back at the condo by 7:30 and stopped by the leather shop. He had already sold one of my "Carl" book bags.

*****

Landscaping at the condo was a bit of a hodgepodge. Ligustrum, Pittisporum, Date Palm, Aleppo Pine, yucca, Arbovittis, Judas Trees, a few olives, Oleander, roses and iceplant. They cut the Bermudagrass lawn at an inch - way too short.

*****

Hale-Bopp comet was bright in the west as we returned from dinner.

*****

101

VIII

0600. At the rate I'm going, I will probably be ready to go to sleep about mid afternoon.

*****

Its Friday already. There was a white heron and several gulls on the lagoon. Migration must be getting started.

We left about nine to find Achillion, the palace of Elizabeth, Empress of Austria. Skirting downtown, we went to Kanalia and took the road south to the turnoff to Gastouri. The road was wide and well maintained since numerous busses took tourists to visit Achillion. The gently winding road passed a number of expensive villas before Gastouri. We parked in the bus turnaround and walked to the entrance.

Elizabeth had first seen this estate in 1861. She finally bought it from Petros Vrailas Armenis in 1889. Two famous Italian architects were hired to do the design and construction, and the house was finished in 1891. During the interval, she saw to the decoration including the frescos on the walls. She purchased or had made a number of statues for the gardens. Here she lived until her assassination in Geneva, on 10 September, 1898.

The estate was abandoned until it was bought by William II, Emperor of Germany. He used it as a summer residence until 1914 when Germany lost the war. It was then used as the military headquarters and hospital by the Franco-Serbian force that occupied Corfu in 1915. The Treaty of Versailles, in 1919, gave Achillion to the Greek government. During WWII, it was again used as a military headquarters and hospital, this time, by the Germans and Italians. In 1962, it was rented to the Greek Casino Company who renovated it. They used the top two floors as a casino and converted the ground floor into a museum. Since 1983, the Greek Tourist Organization (GTO) has run the casino and the museum.

*****

Achillion Yard Art

The structure was impressive but the crowds and the subdued lighting made the museum almost a waste of time. The guide books were available with good pictures provide a much better idea of the history and grandeur of the palace.

The well maintained grounds were impressive except for the many irritating multilingual signs telling people not to pick the flowers. Numerous marble and bronze statues were well placed and, so far, had not shown much damage from air pollution. Many of the legendary views from the estate had been eliminated by the growth of palms and other landscape trees planted on the grounds.

*****

We left Achillion the way we had come and then headed west and south through the oaks and olives to Agios Matheos. Paramóna, with many large new buildings, could be seen two kilometers and five hundred feet down hill on the beach. The south facing hills had sparse vegetation, while those facing north or west were covered with olive and cypress trees.

Agios Matheos was one of the largest towns on the island. It had a lot of nice homes and public facilities but did not appear to cater excessively to the tourist.

Three km south of Ágios Matheos was a turnoff to Gardiki. About a km down the trail, where the road turned south, sat the remains of a Byzantine fort constructed in the 13th century. Built of stone recycled from earlier Roman spring house, the octagonal walls and eight towers covered about five acres. The walls were still standing, and the interior appeared to have had an attempted restoration. A mass of arbutus and other shrubs grew over the floor and on a large rubble pile in the center. The south wall had been incorporated into the adjacent farm complex.

Just past the fort and around the corner was a taverna and a pumping station drawing water from a spring. A large mass of cane was inhabited by magpies (Pica pica), chickens, donkeys, and a Great Tit (*Parus major*) with black wings, yellow sides and white cheeks.

*****

Byzantine Fort at Gardiki

We continued south, past several large greenhouses being cleaned of tomato and cucumber vines that supplied the Greek salads. Another greenhouse had flowers and potted plants with many large ornamentals sitting outside. A tree nursery was growing pines and olive trees. There were also several small potato and artichoke fields.

The road ended crossing the north end of Lake Korission. Two tavernas on the beach were not yet open. Small hard clams and ceriths were on the beach and in the lake. Spike rushes growing in the lake supported a species of land snail.

On the way back, we passed two women taking produce to market packed on a donkey. One of the women wore black with a white scarf, the traditional clothing of a widow. We also passed a large flock of sheep, the first we had seen on the island

*****

We made one more short stop in Corfu for last minute shopping, and went back to Goúvia Bay. We checked out of the condo and reserved a taxi for six in the morning.

On the way to supper, we stopped at the leather shop and met two women that had also been there all week. Surprise. Surprise. We had not seen them before. One was from near San Antonio, and the other was from Washington DC, and they were flying out on the plane with us.

Returning from supper, we packed up and were ready to begin the next chapter of this adventure.

*****

Anything else I would have liked to see or do on Corfu? Maybe more time walking, especially around downtown Corfu and Kanoni. Maybe make it all the way to Kavos. If it was a bit warmer, I'd like to do some snorkeling. The only time we saw any kids was on a school outing - maybe find out what kids do in their off time. Check on the rumors of the tunnels under the old fort? Why not. As an environmental engineer I'd like to look at the water and sewage disposal systems and more into the farming and building processes. I'm just curious. A month to six weeks would be about enough.

*****

Greenhouses and a trip to Market

IX

Its 3 A.M. Thursday morning. Jet lag is supposed to take a day per time zone. I hope not.

*****

It was cold and dark at 0400 Saturday morning. We cleaned out the refrigerator for breakfast and straightened up a little before the taxi arrived at 0545. Checking in with the airline, we had to pay an excess baggage fee for an extra 20 kilos (44 pounds) for the same luggage we brought with us. We had not been charged when we left Athens three times but were charged leaving both Corfu and Rhodes. Maybe this is a local gotcha.

The waiting area was cold and seemed to be full of smokers. After about twenty minutes, they announced our flight and we walked outside into the cold, damp but fresh air, and down the ramp past the armored car to the ground transport to the plane.

*****

I had a window seat this time. Our 0710 scheduled takeoff was on time. We departed over Mouse Island and into the darkness. We were in or over clouds half way to Athens before we left the frontal system behind. The front had been predicted by the previous evening by mare's tail clouds to the north and west.

A day-glo orange sun jumped out of the cottony clouds, painting the cloud tops fluorescent red-orange and shades of violet and gray. Two horizontal slashes of red-orange turned out to be the sun through a crack in the clouds and the sun reflecting off the Saronic Gulf. Mt. Zygos and Mt. Parnassos were easily recognizable, a gleaming white above the clouds. The cold air was clear and dry with fog covering the warmer valleys and the coast. Islands in the mist looked like a Zen painting.

On the approach into Athens, a hydrofoil was approaching Piraeus leaving a wake trail distinctive from the other ferries. The reddish sunrise colored cliffs towards Cape Sounion and Byron's Temple of Poseidon contrasted with the dark mottled green water in the morning sun.

We picked up the bags and checked in to the Hotel London, about a mile from the airport. The hotel had seen better days and was now a $90-a-night $30 hotel by my standards. The room was small with a low lumpy bed, a toilet that ran all night and dim lighting. It had the feeling of hotels on the beach worldwide - damp and on the edge of being moldy. It had a pool that was being renovated and solar heated hot-water heat.

*****

Back downstairs, we booked three tours for the afternoon, evening and next morning. A two dollar taxi took us to the business district of Glifádha (spelled with the revival of old Greek spelling). Thirty-five years ago this was a small village with typical small town Greek stores and a couple villas and small hotels. It was beginning to grow with American families stationed at Hellenikon (Ellinikó) Air Base. Aristotle Onassis had a villa overlooking Glifádha and kept his yacht, the yellow and white converted U.S. Navy cruiser, Caroline, anchored a mile off shore.

Tourist facilities had crept up into the Hymettus foothills and construction covered every possible inch. Dumping construction dirt and debris has added about half a mile of usable land out into the Gulf. The narrow road that once meandered along the beach to Athens had become a six to eight lane divided highway with high speed traffic. The small country town had become a collection of shops much like a mall without big stores to anchor it - fast food franchises; name brand clothing and shoe outlets; a bunch of doctor's offices and clinics; a hardware store; a bagel bakery.

Carol stopped in at a beauty shop for a tune-up. It was just like stateside but the gossip was in Greek.

*****

We were back at the hotel in time to be picked up for a tour to Cape Sounion (Soúnio). Passing yacht clubs and pay beaches, apartments and hotels of all price ranges, we flew along the foothills of Mount Hymettus, the range of hills east and south of Athens. The villages of Voúla and Kavouri flew by. We passed the hot spring called Vouliagmeni Lake where the upper class spend the winter or summer in luxury villas. For the rich, with little less time to enjoy the sun, there was the Astir Palace Hotel.

Southward along the coast, the resort villages of Lagoníssi and Anávissos and the rocky beaches around Anávissos Bay soaked up the late afternoon sun.

Across the bay was the green headland of Akrí Soúnio (Cape Sounion), the southmost tip of Attica basking in the cool spring sunshine.

Looking like a short section of white marble picket fence, the erect pillars of the 5th century B.C. Temple of Poseidon contrasted with the green hillside and the bright blue sky. Sixteen of the original 34 Doric columns are on site. Twelve stand upright.

*****

Akrí Soúnio

The traffic cop to the known world
sat on this point and
reported all that moved
in the Eastern Sea.
A temple was built to assure
protection of the patron saint.

Reconstructed for the umpteenth time,
the point and temple
draw strangers from lands unknown.

*****

A hundred or so visitors on the site and local development projects tend to spoil the moment and make decent pictures nearly impossible. This site, like most in this land with up to 7,000 years of history, contained a mix of Greek, Byzantine and other artifacts. The point had served as a lookout for any shipping in the Eastern Mediterranean and, particularly, any ships approaching or leaving Athens.

The islands of Kéa, Kithnos and Sérifos could be seen to the southeast. The island of Éyina and the eastern shore of Pelopónissos was visible to the west. The sun setting over Pelopónissos through the columns is supposed to be outstanding.

Lord Byron's signature, an example of both modern and royal graffiti, has graced one of the columns since 1810. In his *Don Juan, a* hymn, "Isles of Greece", he refers to Greek independence and commemorated his visit to this beautiful historic site.

*****

Sounio Point

Temple of Poseidon

X

Another hour has flown by, but dawn is still a couple hours away.

*****

We returned to Athens by the same route continuing on to downtown Athens to pick up our tour of Athens by night.

Athens certainly had grown. I remembered a rather slow town of about a million. This has changed to a frenetic town of four million.

We arrived at the terminal of G.O. (Greek Organized) Tours on Amalias Avenue about 7 P.M. with an hour to wait. The street was named after Queen Amalia, the wife of the the first King, Othon or Otto of Bavaria.

The terminal was across the street from the National Garden and the more formal Zappeion. The National Garden had been designed and built for Queen Amalia and has played a prominent role in the social life of Athens. The Zappeion was financed and built by Constantine Zappas, a rich Greek philanthropist who also built schools and other public buildings.

Platía Sýntagma or Constitution Square and the Parliament were a block to the north, both fenced off for the next couple years during the construction of the main subway terminal.

*****

I remember watching *Evzoni*, the distinctive Greek royal (now Presidential) army guards on guard in front of the former Royal Palace. This building has been the center of power almost as long as Greece has been free from Turkish domination. Athens has been the capitol of Greece since 1834 but it was not the first capitol.

After the end of the War of Independence in 1828, Capodistrias, leader of the revolution, suggested establishing the capitol in Náfpilo or Trípoli or Kórinthos (Corinth) or, possibly, Pátra, all on the Pelopónissos. The first National Assembly chose Náfpilo. Capodistrias was assassinated in 1831, and Europe decided Greece needed a king. Othon (Otto), the seventeen year old son of Ludwig (Louis) I of Bavaria was designated and he chose Athens for his capitol. At the time, Athens was on the northern frontier since Greece did not yet control Northern Thessaly, Epirus, Macedonia or any of the Greek Islands other than the Cyclades. The population of Athens was about 20,000 people.

This 19th-century building was built as the palace for King Otto. It was designed, and its construction paid for, by Otto's father. There had been a proposal to build the palace on the Acropolis using part of the Parthenon like the Turks had done, but Ludwig's sense of history and managerial insight prevailed. As historical footnotes: (1) the Athens/ Piraeus area was swampy, as noted by Hans Christian Andersen on his visit in 1841; (2) a stream used to run down what is now Stadiou St.; (3) the Royal planners hung pieces of meat around the area and built the Palace where the maggot count was lowest.

*****

The Sýntagma got its name in 1843, when the irate citizens of Athens gathered in front of the Palace and forced King Otto to produce and sign a constitution or Sýntagma. In the square, on Sunday afternoons under the orange trees, I had listened to war stories of English expatriates and Greek partisans about W.W.II and the Communists. This spot had been the 1944 site of the month-long Battle of Athens, also called the Dhekemvrianá (December Days), the beginning of the three year Communist Revolution. During this period the Free Kingdom of Greece had operated out of the Grande Bretagne Hotel. In 1954, the first demonstrations for enosis, or freedom for Cyprus from Colonial rule, had taken place in this square.

*****

The Grande Bretagne Hotel had been built facing the Sýntagma, in 1862, as a sixty room mansion. In 1872, it was converted into an eighty bed hotel but had only two baths. It is presently a national treasure and an active hotel with 668 beds. The Hotel was the site, on Christmas Eve, 1944, of an assassination attempt on Churchill. It had also been the safehaven where the dictator, Premier Karamanlis, retreated during a coup attempt in 1974.

The Greek-Turkish war ending in 1923, resulted in the resettlement of 1.5 million Greeks from Anatolia and other settlements in Asia Minor on the basis of religion. The Parliament building was used as a refugee shelter until the parliament moved in in 1933.

*****

Hadrian's Arch and the ruins of the Temple of Zeus were a ten minute walk, but it was cool, and we were not really dressed for the weather.

Hadrian's Arch

*****

About 8 P.M., we left to pick up people at various hotels along Panepistimiou and Akademias streets passing the Academy of Science, the University, the National Library and Omonia Square. We also drove down Stadiou St. slowing at Klathmonos (Weeping)

Square whose name could have come from the proximity to the University but is historically linked to a civil servant demonstration near the Ministry of Labor.

Everyone was finally rounded up, and we headed to the Acropolis sound and light show. Seating was outside on Pnyx Hill, about a kilometer west of the Acropolis. The temperature was in the 40's. The sound part of the story was of the founding of Athens while colored lights illuminated the Propylaea and the Parthenon. The 45 minute performance was very well done but seemed to last far too long in the cold. Some of our fellow tourists were in shorts and T-shirts.

*****

We boarded the bus for a short ride to the north side of Acropolis Hill to the Plaka district. This was typical old Athens with hundred and fifty year old one- and two-story stuccoed brick buildings. This area was designated as an archeological site in the 1940's. It had been scheduled for razing in the late 1950's for a new highway but was was saved by the mayor and the Department of Archeology. The area declined through neglect, but since 1974 there has been a turn around. Now the area is considered trendy and choice real estate for shops and apartments.

The bus could not get through the narrow streets of the Plaka. We walked about two blocks through narrow brick streets to a tourist taverna, Vrachos, for supper and a folk dance show. The weather was cool and damp and the streets were not all that well lighted. One of our group from South Africa had to have cigarettes so there was a slight delay in finding him some. He had smoked a pack during the afternoon and would go though this pack before midnight.

We arrived and were ushered upstairs to the loft which overlooked the stage and main floor and seated about 150 patrons.

The low ceiling of the loft was about six feet and tables for six were jammed in as tight as possible to hold another 150 people. Drink orders were taken first. Food was brought and served family style with six servings to a plate. Many of the typical Greek dishes were served - meat balls, spinach rolls, fried fish.

*****

When the meal was well underway, the dancers came out and put on a show of Greek folk-style dances and music with customer participation. The downstairs crowd appeared well lubricated and was really getting into the mood. Three musicians accompanied four male and three female dancers who worked hard for an hour and a half. The show began with Turkish belly dancing.

Other regional folk music and dances included the pre-1830 free Greek resistance music, *paleá dhimotiká,* that do not have Turkish influence. These were followed by Macedonian laments called *mirolóyia* and, finally, drinking songs called *its távlas.*

*****

Sing

Recall ancient wars and the stories of old
sing songs of protest and martyrs bold
sing of storms and weather fine
sing happy songs of love and wine
sing summer songs when the days are cold.
Sing!

*****

They also performed examples of more modern music, the songs of the dispossessed called *rembétika* similar to our protest songs and the *andártika* which are specifically songs of the WWII Resistance. The *rembétika* were banned by the military dictators in the 50's but the style was resurrected in 1974 when the military junta was overthrown.

The stringed *bouzoúki was* played as a part of *amanédhes* style of often impromptu songs that were often enlivened with plate breaking (but not tonight). The *tekédhes* originated from the opium smokers who improvised on a *bouzoúki* or *baglamá.* The *tekes* consisted of a long introduction called a *taksími* often including or were concluded with a *zeibékiko* or wild dance originating in the warrior caste of Turkey. The *rembétika* were banned by the military dictators in the 50's but the style was resurrected in 1974 when the military junta was overthrown.

Hans Christian Andersen described a serenade by itinerant musicians called *rhapodist*. They played Greek laments written under Turkish rule, protest songs written by the Greek poet and freedom martyr, Rhigas, war songs in ancient Greek, a song celebrating the arrival of King Otto and popular European songs. He also spoke of a taverna lunch consisting of an onion and a bottle of retsina.

*****

XI

0500 and all is well. Time for some orange juice then back at it for a little while longer.

*****

In the wee hours of Sunday morning, the US TV show "Hercules" was on television in English with Greek subtitles. Next thing I was conscious of was Sesame Street in Greek and a cold gray light creeping around the drapes.

The shower was a hand-held shower but the water was hot. I dressed and stepped out onto the balcony overlooking an empty pool and enjoyed the crisp wet breeze and the fluttering of doves for about a short minute before retreating back to the relative warmth inside. We packed and I took the bags to the lobby for storage until our afternoon flight. The continental breakfast was weak orange juice, warm coffee or tea, dry toast and boiled eggs.

*****

In this crescent shaped valley, Athens has been occupied for about 7000 years, beginning as a Neolithic settlement about 5000 B.C.. Under the rule of Mycenaeans, the Cyclopean walls were built and the cult of Athena was introduced. In the ninth century B.C., under the Dorians, the Acropolis became the center of the first of the Greek city-states. The Peisistraud tyrants of the seventh and sixth centuries B.C. built their fortified capitol on the Acropolis. The last of these tyrants was deposed and, in 510 B.C., the Delphic Oracle ordered that the Acropolis remain forever the province of the gods, unoccupied by humans.

Legend has it that Athens was chosen as a strategic building site by the Phoenician, Kekrops, leading a colony from Sais. The plain in the curve of Ymitós (Mount Hymettus) is easily protected from invaders and avoids the worst of winter weather. There are excellent anchorages on the Saronikós (Saronic) Gulf which just happen to be situated on the trade routes linking the Middle East, the Black Sea and the Straits of Gibraltar.

*****

The tour bus came by at 8:45 for our tour of Athens. It stopped at several other hotels for passengers then we joined the race down the eight lane Leofóros Syngróu, the widest street in Greece.

We passed the Delta, Athens's only horse racing track. It's name comes from it's location on the alluvial fan where the Ilissós River empties into Fáliro Bay. We arrived at the bus terminal just as the bells of St. Nicholas Episcopal Church were ringing.

The tour proceeded north on Amalias Avenue passing the National Garden and the fenced construction in the Sýntagma and the Parliament Building then turned east on Vassilissis Sofias. This was once millionaires row. Now the classic style buildings lining the street had become commercialized. It was still the address of the the US and Danish embassies, the Benaki Museum with a variety of antiques and the Cycladic Art Museum with the Goulandaris collection which includes items from the Cycladic era (3000-2000 B.C.). The *Evzones'* barracks is across from the Benaki Museum.

We took a turn and passed the pseudo-Renaissance Presidential Palace with *Evzones* in their tasseled boots, white wool leggings, kilts, purple vests and berets. The Palace was built for Crown Prince Constantine in the 1880s and has been the residence of the country's leader since 1933.

At the end of Irodou Attikou Street, we slowed to look at the Stadium located in a valley of Ardittos Hill. It had been constructed in the 4th century B.C., upgraded by Herodes Atticus about four hundred years later and completely restored by George Averoff in 1896 in time for the first modern Olympic Games. This site was not big enough to accommodate the crowds so the new Olympic Stadium was built in the nearby suburb of Kalogresa.

We passed the Zappeion and went through the Pláka, rounded the Agora or ancient market, and parked on Dionysiou Areopgitou Street below the Acropolis along with at least fifty other tour busses. We offloaded and were shepherded across traffic to the steps leading up to the entrance of Acropolis Hill.

*****

The Acropolis of Athens is a limestone block that rises 60 meters (200 feet) above the surrounding hills. The top of the Acropolis is 270 meters (886 feet) by 156 meters (512 feet).

In the past, the Acropolis served as a fortress and, more significantly, as the sacred ground of Athena, the goddess of wisdom. Legend has the Acropolis as the site where the Phoenician, Kekrops, founded a city for which both Poseidon and Athena sought to be the patron. Poseidon, god of the sea, struck the earth and a horse appeared symbolizing all the manly war arts. Athena produced the olive tree symbolizing peace and prosperity. The council of gods chose Athena and the city of Kekrops became Athens, the birth place of democracy and culture.

The Romans defeated the Macedonians and incorporated Athens into the new province of Achaia. Athens relative independence was based on its reputation as a center of art and learning. The Roman scholars, Horace and Cicero, were educated in Athens, and Roman commissions supported many Greek artists.

Athens made several poor political choices. Sulla punished Athens for backing Mithridates by burning the fortifications and looting the treasury in 86 B.C.. Julius Caesar pardoned Athens for siding with Pompey against Rome. Emperor Octavian followed suit by pardoning Athens for sheltering Brutus following the assassination of Julius Caesar.

The visit of the Apostle Paul to Greece and the rise of Christianity marked the change from worship of the ancient gods to Christianity. Athens continued to teach the pagan philosophy, Neoplatonism, until 529 A.D., when Justinian I closed the schools and the temples, including the Parthenon, consecrated them as churches, and designated Athens as an archbishopric.

In the Middle Ages, as a result of the Fourth Crusade, the Franks took over Athens. They established a ducal court on the Acropolis. Athens was back in mainstream Europe for about a hundred years until the Catalan mercenaries, based in Thebes, defeated the Franks in 1311. The Catalans were soon defeated by the Florentines who were routed by the Venetians who were defeated by Sultan Mehet II in 1456.

Many Greek artifacts were "rescued" or destroyed by Europeans. The Venetian, Doge Francisco Morosini, laid siege to the Acropolis in 1687. A Swedish mercenary firing from the hill of Filopáppou or, more likely, a lightning strike, ignited a Turkish powder magazine in the Parthenon and did considerable damage. Around 1800, Lord Elgin removed sculptures from the Parthenon for the British Museum and the French Ambassador, Fauvel, took his share for the Louvre.

The War of Independence began in 1821 with the last Ottoman Turk garrison leaving the Acropolis in 1834.

*****

Off the bus. Cross the street. (Come. Come.) Climb the steps to the ticket booth. The group was hard to keep together. (Let's keep together.) Several made use of the frequent benches on the way up the hill. (Hurry. Hurry.) Vendors had their wares displayed along the steps. Here are your tickets. (puff puff) Explain a little history in English, then in French and then in Greek. Hurry. Hurry in through the Beiulé Gate. A couple thousand tourist shoulder to shoulder, up the trail to the open area below the Propylaia. (Pant. Pant.) Fifteen tour guides speaking at least eight different languages all at once.

*****

In April, 1841, Hans Christian Andersen described the Acropolis with Greek soldiers lounging about as "disordered and wretched… as if an earthquake had shaken the gigantic columns and cornices, one against the other." There were remains of Turkish mud huts and temporary sheds where human bones and artifacts were being stored. Horses grazed the rampant grass. A stack of bricks replaced the caryatid that Thomas Bruce, the 7th Earl of Elgin, British Ambassador to Turkey, had stolen for the British Museum. Every column in the Parthenon had been broken. Andersen said that Athens was a town of white houses with red roofs growing up the side of the Acropolis. He also described the beauty of the snow on Mount Parnasas which we could see to the northeast. A painting by Martinun Rørbye about 1835, called "Greeks Working in the Ruins of the Acropolis", shows the clutter of broken columns below the Propylaia near the pedestal of the Hellenistic King.

*****

When I visited the Acropolis in 1962, on a Sunday in July, there was one bus and very few people. There was no light show and no scaffolding. More people visit the Acropolis on a summer weekend than lived in Athens a hundred years ago.

The first monument is an eight meter (26 ft) pedestal that once supported a statue of the Hellenistic king. Later, after the occupation by Rome, this pedestal held a statue of the the victor of Actium, the Roman General Agrippa, standing in a bronze chariot.

*****

Pentelic Marble

Pentelic marble.
Sexually fluted and curved.
Tan and smooth as summer's maids.
Warm and sensual to the touch.
Eternal.
Cold as sea that hides
the Greek and Persian fleet off of Salamis.
Soothing as a worry stone.
Aesthetically pleasing.
Pentelic marble.

*****

We trudged up a grade, which had probably been a chariot road, to the Propylaia. This gateway to the upper city extends 45 m (150 ft.) across the western edge of the Acropolis. There was period of peace following the Greek victory over the Persian fleet in the Battle of Sálamis in 481 B.C. and the decisive Greek victory at Plataea in 480 B.C.. Pericles commissioned Mnesicles to build the Propylaea as part of the Acropolis complex in 446 B.C.. It took five years to design and build of Pentelic marble to serve as a covered

Acropolis from Plaka

entrance for five gates leading into the Acropolis. The north wing became residence of the Orthodox archbishops in A.D. 630 and the Catholic bishop in 1204. The Frankish Duke, Nerio Acciajuoli, occupied the Propylaial in 1387. He was ousted by the Turks in 1394. They turned the Parthenon into a mosque. In 1640, Turkish gun power stored in the Propylaia was ignited by lightning or gun fire causing collapse of much of the building.

*****

A room in the south wing of the Propylaia had served as a waiting room for the adjacent temple of Athena Nike. The temple, also known as Nike Apteros (Wingless Victory), was built about 450 B.C. in honor of the victory over the Persians. The Athenians portrayed Nike wingless to prevent her leaving Athens. The temple contained a statue of Hecate, the Epipyrgidia. King Aegeus was supposed to have thrown himself into the sea, now called the Aegean, from this temple when the ship carrying his only son failed to give the proper signal. (This site is now about six miles from the nearest water.) The Turks demolished the temple sometime between 1679 and 1751 for building material. Many of the stones were found and a replica was built in 1835. It had to be disassembled in 1939 when the foundation cracked (it had been rebuilt over a Turkish cistern) and it was rebuilt in 1941 after extensive repairs.

Erechtheion

The tourist crowd was directed through the central gate into "upper city". The first view of the Parthenon and the Erechtheion is impressive. The temple of Athena would have been straight ahead. The temple housed a giant statue, the Athena Promachos by the sculptor Pheidias. It stood on a raised dais with a golden spear and helmet visible to guide ships far out to sea.

Bearing to the right, the Sacred Way leads past the remains of the Sanctuary of Artemis to the Parthenon. Along the Sacred Way were once altars and statues of the gods. Foundations of older temples can still be seen. All that remains along the Way is scattered slabs of marble and the bases of some of the statues. The Way bends to the right or south to entrance of the Parthenon.

We sidestepped the crowd for a minute and walked over to the Pelasgian wall and looked down into the Odeon (theater) of Herodes Atticus. Constructed in the 2nd century A.D. by Herodes Atticus as a memorial to his wife, the theater seats 5,000 spectators and is still used for the Athens Music and Drama Festival, for Greek tragedies and for Attic comedies performed in modern Greek.

*****

I was here in 1962. I walked inside the Parthenon. I could see the classical forms taught in design schools - no straight lines, the columns tilted slightly inward, the floor raised slightly in the center of the temple. I touched the marbles and walked the hallowed halls. Now, from air pollution and increased tourist traffic, the Parthenon was restricted and filled with scaffolding being used to replace the corroding iron structural members. Many of the marble works had eroded and the classic details disappearing. Attempts were being made to stabilize the marble against further erosion.

*****

Parthenon

Pericles commissioned Ictinus to design and build the Doric style temple which took nine years to construct. Pheidias was placed in charge of carving the frieze and minor statues and the great statue of Athena Parthenos. Many of the statues were decorated in gold which was part of Athens' gold reserve. The politics and paranoia of Athens lead to Pheidias being charged with shorting the gold in Athena's removable skirt. On weighing the gold he was found innocent. His persecution continued when he was charged with impiety for picturing himself and Pericles on Athena's shield. He either died in prison or was killed in a riot in Olympia.

*****

Against the north wall of the Acropolis stands the Erechtheion, a masterpiece of the Ionic style. This was the site of the contest between Athena and Poseidon for Athens. Poseidon's spring and Athena's olive tree stood on this spot. Kekrops, the legendary founder of Athens, was buried here along with Athena's ward, Erechtheus. The holy olive wood statue of Athena Polias fell from heaven on this spot.

The Erechtheion was burned by the Persians on the eve of the Battle of Salamis. It was rebuilt on the beginning of the Peleponnesian War. The Turkish governor, who lived in the Propylaia kept his harem in the Erechtheion.

Probably the most famous part of the Erechtheion is the south portico with six life-size pillars in female form called the Caryatids. These are concrete copies. Five of the originals are safe in the Acropolis Museum and while the other resides with Elgin's other loot in the British Museum.

*****

It was time for a Coke break, so we stopped outside the Beiulé gate on those hewn steps where Aristotle trod and where Solon had spoken and looked at the cheap souvenirs.

Back at the bottom of the hill we reboarded the bus for the return trip. We had two hours to wait for transportation back to the hotel.

*****

XII

0600. I'm on a roll. Time for breakfast as soon as I type a few more lines.

*****

We walked up to the parliament building and took pictures of two *Evzones* who were being inspected by the sergeant-of-the-guard. Then, being a little after noon, we stopped at the Grand Bretagne Hotel for an outstanding lunch.

It was still a half an hour till the bus so I went down the street to Hadrian's Arch and the Temple of Olympian Zeus. Hadrian's Arch was erected by the Emperor Hadrian about 130 A.D. to mark the boundary between Classical Athens and the City of Hadrian. A frieze on the near side of each reads, "This is Athens, the ancient city of Theseus" on one side and, "This is the City of Hadrian and not of Theseus" on the other. It is a Roman archway with "a Greek superstructure of Corinthian pilasters crowned by an architrave and pediment." The Arch is used for formal occasions such as greeting foreign dignitaries.

Through the Arch, in Hadrian's City, lay the grounds and remains of the Temple of Olympian Zeus. The temple had been begun in the 6th century B.C. by Peisistratus, and finally completed by Hadrian in 131 A.D., complete with heroic size statues of himself and Zeus. There was probably a statue of his friend, Antinous, who, after he drowned in the Nile, was designated a god by Hadrian. The temple was larger than those on the Acropolis measuring 108 m (354 ft) by 41m (135 ft). Aristotle described the temple's size as being in the class of the pyramids of Egypt.

Temple of Olympian Zeus

Hadrian was a frequent visitor to Athens. Besides the Arch and the Temple of Olympian Zeus, he built an immense library.

*****

Tired and cold we returned to the hotel and took a cab to the airport for the trip to Rhodes. I checked the bags in and we found a couple hard plastic seats to wait for the flight to be called.

*****

Mother nature called and I followed the signs to the toilets down stairs. An attendant collected a hundred drachmas and handed out toilet paper. The used toilet paper was deposited in a basket since it was not the soft fanny-and-sewer-friendly tissue Americans are accustomed to. I guess the attendant periodically emptied the baskets. In another public restroom in Athens two invisible women were cleaning the facilities while men came and went. The facilities were regular flush toilets, not the squat down foot pad model. The wash basins were lit with yellowish 20 watt bulbs.

On the subject of bathrooms the water heater in Corfu had been electric and held 50 liters. This was about enough for one hot shower. Water was solar heated on Rhodes and the hotels in Athens. Bathroom lighting in Corfu consisted of four 20 watt bulbs screwed into the face of the mirror which made the mirror practically useless. Lighting was reasonable in Athens. On Rhodes, two fluorescent tubes were at eye level. All the tubs were short and deep with a hand-held shower head. Towels were furnished but no wash cloths were available so we bought a couple small tea towels.

*****

We finally went through the metal detectors. In the departure area were more well-worn hard plastic seats and a lot of smokers. The flight was called and we were bussed out to the plane to stand in the mist and wind awaiting boarding.

The flight was less than an hour in our aisle seats. We were flying out of the setting sun and into the Middle Eastern night.

While we were bussed to the terminal we passed an armored car and several soldiers with automatic weapons. I gathered the bags while Carol rented a car.

We loaded the car and took off into the cold, strange, black of night to follow the somewhat vague instructions on how to get to Sun Beach Club. The instructions said, "Turn left, go to the first and only light and turn left." No map was provided. A couple miles to the left was a traffic light. There was no *clear* indication that this was a divided street so naturally I turned into the wrong way side. This did not matter much since it was late on Sunday evening and there was no traffic.

This oversight was quickly corrected by cutting through the empty parking spaces between the street halves. We proceeded half a mile to the beach and, guess what? No Sun Beach Club. So much for travel agent directions. The obvious road turned to the right and, after almost a mile, it looped back to the main road. We circled back for another shot. The only street to the left was another wrong-way one-way. Since there must be some way around this obstacle, I went up what appeared to be an alley which took us to the beach road. About half a mile and two hotels later the sign for the Sun Beach Club appeared through the car's sun roof from the top of the building. Threading our way through parked busses we finally found the entrance. While Carol checked in I unloaded the car and then drove off to find a parking place.

By now I was cold, tired, hungry, and beginning to get the Ugly American syndrome. It was after ten, and the hotel bar and restaurant and local convenience stores were all closed adding to my aggravation list. There was no such thing as a baggage cart, and the small two-passenger elevator required three trips to get the bags andboth of us to the fourth floor. To make it even better, the heat had come on about 7 P.M. and turned off about 9 P.M. so the room had a definite chill. I stacked the bags in the corner, had a candy bar from my emergency stash, and went to bed cranky.

*****

XIII

That last chapters took more time than I anticipated. It is 0400 Friday morning and, like the frog says, "Time's sure fun when you're having flies."

*****

It was Monday morning and a gray dawn began breaking over the Carian Mountains of Turkey about 0800. By 0900, a platinum sun was trying to break through the cold gray clouds. Weather-wise, it was 15° C (59° F) with high humidity and a 15-20 knot wind blowing out of the north off the Aegean Sea. I went across the road to a minimart for a loaf of bread, a liter of milk and a jar of fresh Rhodian honey. After tea and toast, I was feeling human again. I put on a sweater and a pancho and went for a walk on the beach. In a mile walking, I saw no birds and found no shells or trash or anything other than flat, multi-colored marble pebbles. Swells lapped the beach like a busy kitten cleaning itself. The clicking of a million wave-rounded pebbles and the cool, wet wind off the Aegean Sea were stimulating, but I was getting cold.

Returning, I met an old man and a young boy from Austria with pants legs rolled up were wading in the surf. Brrrrr. The water was not all that cold, it was just the idea.

****

Cold Stony Beaches

Cold morning mist on the shingle beach at Kremasti
and distant snowcapped Carian mountains take me back
to other cold, rocky shores
waiting for the sun.

Cobbles clicking in the surf
at Argentia and Topsail on Newfoundland
with ice flows hidden in the mist.

131

Seastacks peeking from lowering clouds
off a beach of metamorphic stones
on the Straits of Juan de Fuca

Low waves slopping
on volcanic Icelandic beaches
with fishermen's voices carrying through
the Gulf Stream's steamy fog

Waiting.
Waiting hopelessly for a summer sun
to lift the leaden skies
and break the hyperborean spell

I was leaving the beach when some workmen arrived and began hauling small quarter cubic yard loads of sand to the beach in a small truck. They carefully unloaded the sand, one shovel-full at a time, and spread it in a small but expanding square well above the high-tide line. I watched this team of two or three workmen work intermittently all week taking sand to the beach, covering the rocks with sand. By the time we left they had made about a thousand square feet of "sandy beach" for sun bathing when the weather warmed a little. A few hardy souls had used it. All this hand labor could be completely erased by just one late winter storm.

Our assigned hostess knocked. We were invited to a get acquainted party at 1100. We went across the street for a few more groceries and then went down to the lounge for the introductions.

About forty people showed up to sample local wines and cheeses. The hotel staff, between them, spoke enough languages to cover all the guests - a couple from Sweden, several people from Germany and France, newly-weds from Egypt, a few Greeks and a dozen Americans. Surprisingly, no one needed Spanish or Italian but then, Ródhos is at the extreme eastern end of the Med.

Everyone introduced themselves, and the staff explained what was available in the hotel and tours that would be available during the week. They also encouraged everyone to look into the Sun Beach time-share program and wanted to set up appointments.

One of the American couples was living in Saudi Arabia as employees of McDonnel Douglas. He was retired Air Force.

*****

After the party broke up, we drove towards Rhodes Town or Rodos for lunch. Pizza and Cokes. Diet Coke was called Coke Lite in a white can not available yet in the US.

The condo was located on the beach near Kremasti on the north shore about eight miles from Rodos which was to the northeast at the northern-most point of the island. The Filarimos Hills rose inland or south up to the site of the ancient Doric city-state of Ialysos and a monastery of the same name. The first couple miles along the highway was through small strip centers, tavernas, discos and small hotels. Homes and the village itself were inland towards the hills and away for the tourists.

The next political entity was Trianda, on the western tip of the Bay of Trianda. Several big resorts were unloading numerous busses and tourists dominated the beach.

On the eastern end of the bay was the village of Kritiká. A strip of small, one story houses were along the highway. They originally belonged to Cretan Muslim Turks who had been displaced from Crete in 1913 as part of an early and less lethal "ethnic cleansing".

The road trooped over the seaward side of Monte Smith. This hill, formerly Áyios Stéfanos, had been renamed for the British admiral, Sir Stephen Smith, who used it as a lookout during the Napoleanic War. The hill is the site of a 2nd century B.C. acropolis with a theatre, gymnasium, stadium, and a temple to Apollo. The hill and roadside supported a number of Agave plants from Mexico.

*****

Old Moorish Admin and Port Authority

Over the hill were more hotels and more busses. The road became one way Pleletherias Street that ran beside the harbor in Neohori or Newtown as opposed to the older section of town. This part of town had once been called Keratohori or Cockoldville presumably referring to the morality of the Newtown population.

We found a parking place and visited a book store and several leather and umbrella shops which began closing about 2 P.M.. Parking places were designated by blue painted stripes in the street and tickets were purchased at a nearby blue dispenser for 100 drachmas per hour. This trip was largely a recon so we could find things easier later.

As we started back to Sun Beach, the car began to act up. We called the car people who said someone would be out next morning.

*****

I took a late afternoon walk to the west for about a mile along the beach. The tide was out and about two more feet of shingle beach was exposed. The air was warmer but the breeze still had a damp nip. This time I found a broken oyster drill and several land snails. The mountains in Turkey eight miles to the north were shrouded in haze.

Heat was on in the room from 6-9 in the evening so we did a little laundry and used the heat to dry with. After an hour or so the hot water heat had the room reasonably comfortable.

We went out for supper to one of the tavernas on the beach. They must have been waiting for the season to start since the selection was limited and the service were like we were bothering them.

For the evening entertainment, the Sun Beach bar had karaoke and self-proclaimed singer which we watched for one drink or half an hour which ever had come first and crashed.

*****

XIV

Its almost 5 AM. Two more hours until go-to-work time. I should finish this by the week's end.

*****

Tuesday dawned quiet and hazy. The wind had dropped but it was still cool enough for a sweater.

I was taking tea and toast on the patio watching some Mediterranean Gulls (*Larus*) along the beach when a couple crows flew by. These crows were gray with black head and wings. These were the Hooded Crow (*Corvus corone cornix*), a subspecies of the all black Carrion Crow. I also saw them in Rodos and at Lindos.

The car people came a little after 8 and said it was the car's computer but not to worry. Since they were not worried we went to Rodos.

Carol wanted to shop and I wanted to see the harbor and visit Old Town. We parked and parted ways for the day.

*****

I walked a couple blocks north to Papanikolaou Street passing what had been the Hotel des Roses. It was supposed to be refurbished as a Playboy Club in the near future. I turned down Kos Street to the beach.

The beach, up to the high tide line, was pebbles and the tide was out and down about three feet. Sand had been spread above the high-tide line to make a beach for tourist. I walked north on the pebble beach towards the aquarium of the Hydrobiological Institute on Cape Kammborno and found a couple Persian Conchs (*Strombus decorus*).

Harbor Entrance and Base of Colossus

A couple hundred high school students on their graduation trip were waiting to get into the aquarium, so I turned back south along the water's edge. Besides a zillion colorful marble pebbles, I found several a couple more Strombus and a winged oyster (*Pteria hirundo*). Near the Elli Club breakwater boulders I found 2 species of wormshell (*Vermicularia arenaria* and *Petaloconchus subcancellatus*), a limpet (*Fissurela reticulata*) and at least one species of chiton. On the other side of the yacht club, I combed the beach from the boat ramp to the seawall but found nothing.

*****

One side of Eleftheris Street was a promenade along the harbor. Across the street were the Mosque of Murad Reis built in 1522 and Lawrence Durrell's Rhodian home, Cleobolus. The pseudo-Venetian pink and tan Post Office and Port Authority, and the Church of Evangelismus (the Annunciation) and the Bishop's Palace with date palms occupied most of the street. The bulk of Old Town loomed in the background.

The water visibility in the harbor was a good ten feet. Some of the concrete jumble from WWII was probably still littering the bottom.

137

A stone mole lead out to a column with an iron deer on its top that had a twin on the other side of the harbor entrance. These were supposed to be the historic bases for the Colossus of Rhodes, one of the Seven Wonders of the World. This is unlikely due to the engineering problems involved not to mention earthquakes and WWII damage. The statue probably stood above the town on the hill near the tower of the Grand Master. This was the site of the Temple of Helios and had good visibility from all three harbors. It is also unlikely that the entrance to the military harbor could have been closed for the 12 years it took to construct the statue.

*****

This heroic statue and lighthouse had been 31 meters (100 feet) tall. This bronze statue of Helios, the sun god, was financed by near defeat. Antigonus tried to get an alliance with Rhodes against Ptolemy and Egypt. Since Egypt was a good trading partner and Rhodes was trying to be essentially neutral, they declined. Demetrius, son of Antigonus, had beaten Ptolemy and Cassander and was trying to reassemble Alexander the Great's empire. He arrived off Rhodes in 305 B.C. to "reason" with Rhodes accompanied by 200 men-of-war, 170 troop ships with 40,000 infantry and many supply ships of various kinds not to mention a fleet of "vulture boats". After several attacks, they gained a foothold but were harassed by the more agile Rhodian fleet. Demetrius captured a hill (Monte Smith?) and built giant catapults that could throw round stone projectiles up to 600 pounds or darts up to 12 feet long a distance of up to 3,000 feet. After several infantry assaults, a siege-engine was constructed reported to be 150 feet high. This colossus, called the Helepolis, made one partially successful attack and breached the wall, but had to withdraw for repairs. After a lot of internal politicking on both sides, Demetrius received a letter from his father telling him to make peace with the Rhodians and come home. This saved face for both sides. Rhodes remained free but signed an alliance with Demetrius against any enemy but Ptolemy. Demetrius gave all the war equipment to Rhodes to sell provided they would use the proceeds to erect a suitable monument to commemorate the siege.

The bronze statue was erected over a wooden frame by Chares of Lindos about 293 B.C. It cost about three hundred talents of gold

($300,000 US). The statue was toppled by an earthquake in 227 B.C. and decorated the waterfront for 900 years. It was eventually broken up by the Saracens and shipped to Syria. There it was loaded on 980 camels and finally delivered to Édessa. Several of Rhodes' neighbors had donated money and resources to help reerect the Colossus, but this was never accomplished. Some sources said it was beyond the engineering talent of the day to reerect it. Others sources said the Oracle of Delphi predicted worse evil if the Colossus were reerected. Anyway, the Rhodians used the gifts for the repair for other things.

*****

Rhodian mythology has the amphibious demonic Telchines as the first inhabitants (they had been expelled from Crete). According to Diodorus of Sicily, the three Telchines were Chrisos (gold), Argyos (silver), and Halkos (Bronze). They taught men the crafts of stone and metal working. They made Kronos the sickle used to cut up Uranus. They also crafted Poseidon's trident. Their sister, Alia or Amphitrite, married Poseidon, and had six sons and a daughter, Rhodes. Helios, the sun god, was attracted to Rhodes and their children, the Iliads, became sailors and merchants. Pindar's story of the founding of Rhodes is similar but it does not mention the Telchines. That, dearly beloved, is how Rhodes got its name and who Helios was. (Actually, Rhodes or Rodos was more likely named for the wild hibiscus flower.)

*****

Historically, the island was first inhabited about 7,000 years ago in the Neolithic period. Early inhabitants included Carians, Phoenicians, Lydians and Minoans. The first Greeks were Myceneans from Argolid around 1400 B.C.. Rhodes has lived under the several names: Kleovoulou, Doriea, Ethrea, Atavyria, Oloessa, Ophioussa (land of snakes), Piessa, Pelagiou, Stadia, and Telehina. So, when you run across these names in your ancient Greek or Biblical history, you will know the term is referring to Rhodes.

The plan for the town of Rodos was established in 408 B.C. by Hippodamus of Milesia. This new town was to be the common administrative and religious center for the three original Dorian cities of

Ialyssós, Kámiros and Líndos. This new city quickly became the financial and cultural center for the eastern Mediterranean.

*****

Across and inside of the harbor or Mandraki ("a sheepfold" in ancient Greek) were the hydrofoil ferries and the castle of St. Nicholas. The castle was built in 1464 to guard the entrance to the harbor. The castle is connected to the mainland by a causeway on top of the breakwater now called Akti Boumbouli Street. Many yachts were berthed along the inside of the causeway. The castle was converted to a lighthouse that is still in operation. Three former Byzantine wind-powered flour mills were built along Akti Boumbouli to take full advantage of the wind. These mills were virtually destroyed during the liberation from German occupation. The restored mills no longer work and have been converted into trendy Yuppie apartments. Several other mills in modern Rodos have been similarly renovated.

Old men sat on benches in the sun claiming ancestral spots where the shade of Judas Trees would be when the weather warmed. Some remember fifty years ago when the harbor was fenced in barbed wire and manned by Italian soldiers or, after WWII, the ordnance disposal that provided a daily spectacle on Monte Smith.

Along the brick paver walk, a war memorial marked the beginning of the tour boats. The tour boats were available to provide day trips to secluded beaches and tours to other local Greek islands and to Turkey. Dive boats required a check dive and local certification (at your expense) before they would take you out.

*****

I walked around the south end of the harbor where the Coast Guard cutter was moored and then along Akti Boumbouli admiring some of the yachts. Tourist were posing with the windmill and the boats. The sails were displayed mounted on the mills on holidays.

Hooded crows scoured the coquina boulder riprap along the outside of the breakwater. There is a legend concerning the crows. About 1500 B.C., Phalanthou, leader of the Phoenicians occupying Rhodes, was confronted by Iphicles, the leader of the Acheans. An oracle told

Phalanthou that the Phoenicians would loose Rhodes when the ravens turned white and there were fish in the wine jugs. When Iphicles heard of this prophesy he had some ravens painted white and bribed his opponent's wine steward to put fish in the wine jugs. Awed, Phalanthou requested safe conduct to withdraw from Rhodes. The ravens have been partially white ever since.

Actually, the hooded crow is a now permanent resident on Rhodes. The Phoenicians may not have previously observed this bird or the bird may have just returned from its winter migration to Africa or its could have recently expanded its range into Rhodes. It is a natural subspecies of the all-black Carrion Crow.

*****

I continued to the castle and the pedestal for the right foot of Helios to look at the hydrofoils. Returning along the riprap at water's edge, I found Rosemary, Tall Melilot, one of the mint family, a plantain, Smooth Sow-thistle, Long-beaked Stork's-bill, and a small purple mallow all growing wild in the riprap. I crossed the end of the moat below St Paul's gate and followed the beach below the outer wall. There were no shells, but a couple couples were taking advantage of the sun. I did not go all the way out to the Naillac tower on the end of the seawall protecting the opening of the commercial harbor.

*****

Retracing my steps to Neoriou Square, I stopped for a soda then entered Old Town through the Eleftherias gate into Symi Square. Limited traffic squeezed through the square through the Arsenal Gate from the smaller yacht basin and the commercial port. Most of the traffic was taxis carrying tired tourists from the Marine Gate.

An archeology site, the Temple of Aphrodite, was still being worked on the edge of the square. The sidewalk around the square was constructed in a style called *hokhláki*. It was hard and slippery consisting of flat marble pebbles stood on end and arranged in colored mosaics. This amenity was usually reserved for courtyards. There was little vehicle traffic so many of the streets were brick or marble flagstones.

Apelou Street began at Symi Plaza running southward for half a mile to Platonos Street passing through several plazas. The first of these, Plaza Argyrokastrou, stretched about a hundred yards from the current art gallery and bank to the gate near the old infirmary, which contains the folk museum, and the Inn of Auvergne. Like most of the buildings in Old Town, the Inn contained offices or shops.

Large stone balls were stacked in pyramids or used singly to control traffic. These were catapult stones and came in several weights from about a hundred pounds to close to a thousand pounds. The weight classes were marked on the stones.

A lady police person was controlling the limited traffic through the gate into Alexander the Great Square with St. Mary's of the Castle church. A shop selling replicas of antiques was on the corner of the square and Odhós Ippotón (Street of the Knights).

*****

I crossed Odhós Ippotón into Plaza Moussion with the Inn of England and the Hospital which housed the archeological museum. Jewelry stores, fur and leather goods, and art and craft shops abounded.

It's hard to believe that the Italians did archeological research and fought a war at the same time.

Apelou crossed Protogenous and Evdimiou on the left which changed to Agisandrou and Polydorou on the other side of the street. I turned left through a small park to the Chardevan Mosque with its large, rounded dome. Behind the mosque sat Ippokratous Square, with its portalis and arched doorways. A stone fountain with a centerpiece like a minaret occupied the center of the square. Several hundred students were posing for pictures, sitting around smoking, or otherwise holding the fountain down.

Rounding a corner, I found myself near the Marine Gate. Through the Marine Gate was the commercial port and a taxi stand with thirty taxis each with its santos or blue beads on the dashboard to ward off evil.

Returning through the gate and the cool shade and vendor's stalls, I found the Street of Socrates. Window shopping my way along through the students on holiday I came to the Mosque of Suleiman and the clock tower.

Nearby was a taverna for lunch with a courtyard and lemon trees in bloom. The crescent moon matched the crescent moon on the red dome of the mosque against a dark blue sky all framed by a wreath of lemon blossoms. My lunch was squid and fries with ouzo.

Sacratous Street became Apollonion Street as it approached the Tower of St. George. This part of the old wall was an active archeological excavation site and not accessible. I retraced my steps to Orfeos Street and turned left into Revolution Square passing in front of the Palace of the Grand Masters. Time had flown and it was 3 P.M., time for the Palace to close to tourists.

I left Old Town through St Anthony's Gate passing a gaggle of street artists and T-shirt vendors to D'Amboise Gate. There, I caught a taxi back to Sun Beach.

*****

Mosque and lemon tree

When Carol returned, we decided to turn the car in and take some tours instead.

I took another long walk on the beach before going down to the condo's Greek Night feast and folk show. After all the walking some ouzo and a big dinner had me dozing before the dancing started.

*****

XV

Its 6:30 A.M.. I have another hour before I have to leave for work. Just think. Tomorrow is Saturday and I should get this finished.

*****

The Wednesday tour left at 0800, so we were up about 0600. I went for a walk on the beach and found several shells deposited over night. A fishing boat was setting gill or trammel nets about 200 yards off of and parallel to the beach. I don't know what they intended to catch setting nets for daylight fishing.

After tea and toast, we went down to catch the tour bus. The tour followed the road into Rodos and cruised the harbor stopping only briefly at Old Town. Our driver and guide par excellence, Michael, was born on Rhodes and had lived in Texas. His knowledge of Rhodian history was excellent and his presentation, in several languages, was outstanding.

We turned on Papagou then on Dimokratias then onto Papalouka on the way to Monte Smith. An overlook showed clearly why Smith had used this as a lookout. The town, designed by the architect, Hippodamou of Milesis, was laid out below us to the north and northeast. To the west and northwest a view of the shipping lanes and nearby islands was superb. The Turkish coast and snowcapped mountains were plainly visible. Agave (<u>A. americana</u>), red poppies (<u>Papaver</u> <u>apulum</u>), and other wildflowers cloaked the hillside. Further on, we passed Hellenistic Rhodes park where a light show was put on at night during the tourist season.

There was a restored small Greek theatre on the hill and an Olympic stadium where naked wrestlers and boxers had beat upon each other. Women were excluded under penalty of death until one woman, whose husband and son were both national champions and participants, slipped in in disguise. She revealed herself as a woman when she ran down to congratulate her son on his victory. They decided not to kill the mother and wife of national champions and after this incident athletes began to wear minimal clothing and women were allowed to watch.

Above the stadium, originally built in the 2nd century B.C., was an archeological restoration on the site of a temple of Apollo. Temples to Athena Poliados and Zeus Polieos have also been discovered.

Stadium

*****

We left Monte Smith passing through more olive groves and reentered the city. Every construction site on Rhodes hits new archeological remains like buildings, sewers, roads, etc., but this does not stop building. Finds are recorded and charted and left in place.

We passed the new Aegean University near where Cicero, Pompey, Brutus, Cassius, Artemisia, and Demosthenes had studied rhetoric.

We headed south passing a large cemetery. Many of the Rodians were so dedicated to their politics that their graves were in the colors of the party. There were many blue or green markers and some of the tombs were freshly painted these colors.

*****

The beach road lead to Agia Marina and Reni Koskinou then to Vodi Point on the northern end of the Bay of Kallitea. Curving around the bay to Faliráki, we joined the main highway. Near Kolýmbia and Vágia Point was the Byzantine Monastery of Tsambika where, on the 8th of September each year, childless women climb to the Monastery to cure their barrenness. Children resulting from this pilgrimage are dedicated to the Virgin and are often named Tsambikos or Tsambika. These names peculiar to Rhodes and surrounding islands.

*****

I noticed many of the homes had the iron reinforcing bars extending from the top of the structures. In the Latin world, this was a sign that the structure was not yet completed and, therefore, could not yet be taxed as a completed structure (it might never be finished). In Greece, it indicated only that the structure is not yet completed. Parents built the daughters a home for a dowry. Most were built out-of-pocket as the money became available. The home was usually completed by the time the daughter married. The rebar allows continuing work so the cement will be tied to the existing structure and the family can add rooms as necessary. Sons were out of luck. Property passes to the daughters. Sons have to work for a living and buy property or marry a house and property.

Most of the homes had solar water heaters. Much of the clothes washing was done by hand with a tub and scrub board but, at least, they did not have to heat the water.

Many houses had once had wooden windmill power to pump water, grind flour, and press grapes and olive oil. Under the Italian administration, metal windmills, many from America, replaced the older wooden windmills. Electric pumps have replaced wind power and the poor storks that once roosted on the windmills must make do with TV antennas or solar collectors.

*****

We passed a former military airfield. This was one of four built by the Germans to support their war effort in North Africa. One of these had been the island's commercial airport until the present airport had been built.

The road passed through the Kalavarda valley where fields and orchards produced apricots, carob, grapes and olives. The wildflowers were spectacular. Large white composites with yellow centers predominated mixed with yellow mustards and highlighted with bright red poppies.

The road passed several miles inland of Archangelos, the ruins of Castle of Faraklos (a 14th century Byzantine castle) stood on the hill overlooking the village of Agnathi, Charaki and Malona with the church of Agia Agathi overlooking Vlicha Bay and Massari where the Knights had a sugar refinery.

Many of the homes we saw had outdoor ovens fired with sticks and crop waste. The ovens were clay over a metal frame.

In old Greece, the bed was the dominant piece of furniture in the house and the most elaborate family possession. This was not from excess passion or opulence, but because the bed could not be seized for taxes like the goat or the water bucket.

Oven

A number of small dry river beds crawled out of their canyons and under the road. Some had a little water resulting from artesian springs including the Mangazi which drained some of the Psiothos mountains, and the Makaris which emptied into the the Bay of Vlihia near Amalona.

The ruins of Ferrklós castle. The Turks captured and destroyed this last last Knight stronghold in 1522.

*****

The first view of Lindos, on Aghios Emilianos Point, was impressive in many ways: contrasted against the blue sky and bluer sea; the red roofed white Cycladic sugar-cube houses of Lindos village below the acropolis with its Byzantine walls; the hundred busses trying to get close to the site; and the several thousand people climbing hill or on the promontory. Lindos was the most important of the three ancient Dorian cities of Rhodes. It was first settled about 2000 BC.

We turned off for Lindos at the village of Pilonas, 55 kms south of Rodos. Busses of all sizes were negotiating the hill to the village. There was a turnaround around a big tree where the large busses were forced to return after discharging passengers. Smaller busses, like ours, made a tight turn and drove a couple hundred feet downhill to the beach. We stopped at a taverna on the beach for lunch before making the nearly 500 foot climb to the acropolis.

I walked the beach, while waiting for lunch, and found several shells. I found what I thought to be a necklace stone, a stone pierced by burrowing clams, like I had found near Athens. It turned out to be a shard from a Paleo Period jug with a hole where a thong handle had been strung. Its was several thousand years old.

Here they were also trucking in sand to make a nice tourist beach.

After lunch, we started up the hill through the maze of the village of Lindos. The narrow streets were filled with donkeys and tourists and an occasional motorcycle. We finally found the proper turn and began the switchback climb. Looking back to the north was Mount Ataviros, the highest peak on Rhodes.

The tomb of the 6th centuary BC benevolent tyrant Cleobolus was supposed to be on the point of land on the other side of the little harbor. He was one of the Seven Sages of Greece and a personal friend of Solon. His father, King Evander, built the reservoir and water supply tunnels used by Lindos until recently.

Lindos had begun with an Egyptian temple erected in 1510 BC on a heavily wooded promontory. The sacred groves had been well tended up until the 4th century AD. Probably the destruction or conversion of the temples and the cutting of the sacred groves came with Christianity.

Lindos Bay

Achean and Dorian deities predated the Greek Athena. This temple was unique in not having an altar. One story was that the temple had been built by Heliades, a direct descendent of the sun god. He forgot to bring fire with him when he climbed the cliff to make a offering to the Lindan Athena. Their offerings were grains, fruit, sweets and other agricultural products not needing fire. This act set the procedures for this temple.

Another story relating to the site concerned Danos, the father of all true Greeks, and his daughters as they fled Egypt. They stopped at Lindos and built a temple to Athena with her statue as a plain piece of wood. Wooden images were used until the first carved statues representing Athena appeared in the 8th century B.C.. Marble statues were first used in the 4th century.

*****

The first temple to Athena was constructed in the 8th century B.C.. A new temple was begun by the tyrant, Kleovoulos, in the 6th century B.C.. It was completed over the next two hundred years. Burned in 342 B.C., it was replaced by the Lindians. Near the temple site, the Dorians built a stoa in 200 B.C.. A temple to Psithirou, their god of prophesy, was built in 200 A.D..

The Byzantines fortified the acropolis and built a church to St. John. The Knights expanded their fortifications by building another castle and a palace for the Keeper of the Castle.

This acropolis retained the mix of cultures rather than being sanitized to one period like the acropolis in Athens. In many ways, this is more meaningful as living history by showing that things change and how change was made. Without a good guidebook and a lot of time, the site appears to be a jumble of columns and cut stones.

The marble steps up the hillside had been polished by years of foot traffic. These possibly slippery steps had been chipped with a jackhammer to improve traction. There were no hand rails or resting places along the climb to the main gate. The entrance fee was 1200 drachmas (about $4 US).

Beyond the gate, more steps lead to a small landing or square. The stern of a Phoenician triene was carved in bas relief into the wall by Pythourito of Timoharou, in 180 B.C.. The carving, 4.5 by 5.5 meters, shows much detail of ancient ship building. This plaza also contains remains of an altar and some Byzantine cisterns.

Eighty more steps lead to the domed entrance into the administrative building and home of the Keeper of the Castle. This area was serving as a storage place for large artifacts.

We turned left and proceeded through the ruins of the Church of St Johns and the Doric stoa and into the Great Arcade. In the center of the arcade were 36 steps leading to the remains of the Propylea which, in turn, lead to the temple. Not to downgrade the site but the hundreds of people make it difficult to see and appreciate the site or photograph it, and climbing over the polished marble ruins is hazardous particularly with a bunch of teenagers on their normal public behavior.

*****

Dream of Lindos

Dream of Lindos at moonrise.
The beach with lapping waves
whispering to fishing boats
leaving with lanterns lit.
And dreams of Lindos town
below the Acropolis,
waking from siesta
preparing for the evening
its white walls glowing in the moonlight.
Dream of the Acropolis
columns and walls
losing themselves
against the black sky
as scud crosses the moon.
Dream of night swimming
in St Paul's harbor
with a candle in the chapel
to guide you back to shore
The Acropolis
backlighted by the rising moon.
Lindonian dreams.

*****

I walked back to the far corner of the acropolis and looked over the wall. St. Paul's bay was tucked in under the promontory. Several Elenora's Falcons were riding the updraft along the cliff face. Far below, Hooded Crows were patrolling the beach. Oxalis and Gallium were among the weedy plants on the acropolis.

*****

The trip back down the hill again passed through the village. One of the strange sights was a combination laundromat and lending library in one of the stalls along the main thoroughfare.

Back down on the beach, they were still hauling sand.

*****

The bus climbed the hill and drove around to the Harbor of St Paul (St Souls) where the Apostle Paul was thought to have landed about 58 AD. Paul was supposed to have walked the island preaching and performed a miracle near Soroni, about 15 miles away. A chapel, Aghios Soulas, was built on the hot spring where the miracle occurred. The miracle was healing some sponge divers with a skin affliction common to sponge divers. It usually goes away when the diver leaves the sea for a few days or takes a mineral bath treatment.

This was a pretty little cove with a couple beaches and a small chapel. The west side of the acropolis face was used to film "The Guns of Navarone".

Along the road were small karst caves used to shelter donkeys, other livestock, and equipment. Caves had been used to shelter animals at night and over the winter for as much as 6,000 years. A similar cave is possibly the "inn and manger" where Jesus was purported to have been born in an area outside Bethlahem commonly used for stabeling livestock.

Harbor of St Paul (St Souls)

The road lead above Lardos and then through olive groves to Laerma. Nearby was Moni Thari founded in the 9th centuary with the church of Áyios Yióryios that contained some 14th century frescoes. We turned south for 2 km to the monastery of Thari, dedicated to the Archangel Michael, the encourager. The small domed stone church or kathólikon contains many frescoes dating from 1300 to about 1450 A.D. displayed on the walls of the nave and in the barrel vaulted dome. Many of the frescoes had been recently cleaned thanks to agrant from a rich Texan but many others were dark with the accumulation of smoke from votive candles and the humidity. The lay sister, who acted as cook and caretaker for the monastery and its 15 monks, was formerly a public health instructor at Harvard.

Monastery of Thari

There were many burned-over areas through the forest of Alepo pines, oaks and some eucalyptus. Ilex and arbutus were among the understory shrubs and trees. There was also a Nazi vacation site.

We made a final stop at a ceramic shop that produced very good work then back to the Sun Beach for the evening.

*****

The hotel dining room took 45 minutes to cook and serve a pizza. At the thirty minute mark I asked what was taking so long and the manager said I should relax and enjoy my vacation as if my vacation was an excuse for their inefficiency.

*****

XVI

It's 5:30 A.M. and I'm finally back on schedule. Only three day of diary left and I hope I can finish it today.

*****

The Thursday tour was to be down the west side of the island. Rain clouds obscured Rodos and the Turkish coast.

During breakfast on the terrace, a Greek Navy amphibious landing ship (LST) dropped anchor off Trianda, opened its well door and dropped its ramp. It sat there, swinging on its anchor, for about an hour. They were probably running drills of various kinds. It finally closed up and left. An Army Huey helicopter flew south along the coast right on schedule as it had every morning. With a crisis in Albania, security was a little tighter.

While waiting for the tour, I discussed the hotel landscaping with the manager. The grass was being cut too short. There was lack of a central landscape theme. Most of the shrubs were inappropriate for their intended use such as using Pittisporum and hibiscus as closely pruned hedges along the walks. He said that was the way Greeks landscaped. I told him that appearance was a big selling point in getting return business and that a good landscape would enhance his reputation. He replied that they were booked solid. I guess you can't argue with success or with someone who does his own landscaping.

The tour group was the same as on the previous day, but the bus was a little smaller. We would be on some rougher roads with less maneuvering room. This time we took the highway heading west.

*****

Near the airport, we met a small Army convoy. Several military installations were on the island. All Greek males were required to put in 18 months of military service.

We passed the airport at Paradissi and turned inland to visit the Petaloudes Valley, also known as the Valley of the Butterflies. Our small bus made the tight turns easily to the concession stands where the stream began near the head of the valley. This stream, called the Pelican River, began below the Kalopetra Monastery. It rushed down a narrow, steep-sided valley through a thick hardwood forest. Common trees and shrubs included "maple" or Plane Tree, *Phillyrea latifolia*, Oriental Sweet Gum "balsam tree" or Zithia (*Liquidamber orientalis*), Storax (*Syrax officinalis*), and an oak (probably *Quercus coccifera*), the mastic tree or lentisc (*Pistachia lentiscus*), arbute or strawberry tree (*Arbutus unedo*), carob or locust tree (*Ceratonia siliqua*), laurel or sweet bay (*Laurus nobilis*), olive (*Olea europea*), Phoenician juniper (*Juniperus Phoenicea*), European holly (*Ilex aquifolium*), sage-leaf cistus (*Cistus salvifolius*), Tree Heath or heather (*Erica arborea*), Hairy Thorny Broom (*Calycotome villosas*), Gorse (*Genista acanthoclada*), thyme (*Thymus capitatus*), savory or satureia (*Sateurja thymbra*), Stink Aster (*Dittrichia vicosa [Inula vicosa]*), and sage (*Salvia officinalis*). A relatively rare endemic of Rhodes, the Rhodes Spring Sowbread (*Cyclamen reptandum rhodense*) was found in the valley. It is recognized by a delicate light pink or white with a pink ring around the mouth.

The cool stream water moderates the temperature and humidity in the valley to within the range needed for the a large population of the Jersey Tiger Moth (*Panaxia quadripunctaria* Poda) to thrive. This is not the only place in Europe or on Rhodes where this moth occurs

Petaloudes Valley

but the only place it occurs in such a large population. We were about a month early to see any of these moths. Eggs are deposited about the end of September and hatch in a month. During the wet winter season the caterpillars feed on understory shrubs such as arbutus (*Arbutus Unedo*) and myrtle (*Myrtus communis*). They molt six times before early May when they pupate on or under ground. The adults emerge in early June and begin a migration to this and several similar valleys to form mating aggregations in August. The females dispurse up to 30 km to lay eggs. The adults do not feed.

The adult moth wing is an equilateral triangle about an inch on a side. A pink stripe bisects the moth from head to tail. The wings are brown-black with two cream color bars slanted to the rear on each forewing. They react to ultrasonic noise This probably evolved from avoiding bat sonar.

*****

Several of the group walked down the stream and were picked up at a taverna at the bottom of the hill.

Back to the coast road and past Theologos, we came to Soroni with the Island's main power plant, an old diesel powered unit, that was being replaced. It must have been water cooled since it sat right on the beach. We later saw the 30 ton unit being moved along the highway. Two tractors pulled it on a trailer with 110 tires. Large wooden load spreaders were used to protect the road.

Most of the drinking water was pumped from shallow wells and distributed with no treatment. There did not appear to be much sewage treatment other than septic tanks and ocean outfalls.

The coast road was lined with orchards of peaches and apricots and olives. Many fields were being prepared for planting. A few of the cold weather crops, like cabbage, were still in the ground. Wild flowers, especially the yellow mustard and a white composite, were rampant. Greenhouses were raising tomatoes and cucumbers growing in the ground but strung on trellises.

We made a pit stop at Mandirko. I looked at the greenhouses and around the harbor, then bought a Coke and joined the rest of the group at the local taverna. Several fishermen were just getting in off the water and having fish for breakfast.

Just past Skála Kamírou was the ruins of a Knights fortification which was not easily accessible by road. Looking to the north across the multi-hued blue water were the island of Sýmé (Simi) and the tip of the Turkish Dracya peninsula.

The road turned up the Lirono River valley to Kritinia with a cemetery being decorated for Easter. Blue and green crypts were visible. Southward through the wooded hills was Siana, the island honey center. The mix of pine and sage produced a reddish, aromatic honey.

The forested bulk of Akramillis Mountains blocked the view of the sea and the islands to the north. A roadkill badger was lying along the roadside.

Akramillis Mountains

As we approached the village of Monolithos, a Knights castle on the monolith became visible. I guess this is where the definition the term "monolith" came from. The castle sits on what looks like a light gray volcanic plug. It is contrasted against a deep blue background that was fading to a misty bluish-white. The small island of Hálki hovered in the background.

Near Apolakia, we took a small road through the hills. The road wall lined with small white composite flowers and hundreds of bee hives painted blue. Mixed hardwood and Alepo pine forest provided shade for cyclamens, stork bill, several mallows and other early spring flowers. We finally stopped for lunch at Plimiri in the cool sunshine.

*****

Returning by the coast road we stopped to look at Monolithos castle then stopped at Siana at the Emory winery. The winery produced several nice wines and a selection of a dozen brandies. Fermentation vessels were modern steel. The wines were aged in wood. Bottling was a combination of man and machine.

Two birds seen locally were what looked like the Woodchat Shrike and a Pied Flycatcher.

*****

The road east from Siana circled around the east side of the Ataviros mountains, through thick green Alepo pines. The road was very good. It had been built by the Italians during their occupation and lead to the villa of the Italian commander. Italians and, later, German soldiers used this area as a recreation site. An abandoned private school and the Deer and Roe Hotel sit waiting for restoration and exploitation.

The 15th century church of St. Nicholas Foundoukli was small and dark with a sweet water spring and old olive and fig trees. It was one of the many private chapels built and maintained by a family. We passed near the retreat of Profítis Ilías (Profit Elias). Near Trianda, we climbed 5 km to the Fileramos Monastery on the site of the ancient city of Ialysos. Ialysos was the least important of the three Dorian cities inhabited by the Phoenicians. The acropolis was built atop Mount Filerimos in the 15th centuary BC. John Cantacuzene used it as a Byzantune fortress against the Genoese in 1248. Suleiman the Magnificent occupied it and used it as a fort against the Knights in 1522. A third centuary BC Temple of Athena Polias and Zeus Polieus lies under the Byzantine church. Little remains of Ialysos but the monastery was in good repair. It covered the hilltop and had a spectacular view of the plain below. A Sparrowhawk was working the open grass.

Webworms and spittle bugs were attacking some of the pine trees along the road. I had noticed this in several localized areas during the trip.

*****

The last stop was at the studio of the impressionist artist, Gustave Alhadeff. Carol wanted something from Greece so we picked a painting of an old-style fishing boat. This boat still worked the waters off Lindos.

In the evening we went out to supper with Michael and Mary Bikaris and Gustave Alhadeff. Good food, a couple bottles of retsina and stimulating conversation.

*****

XVII

Friday was not starting off well. We were supposed to verify our return flight three days in advance. I had verified both the legs to Rhodes and Rhodes back to San Antonio before we left Corfu. No problem. I called Olympic Airlines just to check. They said we were not in the computer so tough luck. They did not care that we had valid tickets. I called our RCI travel agent and found they did not have an emergency number - call back in 8 hours. We got the hotel travel person on line and Olympic Airlines said to come down to their office so they could see the tickets.

We took a taxi down town to the airline office and got to see the local manager within a few minutes. He did not have any record of our reservations or, for that matter, how we got to Rhodes. Our tickets for Sunday morning were no good because we were not in his computer. He could get us out Monday, but since he was a good guy and we had paid tickets and an international connection to make, maybe he could get us on the plane Saturday night. They had 2000 high school students to get back to their parents Sunday. (I took his offer and finally got through to our RCI travel agent located in Michigan who said they had contacted Olympic Airlines and, not to worry, the reservations were still good for Sunday. This has resulted in several letters and phone calls but no reply or explanation from the airline. RCI offered a settlement which they never paid.)

We called a local travel agent who checked the reservations. She recomended we take the Saturday flight. She also arranged a hotel for this unplanned overnight stay in Athens.

That settled, we went to Old Town and spent the afternoon seeing the sights and visiting the archeological museums in the Knights Hospital and the Palace of the Grand Master.

*****

We entered at the Eleftherias Gate, passed through Symi Square and Argyrokastrou Square with the art museum and bank and the Knight's infirmary housing a folk art museum into Alexander the Great Square. Crossing Ippoton St. into Mouisson Square we entered through the massive doors of the Hospital. It was a huge square two story cut coquina stone structure with a 10,000 square foot mosaic courtyard surrounded by a portalis with an arched colonnade rebuilt by the Italians. The portalis was dark and cool in the crisp noon sun, with four curved beams meeting in a point between the columns. This area held many artifacts awaiting disposition. The courtyard was covered with hokhláki (a stone mosaic), and sported an ancient stone lion and pyramids of catapult stones. The arches in the second floor portalis were shorter than the ground floor. Inside of the portalis were open wards lined with private rooms no more than 4X8 feet. Some of the larger rooms were being used as display rooms for collections of pottery, glass and bronze artifacts and Greek and Roman marble statues, busts, funerary steils and pieces. One of the statues was a Hellenistic statue of Aphrodite that had been dredged up in a fisherman's net. Durrell had called this his Marine Venus.

Window shopping our way along Socratous Street we looked at gold jewelry that were bargains. With a little bargaining, they all offered to pay the duty. We stopped a several art galleries and stopped to watch a weaver work on a Persian rug. Dozens of shops had leather goods, ties and scarves, and furs. Lunch was at a taverna near the Mosque of Suliman and the clock tower.

*****

One older lady shopkeeper greeted me, "Kaliméra" in demotic or common vernacular Greek. I replied with the more formal, "Kaliméra sa". She changed gears and launched into kathomilouméni which is pretty close to classical Greek and sounds different from street Greek. So much for showing off. I told her my Greek was poor and she was speaking too fast and we went back to English.

*****

Around the corner was Revolution Square and the Palace of the Grand Master. This fourteenth-century fortress was built for the elected Grand Master of the Knights of the Order of St John of Jerusalem. The Order had been founded during the Crusades in the 11th century. After the Crusaders were driven out of Palestine, they settled on Cyprus. In 1309 the Knights bought Rhodes and ruled the island for about 200 years. They were defeated by the Turks and made a negotiated retreat on 22 December 1522.

The original structure was destroyed in 1856 while being used as an ammunition depot. It was rebuilt by the Italians as a summer home for Mussolini and Vicktor Emmanuel III, King of Italy and Albania and Emperor of Ethiopia. The dimensions were about twice those of the Hospital.

An exhibit called "Ancient Rhodes" was on display. I found that the shard from Lindos was a string handle from a middle to late neolithic form Kalythies (500-3700 B.C.) jug.

The second floor was furnished in period items. Roof top terraces held fountains and numerous marble statues and busts and catapult stones.

We took the Ippoton or Street of the Knights to the gate we had entered and caught a taxi to Sun Beach.

*****

Within an hour of sunset, a dozen or so flocks of about a hundred small brown finch-like birds came in from the east and hit the shrubs along the beach for a few minutes. Then they headed west out over the Aegean. The weather had cleared so the snow-covered mountains of Turkey were visible. The birds were taking advantage of the high pressure and clear weather to jump to mainland Greece.

*****

Our painting was delivered ready to ship. I had the hotel call their UPS equivalent who eventually refused to ship it. Another minor panic.

*****

VIII

Home stretch.

*****

The Saturday morning sun came up a red orange ball out of the blue mountains in Turkey. Flocks of little brown birds were still heading west into the cold weather in central Europe. A single bird about the size and sound of a Mockingbird sat on an oleander. It was a Jay (<u>Garrulus</u> <u>glandarius</u>). My morning walk on the beach was at low tide with a flat sea and no wind. I found several shells and several kinds of algae. Turtle grass had been washed ashore, and I found a small sea hare, gray about 2.5 inches square with dark gray stripes, wrapped around a turtle grass stem.

Since we could not ship the painting, we headed downtown again for last minute shopping and to buy a suitcase big enough for the painting. Back by noon, we packed and went out for supper. We checked out about seven in time for a ride out to the airport. The plane was an hour late.

*****

We were met at the airport by the travel agent representative who took us to the Hotel Fenix in Athens. This hotel was a welcome change with hot water and enough pressure for a good shower and lights bright enough to read by.

*****

Sunday morning TV was a choice of several religious broadcasts in Greek or Italian, CNN or Fraggle Rock in Greek. I watched swallows swooping and listened to sparrows chirping while Carol dressed. I got the bags down and we sat down for a miserable continental breakfast of burned toast and warm tea. Transportation to the airport arrived about 0900.

We went through customs and two metal detectors. The carry-on bags went through a computer enhanced x-ray that produced a

165

color-coded picture. A little after eleven, we were bussed out to our plane. This time the weather was clear and sunny but still cool as we waited to board our Boeing wide body jet for a ten hour flight across eight time zones.

The weather was clear for the first half-hour of the flight, then patchy clouds appeared over the Adriatic. It was cloudy half way across France. North of Avignon, lunch was served. The plane's speed was 477 mph at 37,000 ft with an outside air temperature (OAT) of -54ºF. Our location was shown on the projection TV monitors.

Across France, the farms and small towns looked like a very difficult giant jigsaw puzzle of irregular green or tan pieces. All towns and cities, large or small, were either on major road intersections or on rivers.

I dozed off while the movie ran and woke about 700 miles west of Cliffden, Ireland, in time for supper. The north Atlantic was overcast all the way to Nova Scotia where snow was still on the ground.

*****

We arrived a Kennedy Airport in New York, in late afternoon and had a couple hours' wait for our plane to St Louis. Takeoff was about dark. After a bumpy ride, we made an approach, but took a waveoff at St Louis about 9 P.M. due to a severe thunder storm.

*****

We flew around for a couple hours and had to land in Kansas City to refuel finally arriving at St Louis about 0100.

We got the baggage and waited for the hotel shuttle. It arrived a little after 2 A.M. We were up at 0500 to catch the shuttle back to the terminal to catch our plane to San Antonio.

*****

It was about 1100 when we walked in our front door. I had enjoyed about all I could stand - till next time.

*****

XIX

Overview

Looking back on the trip there have been many changes in the intervals between 1841, 1937, 1962 and present. The weather has remained a constant and politics, if constant means continuous change, is unchanged.

Compare this poem of the GLIFA'DHA BEACH today with the GLIFA'DHA BEACH of 1962 at the beginning of this book.

*****

RETURN TO GLIFA'DHA BEACH

For forty years
    tourists,
    developers,
    soldiers,
    and politicians
    trod this beach.

Their eyes have coveted those
    hills covered with oak and olive trees for condos
    good anchorage in the Saronic Gulf for pleasure craft
    and the fair country girls of myth
    as they approach
    from Athi'nai to the north.

The forty civilizations
    that spilled their blood
    for this beach and these hills
    have been replaced
    with the greed and trappings
    of yet another culture.

In 1962, I had come as a warrior.
My summer had been spent in peace
    in a small family hotel on the beach
    looking south and west across the Gulf.

In 1997 the hotel is gone
    beneath a resort complex.
    The quiet road has become
    a six lane divided high speed highway
    lined with high-rise buildings.

The beach has been extended half a mile
    the rubble of demolition
    covered with sand, hotels,
    and expensive homes

Up each day to catch the morning,
    awakened by the soft knock of the maid
    who left croissants, jam
    and tea on the terrace.

This time
    I was wakened
    by a computer driven telephone
    and the noise of traffic.

I watched a cold April morning sky
    lighten with no softening drape of fog.

The yellow and white Caroline was gone
    along with Aristotle and Jackie O.

The quiet beach and fishing boats
    are gone.

My war went well.
I have returned as a visitor

The quiet village
    is a bustling city of malls and botiques.

Athens has grown from less than a million
    to over four million souls.

The slum called the Plaka and set for razing,
    was saved and has become the yuppy dream,
    a place of quaint housing
    and trendy tavernas.

Today's flight is on Olympic Airlines
    from the same airfield
    I flew from in 1962.

Nights of
    Ouso and racci and retsina
Afternoons of
    white goat cheese, raw squid, and fish
are still available - for a price -
    but the spreading oaks are gone.

Pizza and Greek salads
    have replaced bif stek and
    stuffed grape leaves
    in the bars and restaurants.

Greek, German, Italian, and English
    are widely heard
    and the drachma
    is a stable currency.

Carl April 97

Would I make this trip again? In a heartbeat. Would I stay longer? Please don't throw me in that briar patch! A couple months at different times of the year would work. We saw a lot but had to leave a lot for next time. The homework helped but the desire to see and do things was constrained by season, weather and time.

Birds of Greece

April 4-17 1997

Identifications were best guess using picture keys and distribution maps.

Herons, Egrets and Bitterns:
Arideidae:Hawks: Accipiter

Accipiter <u>*nisus*</u>	Sparrowhawk	Rhodes

Falcons: Falconidae

Falco <u>*eleonorae*</u>	Eleonora's Falcon	Rhodes

Gulls: *Laridae*

Larus <u>*audouinii*</u>	Audouin's Gull	Corfu, Rhodes
Larus <u>*melano- cephalus*</u>	Mediterranean Gull	Rhodes

Pigeons and Doves: *Columbidae*

Streptoptopelia <u>*decaocto*</u>	Collared Dove	Corfu

Swallows, Martins: *Hirundinidae*

Hirundo <u>*rustica*</u>	Swallow	Corfu

Accentors: *Prunellidae*

Prunella <u>*modularis*</u>	Dunnock	Corfu

Turdidae

Saxicola <u>*torquata*</u>	Stone Chat	Corfu
Turdus <u>*totquatus*</u>	Ring Ouzel	Corfu

Warblers: *Sylviidae*

Acrocephalus <u>*scirpaceus*</u>	Reed Warbler	Corfu

Flycatchers: Muscicapidae

Ficedul <u>*hypoleuca*</u>	Pied Flycatcher	Rhodes

Penduline Tits: Remizidae

Remiz <u>*Pendulinus*</u>	Penduline Tit	Corfu

Tits: Paridae

Parus <u>*major*</u>	Great Tit	Corfu
Parus <u>*ater*</u>	Coal Tit	Corfu

Shrikes: Laniidae

Lanus senator	Woodchat Shrike	Rhodes

Crows: Corvidae

Pica pica	Magpie	Corfu
Corvus corone cornix	Hooded Crow	Rhodes

Starlings: Sturnidae

Sturnus vulgaris	Starling	Corfu, Rhodes

Sparrows: Passeridae

Passer domesticus	House Sparrow	Corfu
Passer hispaniolensis	Spanish Sparrow	Corfu

*****

Seashells of Greece

Collected April 1997

Best guess identifications were made based on picture keys, keys, checklists, and maps.

Phylum Mollusca
   Class Gastropoda
      Order Opisthobranchiata
         Suborder Nudibranchiata
   Family Dorididae

Cryptobranchiatae   Sun Beach
                    wrapped around the base in Turtlegrass
Order Prosobranchiata
Family Fissurellidae: The Keyhole Limpets
Fissurella reticulata   Reticulated limpet: Kamborno pt
Family Pattellidae: The True Limpets
Patella ferruginca   Ribbed Mediterranean Limpet:
Gouvia Bay, Sidari, Glyfada Beach, Athens, Lindos
Patella cerulea   Rayed Mediterranean Limpet: Gouvia Bay
Family **Trochidae:**The Monodonts
Gibbula albidum   Whitish Gibbula: Lake Korissia, Gardiki
Bch, Athens, Lindos, Sun Bch
Family **Turritellidae:** TheTuritellas
Turritella communis   Common European Turritella: Govia Bay
Turritella mediterranea   Mediterranean Turritella: Lake Korissia
Family **Vermetidae:**The Worm-shells
Petaloconchus subcancellatus   Variable Worm-shell: Rhodes
Vermicularia arenaria   Gouvia
Bay, Athens, Kammborno pt

Family **Cerithidae:**The Ceriths

Cerithium vulgatum	European Cerith:	Gouvia Bay, Gardiki Bch, Sun Bch

Family Strombidae:True Conchs

Strombus decorus	Persian Conch:	Gouvia Bay

Family Naticidae: The Moon Shells

Payraudcautia intricata	European Gray Moon:	Lindos
Natica filosa	Flamed Moon:	Sun Beach

Family**Muricidae:** The Murex Shells

Bolinus brandaris	Purple Dye Murex;	Gardiki Beach

Family **Columbellidae:** The Dove-Shells

Columbella rustica	Rustic Dove-Shell:	Gardiki Beach,

Lindos, Sun Beach,

Family **Fasciolaridae:** Tulips and Spindle Shells

Fusinus sp.	Lindos

Family **Cancellaridae:** The Nutmegs

Cancellaria sp	Gouvia Bay

Family **Conidae:** The Cones

Conus ventricosus	Mediterranean Cone:	Lindos

Class Pelecypoda (Bivalvia)

Family Arcidae: The Ark Clams

Arca noae	Noah's Ark:	Glyfada Beach
Barbatia barbata	European Bearded Ark:	Glyfada Beach

Family Anomiidae: The Jingle Shells

Anomia ephippium	European Jingle Shell:	Athens

Family Pteriidae: The Wing Oysters

Pteria hirundo	European Winged Oyster:	Kammborno pt

Family **Ostreidae:** TheTrue Oysters

Ostrea sp   Gouvia Bay

Family **Cardiidae:** The Cockles

Acanthocardium tuberculata Gouvia Bay,
Tuberculate Cockle:
Gardiki Bch, Lindos, Sun Bch

Cerastoderma edule   Common European   Lake Korissia, Glyfada
                                              Cockle:

Family **Donacidae:** The Donax and Bean Clams

Donax trunculus   Truncate Donax: Paleokostritsa, Glyfada

Family **Veneridae:** The Venus Clams

Venerupis decussata   Decussater Venus: Govia Bay

Venerupis aurea   European Aurora Venus: Gouvia Bay

Dosina exoleta   Mature Dosina: Gardiki Beach

Pitar rudis   Rough Pitar Venus: Paleokostritsa

Callista chione   Smooth Callista: Lindos

Family *:***Ungulinidae:** The Diplodon Clams

Diplodonta rotunda   Rotund Diplodon: Govia Bay,
                                             Gardiki Bch, Paleokostritsa

Family **Pholadidae:** The Pholads and Piddocks:

Pholas dactylus   European Piddock: Gouvia Bay,
                                             Gardiki Bch, Athens, Kammborno pt, Lindos

Land snails

Family **Helicidae**:

Trochoidea cretica	Cretian Land Trochus	Paleokostritsa,
Kammborno pt		
Helix aspera	Speckled Escargo:	Sun Beach

Family **Subulinidae**

Rumina decollata	Decollate Snail:	Paleokostritsa,
Sun Bch		

Family **Clausiliidae**: The Door Snails

Albinaria coerulea	Bluish Door Snail:	Paleokostritsa

Three other unidentified land snails

Class **Cephalopoda,**
Subclass **Dibranchiata**

Sepia sp.	Cuttlefish (cuttle bone).	Corfu, Rhodes

Miscellaneous Animals

The following were seen and tenatively identified.

Phylum **Coelenterata**

Order **Actiniaraia**

Family **Cribrinidae**

Anemonia sulcata	Snakelock Anemones	Gouvia Bay

Phylum Arthropoda

Class Crustacea

Order Cirripedia: Barnacles

Suborder Lepadomorpha: Gooseneck Barnacles

Suborder Balanomorpha

Family Barnacles**: Cirripedia**

Balanus sp.	Acorn shells:	Lake Korissia

Butterflies

	Frittillary	Corfu
	Yellow sulfer	Corfu
Panaxia quadripunctaria	Jersey Tiger Moth:	Rhodes

Glass-Snake Lizard Road kill

Family Anguillidae

Ophiosaurus sp	Corfu
	Road kill

Order Carnivora

Family Mustelidae

Taxidea sp	Badger	Rhodes
	Road kill	

Trees, Shrubs and Wildflowers

These trees, shrubs and herbs were those seen in flower or that could be otherwise identified using keys, checklists, and other sources. Common vegetable crops are not listed but include potatoes, and salad crops such as tomatoes, cucumbers and lettuce grown in greenhouses and greenhouse grown ornamental plants and table flowers. Plants around Athens are not included.

Gymnosperms

Pinaceae: Pine Family

Pinus halepensis	Aleppo Pine	Corfu, Rhodes
Pinus nigra	Austrian Pine	Corfu

Cupressaceae: Cypress Family

Cupressus sempervirens	Italian Cypress	Corfu
Juniperus phoenicea	Phoenicean Juniper	Rhodes

Angiosperms

Gramineae: Grasses

Arundo donax	Giant Reed	Corfu

Palmae: Palm Family

Phoenix dactylifera	Date Palm:	Corfu, Rhodes
P. canariensis	Canary Palm:	Corfu, Rhodes

Liliaceae: Lily Family

Muscari neglectum	Common Grape Hyacinth	Corfu
Smilax aspera [S. mauritanica, S. nigra]	Common Smilax	Corfu

Agavaceae: Agave Family

Agave americana	Agave, Century Plant	Rhodes
Yucca gloriosa	Yucca	Rhodes

177

Fagaceae: Oak Family

Quercus aegilops (Q. macrolepis)	Valonia Oak	Corfu
Q. coccifera	Kermes Oak	Rhodes

Ulmaceae: Elm Family

Ulmus canescens	Mediterranean Elm	Corfu

Moraceae: Mulberry Family

Ficus carica	Fig	Corfu, Rhodes

Chenopodiaceae: Fathen Family

Salicornia europaea	Glasswort, Sea Samphire	Corfu

Aizoaceae: Aizoon Family

Mollugo cerviana	Mollugo	Corfu
Mesembryanthemum crystacrystallinum	Ice Plant:	Corfu, Rhodes

Lauraceae: Laurel Family

Laurus nobilis	Laurel, Sweet Bay	Rhodes

Ranunculaceae: Buttercup Family

Anemone coronaria	Crown Anemone::	Corfu

Papaveraceae: Poppy Family

Papaver rhoeas	Common Poppy	Rhodes
P. apulum	Common Poppy	Rhodes

Cruciferae: Mustard Family

Brassica fruticulosa	cabbage:	Corfu, Rhodes
Lepidium spinosum	Pepperwort	Corfu, Rhodes

Platanaecae: Plane Tree Family

Platanus orientalis	Plane Tree	Corfu, Rhodes

Pittosporaceae: Pittosporum Family

Pittosporum tobita	Pittosporum	Corfu, Rhodes

Rosaceae: Rose Family

Prunus dulcis (Amygdalus communis, A. dulcis, P.communis)	Almond	Corfu, Rhodes
Rubus sanctus(R. ulmifolius)	Bramble or Balckberry	Corfu
Rosa sempervirens	Wood rose	Corfu

Hamamelidaceae: Witch Hazel Family

Liguidambar orientalis	Oriental Sweet gum, maple, zithia, balsam tree	Rhodes
Leguminosae: Pea Family		
Acacia cyanophyla	Blue-leaved Wattle	Corfu
Ceratonia siliqua	Carob, Locust Tree	Corfu, Rhodes
Cercis siliquastrum	Judas Tree	Corfu, Rhodes
Calycotome villosa	Hairy Thorny Broom	Rhodes
Genista acanthoclada	Gorse:	Rhodes
Melilotus altissimus	Tall Melilot	Rhodes
Trifolium speciosum	Clover	Corfu
Vicia villosa	Fodder Vetch	Corfu
Oxalidaceae: Oxalis Family		
Oxalis europaea	Oxalis:	Corfu
Geraniaceae: Geranium Family		
Geranium tuberosun	Tuberous Cranes-bill	Corfu
Erodium gruinum	Long-beaked Stork's-bill	Corfu, Rhodes
Erodium hoeftianum	Stork's-bill	Rhodes
Euphorbiaceae: Spurge Family		
Euphorbia characias	Large Medeterranean Spurge	Corfu
Aquifoliaceae: Holly Family		
Ilex aquifolium	European Holly	Rhodes
Rutaceae: Rue Family		
Citrus limon	Lemon	Rhodes
Vitaceae: Vine Family		
Vitus vinifera	Grape	Corfu, Rhodes
Malvaceae: Mallow Family		
Lavertera cretica	Cretan Mallow:	Corfu
Cistaceae: Rockrose Family		
Cistus salvifolius	Sage-leaved Cistus:	Rhodes
Tamaricaceae: Tamarix Family		
Tamarix tetrandra	Tamarisk:	Rhodes

Myrtaceae: Myrtle Family

Myrtus communis	Common Myrtle	Corfu, Rhodes
Eucalyptus globulus	Blue Gum:	Rhodes

Ericaceae: Heath Family

Arbutus unedo	Strawberry Tree, Arbutus:	Corfu, Rhodes
Erica arborea	Tree Heath	Rhodes

Primulaceae: Primrose Family

Cyclamen repandum rhodense Spring Sowbread		Rhodes

Styracaceae: Storax Family

Styrax officinalis	Storax	Rhodes

Oleaceae: Olive Family

Ligustrum lucidum	Chinese Privet	Corfu, Rhodes
Olea europaea	Olive	Corfu, Rhodes
Phillyrea latifolia	Rhodes	

Apocynaceae: Oleander Family

Nerium oleander	Oleander	Corfu, Rhodes

Rubiaceae: Bedstraw Family

Gallium heldreichii	Bedstraw	Corfu
Gallium mollugo	Hedge Bedstraw:	Corfu

Labiatae: Mint Family

Marrubium vulgare	White Horehound	Corfu
Rosmarius officinalis	Rosemary	Rhodes
Thymus capitatus	Thyme	Rhodes
Salvia officinalis	Sage	Rhodes

Solanace: Potato Family

Lycium schweinfurthii	Tea Tree:	Corfu

Passifloraceae: Passion Flower Family

Passiflora caerulea	Passion Flower	Corfu

Compositae: Daisy Family

Anthemis arvensis	Corn Chamomile	Rhodes
Cynara scolymus	Globe Artichoke	Corfu, Rhodes
Sonchus oleraceus	Sawtooth SowThistle:	Rhodes

Greek food. Greek dancing.

Seen through Hellen of Troy's rainbow.

A Dickens Christmas London

December 2000

By

Carl Lahser

A New Kind of Vacation

A few years ago we saw an article on a new kind of vacation - home exchanges. Over the past twenty years we looked at several less expensive ways to vacation. Club Med did not offer activities or locations we were particularly interested in. Holiday licenses were out since we are not campers or RV people. We did purchase a couple of timeshares and have traded timeshare periods to several locations for ski or beach weeks in the US, Mexico, and Greece through RCI. This new home exchange idea sounded interesting.

Surfing the Internet turned up some information on home exchanges. It appears organized home exchanges have been around since 1965 in England and Europe. They have been available on the Internet since about 1985. As of January 2001, there were seven home exchange web sites. Several were listed more than once and under different names on different search engines. Some of the websites and fees are as follows:

www.apartmentswap.com	New York City. Free.
www.digsville.com	Free and friendly
www.holi-swaps.com	English. About $40/yr
www.homebase-hols.com	London-based. $60-120 US/yr
www.homeexchange.com	Charges $30 per year but guarantees a free year if you can't find a swap.
www.homelink.org	Free but not user friendly
www.trading-homes.com	$65-95/yr depending on services
www.vacation-homes.com	also charges $30/year.

We signed up for Home Exchange.Com. Over the first year we got several inquiries from Mexico and Canada and one for two weeks in Paris in July. The first year was almost up when we finally hit on one that fit our schedule. A couple working in London called. They wanted to come to San Antonio over Christmas and New Years.

We discussed this possibility for a couple days and decided to try it. Friends made numerous suggestions and thought a Dickens Christmas in London sounded fun. Carol had had a double hip replacement about two years previous but decided it would not be a hindrance.

Several e-mail messages were exchanged before we reserved tickets to London. We bought e-tickets choosing to fly on December 14th because the fare doubled on the 15th. Continental Airline was chosen because it flew direct from Houston to Gatwick and might be less trouble than winter flying out of Atlanta or New York or St Louis. We were to return on 2 January 2001. The flight was scheduled to leave San Antonio about 3 PM and Houston about 6 PM to arrive at Gatwick airport about 9:30 on the 15th. The Internet also found a limo service to move our five suitcases and us from Gatwick right to the front door.

One thing we did in preparation for the swap was to prepare an operating manual for the house. This was probably not necessary but it pointed out features that might otherwise be missed, covered items like the garbage pickup schedule and emergency phone numbers. It also provided information such as where the fire extinguishes were located.

A couple days before we left we began to childproof the house since they had a year old son. It was surprising how much hazardous stuff was under the kitchen sink and otherwise within reach of a toddler. We were years out of practice and probably did not do a super job.

One car was moved out of our two-car garage so our guests could drive into the garage. The garage door opener, security code and key were left for them to pick up at the neighbors next door. We were to pick up their key at the school where they both worked.

London Bound. Thursday the fourteenth of December arrived and Carol had a panic attack when the taxi arrived fifteen minutes early. She still had two bags to close and makeup to complete. The driver and I loaded the packed bags and talked about his trip to London while she finished. He was a retired Marine and he and his wife traveled quite a bit.

We checked in at the Continental Airline counter about two hours early. Our tickets were electronic tickets bought on-line. This was the first time we tried this method. It worked like promised and check in was very easy. By the time we had lunch (the last BBQ for a couple weeks) and walked to the gate we still had over an hour before boarding. Flight CO4, an MD-80, left San Antonio fifteen minutes late. The cabin safety briefing was in seasonal rhyme. There was a two-hour wait to change planes in Houston before the nine-hour flight to London Gatwick. Our new plane was a Boeing 777 and took off 45 minutes late.

Our great circle route took us over or near Hot Springs, Memphis, Cleveland, Toronto, Montreal, Presque Isle, and Gander, then across the Atlantic for a landfall on the west coast of Ireland.

Each seat on this plane had a neat little TV screen with movies and games to entertain the passengers during a nine-hour flight. A flight path video showed where we were which was good since it was cloudy all the way to Ireland. There were also a dozen music channels. Supper was lasagna served over the Middle Atlantic States at 39,000 feet and 687 mph including a 200 mph jet stream.

I woke up with the dawn breaking over a layer of clouds.

North Atlantic Dawn

Screaming eastward at 1000 kph
still in the world of night
the false dawn begins
defining the horizon
as the stars wink out.

A spot of sunlight slides down the wing
Merfolk below might have seen
a silver meteor
heading southeast

two hours before their dawn.

The cloud deck was still under us as we passed over the Cliffden radio beacon and central Ireland. The clouds parted for a couple minutes near Waterford, Ireland, on St. George's Channel. A green glimpse of the eastern coast of Ireland was overcast with no sun. England became visible through the clouds over Wales between Swansea and Cardiff. We crossed the Bristol Channel near the mouth of the Severn and across Somerset and Dorset counties to the Isle of Wight in the English Channel.

It's funny how you can be disoriented. I had thought France was east of England but there it was hiding under the clouds about forty miles across the English Channel to the south.

We turned north across brown, tan and green fields divided by hedgerows of Plain trees with houses highlighted in the early morning sun. There were long low hills and small lakes full with the recent rain. Haystacks and cattle occupied some of the fields. Water was standing in many of the fields as we crossed Hampshire and Berkshire counties to Gatwick about 30 miles west of London. Touchdown at Gatwick was right on schedule Friday morning.

No birds were visible on the approach but rooks were plentiful perched on aircraft and around the terminal area.

We got off the plane with a couple hundred other passengers. Carol had had hip replacement surgery and must have looked in distress because a courtesy cart picked us up. They collected our passports and rushed us through immigration and to the baggage area. I found all but one bag with my pink tape on the handles and found the last one on someoneelse's cart. We loaded the bags and were taken to customs. Along the route we spotted our taxi driver with a big sign. He said he would meet us at the pickup area. We breezed through customs and were out on the sidewalk in nothing flat.

It was about 10 AM, cloudy, and in the upper forties (this was about ten degrees C). Our driver pulled up in a 1997 Austin London cab dressed in a short-sleeve yellow shirt. We had reserved the cab over the Internet for a fixed price of £75 (the rate of exchange was $1.44 to a £ or pound sterling) from the airport thirty-five miles to pick up the key then on to the address. During the trip we discussed recent changes in London, fuel prices, housing costs, the British job market, Millennium Park, classic British cars, and the decrease in smoking in England.

If we had known how to get where we were going and had not had four suitcases plus our carry-on bags we could have taken the train for £10 each to Victoria Station then another £1.90 each on the tube (subway) or bus to the St. John's Wood stop on Wellington Road about three blocks from the address.

I'm glad someone else was doing the driving. We were on an interstate (the M4, I think) and crowded roads through the countryside, more crowded streets through small towns and, finally, London traffic all on the wrong side of the road. About an hour later we stopped at a moneychanger to convert some US dollars to pounds (£). A few more minutes got us to the American School to pick up the key and a few more minutes to the address about 2 PM.

At home in London. Our home for the next two and a half weeks was a nice third floor two-bedroom walk-up apartment (flat) a block from Regents Park in St. John's Wood. The flat was on a small street midway between St. John's Highroad and Wellington Road. It also had a living room, bath, kitchen and utility room and totaled about 900 square feet. It had a gas range and oven, apartment size refrigerator and freezer, and an electric oven. There was an apartment size washer and dryer. Heat was from a small gas boiler on a timer that fed hot water radiators. The boiler was on from 7 to 10 AM and 4-10 PM and kept the place at 60-70 F since many of the windows did not close well. This was much as I remembered London from trips 15 and 20 years past. The bath had a hand-held showerhead and a hot water heated towel rack.

TV was on cable and consisted of six channels but only five stations. We saw numerous satellite dishes on houses and apartment buildings that picked up a hundred or more stations from all over Europe and even the US and Asia.

This apartment building may have been Council housing at some time in the past but not currently. Council housing is low rent public housing complexes. Much of this housing had been built by the government between the end of WWII and the early 1950s. Over the past few years privatization has gained a foothold in England and many of these apartment buildings have been sold to private enterprise. The new owners are expected to upgrade them as rental property rather than upgrading them at government expense.

We looked in the realtors' windows in various parts of town and found one-bedroom apartments beginning about £1000 a month. A three bedroom house with parking went for £3000 a month and up depending on location. Entry-level jobs such as management, secretarial or accounting began at £12,000 to £17,000 a year.

First Time Out. After getting settled we walked past St. John's Churchyard to the St. John's Highroad. We found a green grocer, several small food stores, a small supermarket, several bakery/coffee shops, a butcher shop, several restaurants, two pubs, three newspaper stands, and various small shops within a half-mile. The neighborhood consisted mostly of blocks of apartment buildings. There were no individual homes. Grocery and restaurant prices appeared to be about twice San Antonio prices.

Lunch was in a teahouse. They advertised a roll and coffee or tea for about £2 ($3). I had Welsh rarebit and tea (£8) and Carol had the equivalent of a hamburger, fries, and a coke (£9). This came to about £21 ($30). Eating was going to be expensive.

We bought a few groceries and returned home. A quart of orange juice was £2.5. A small loaf of bread was £2. A jar of strawberry preserves was £3. A quart of milk was £1.75. With a box of cookies the bill was about $15 US.

We watched some TV. *Who wants to be a Millionaire?* That paid off in pounds sterling and left contestants hanging over the commercial to find if they answered correctly. *Wheel of Fortune.* A new show called *The Weakest Link* where the belittled contestants voted off their fellow players who missed questions and moderated by a cranky woman. A James Bond movie. Some local sitcoms. The news said it would be about 2 overnight and about 8 tomorrow. That is low 30s to low 40s. It was cool enough to wrap up in a blanket until the boiler went off at 10 PM. The featherbed felt good in a 60° bedroom.

Saturday. We slept until about eight. The sun was barely up and daylight was not making much headway. Clouds took over the sky but no rain was expected. Pigeons and starlings were feeding in the street and perching on neighboring roofs.

A small back yard contained a couple fig trees under a large crabapple with buds almost ready to pop. A Great Tit landed in the crabapple followed by two others.

A variety of architectural styles and materials were visible for the windows. Brick or stucco were common materials with a few cast concrete structures.

I put on water for tea and discovered I had to push the igniter button and then turn on the gas. Another peculiarity was the kitchen faucet – although it had hot and cold water handles the water did not mix but came out in separate streams. This applied to the bathtub as well but the flows mixed in the hose to the showerhead.

We discussed where to go for the day over breakfast. One of Carol's friends had recommended that we visit the Victoria and Albert Museum and it seemed like a good place to start. We bundled up and off we went.

It was a cold three blocks to the tube station even with a sweater, coat, muffler and hat. Signs in windows said "recruiting" for hiring and "letting" for renting. We bought roundtrip tickets for £3.5 each and took the escalator down about 50 feet to the train. The escalator ran much faster than we were used to. The Jubilee line took us to Westminster station where we transferred to the Green line to the South Kensington station.

The St. John's Wood station was fairly friendly with a short tile lined tunnel to the train platform. It had a couple benches, a candy machine, lots of billboards, and a tile sign indicating "Way Out". Even the wall around the escalators was covered with playbills for shows like "Fossy" and "The Beautiful Game" and travel agencies. The South Kensington station exited on to Cromwell Road near the Science Museum and the Natural History Museum. An arrow pointed to a tunnel leading to the Victoria and Albert.

The Museum has about 7 miles of galleries. We may have covered about two miles. The museum was established after the Great Exhibition of 1851 as the Museum of Manufactures in 1852. Its purpose was to collect examples of the world's craftsmanship as an example and inspiration to students of design. The eclectic collection includes examples of metalworking, glass and ceramics, textiles and clothing, jewelry, woodcarving, furniture, paintings, prints, drawings, and photography. The six-level building itself is a work of art. Items range from Asian art to forgeries to Doc Martin boots. Two galleries contained castings from plaster casts of statuary and architectural examples. Private collections are on display such as the Nehru Gallery of Indian Art, the Toshiba Gallery of Japanese Art, the T.T. Tsui Gallery of Chinese Art, and the Samsung Gallery of Korean Art. European art includes painting by Constable and figures by Rodin. I was particularly interested in the first teapot. We finished the Frank Lloyd Wright exhibit and left.

Returning to the tube station we found it closed. It was after sundown and getting cold so we took a taxi home for £9.

The Tube

Victoria and Albert Museum

Sunday in Trafalger Square. The overnight low was near freezing. The predawn sky was a muddy orange color that faded to gray as a cloudy day dawned.

We discussed the day's excursion and decided on the National Gallery and the area near Trafalger Square.

We left for the underground about 10 AM. We changed trains at the Baker Street Station. The tiles in the walls of this station had a picture of Sherlock Holmes. The Bakerloo train took us past Oxford Circus and Piccadilly Circus to the Charing Cross station. We emerged near South Africa House just east of Trafalger Square.

Trafalger Square was designed and built by John Nash in the 1830s as a memorial to Admiral Lord Nelson who died in the Battle of Trafalger in 1805. A 165-foot column topped by a statue of Nelson dominates the square. The four lions guarding the column's base were designed by Edwin Landseer were added about 1867. A large lighted Christmas tree stood in the square. It could be called "Pigeon Square" by virtue of the couple thousand pigeons fed by tourists and sitting on everything available.

Trafalger Square

We crossed Duncannon Street to St. Martin-in-the-Fields church where services were being held. This is also known as the Royal Parish Church. A church has been on this site since the 11th century. The present church was designed by James Gibbs (a student of Christopher Wren who designed Westminster). It was completed in 1726. The church is famous for its music and for caring for the homeless.

We crossed Charing Cross Road to the National Portrait Gallery. It was just passed noon and the gallery had just opened. Historic portraits included most of the Royal Family since the 14th century and other famous and infamous people in English history like Shakespeare, Tennyson, Dickens, Shaw, the Bronte sisters and a lot more. An exhibit of early female writers was being presented.

We went literally next door to the National Gallery. This is one of the world's great galleries with over 2,200 masterpieces. The collection is selective rather than comprehensive since all its pieces are on view at all times.

The collection began in 1824 when Sir George Beaumont talked the government into buying the collection of John Julius Angerstein after Angerstein's death. There were 38 paintings including Rembrant's *Women Taken in Adultery* and *Adoration of the Shepherds*, Ruben's *Rape of the Sabine Women*, and Titian's *Venus and Adonis*. Additions and gifts have included Leonardo da Vinci, Giotto, Picasso, Botticelli, Holbein, Bellini, van Eyck, Constable, Diego Velazquez, Renoir, Monet and Van Gogh.

William Wilkins designed the main building in the neoclassical style. Construction took place between 1834 to 1838. Just to prove not everything in London is old the Sainsbury Wing was added to the museum in 1991 financed by the Sainsbury grocery family. This wing has some early painting but is used mostly for changing exhibitions and houses the Micro Gallery, the Gallery's database.

Seeing the Old Masters in real life is awesome. They hang in rooms at least fifty feet wide with thirty-foot ceilings. There are guards in the galleries and some electronic security but the pictures are not under glass. Humidity, temperature, and lighting are controlled and no photography is allowed.

We left at closing time about 4 PM. The temperature had dropped to about 40 under a heavy overcast sky.

We went a few blocks north on Charing Cross Road to the *New World* Chinese restaurant on Gerrard Street in London's Chinatown. We bypassed Leicester Square with the statue of Charlie Chaplin standing in the dark rainy plaza and passed by Cecil Court with its bookstores mostly closed for the holidays and the Hippodrome that is one of the world's largest disco nightclubs.

The *New World* was a dim sum restaurant and I tried seaweed and an order of stuffed tofu.

Gerrard St

Outside the *New World* we saw a McDonalds sign a block away on Shaftsbury Avenue. They're everywhere.

A taxi took us home. We remarked about the drizzle and asked about the famous London fog. When I was in London in 1967 the fog cut the nighttime visibility to a hundred yards or less. The next trip to London was in the late 70's after England switched from soft coal and was water-blasting the years of soot accumulation off of everything for the Silver Jubilee. The driver said the fog was rare after they changed coal.

The best thing on TV was the Royal variety show on BBC1. The best comedians and other artist in Britain were showcased.

Monday at the Tate. We were up and ready to go by 10 AM when the maid arrived. She was scheduled every Monday for two hours.

We took the tube to Green Park station to change to the Victoria line. The Green Park station was about a hundred feet down and not as user friendly as some of the other stations with several short flights of steps and long tunnels between train lines. There was an elevator for the handicapped but you had to find one of the staff to operate it and there were still steps to access the elevator.

At Pimlico station we took the escalator to the surface. Following the arrows we found Vauxhall Bridge Road then down to the Thames. We turned right on Millbank and walked the two blocks to the Tate Gallery.

I crossed this heavily traveled street for a view of the Thames. The tide was in and the orange Vauxhall Bridge stood out against the overcast sky. Down stream was the more traditional Lambeth Bridge that leads to Lambeth Road and Lambeth Palace.

The National Gallery had more paintings than it could possibly hold. In 1897 Sir Henry Tate, a rich sugar broker and art collector, contributed £80,000 to establish a new museum. He is famous for inventing the machine for cutting sugar cubes. He convinced art dealer Sir Joseph Duveen to contribute additional resources to build the museum on the site of the old Millbank Prison.

Thames River

The museum opened with 282 oils and 19,000 watercolors from the National Gallery plus Tate's own collection. The national collection of modern art moved in 1916. The space was expanded by 50 percent in 1979 and the Clore Gallery for the Turner collection was added in 1988. The Tate opened a gallery in Liverpool, the hometown of Sir Henry Tate, in 1988. As a part of a £32 million expansion and modernization the Tate acquired the abandoned Bankside Power Station, which was remodeled and opened as the Tate Gallery of Modern Art in 2000.

The main entrance to the Tate was a Greek style portico and had a course of steps. The handicapped entrance was on the ground floor in the Clore Gallery addition and past the gift shop. The elevator took us up to the first floor and into the spaces of the Turner Bequest.

J.M.W. Turner (1775-1851) was a landscape artist and watercolorist. Many of his pieces are in other museums but his largest and most complete collection came from his bequest with the condition that they all remain together. A suite had been set aside in 1910 to display his principle works but it was not until the Clore opening in 1987 that all of his material was housed together. Other Turner paintings I had seen gave the impression of dark and heavy subjects but here were beautiful seascapes, ships and shipwrecks, several almost abstracts, architectural works and some lighter works. His painting kit, fly rod and ship models he had built were on display.

Tate Gallery

We wandered through many of the 29 rooms of priceless art. Several horse paintings by George Stubbs. Lucian Freund's nudes. John Constable's landscapes in light and shadow. Formal portraits beginning in the 16th and 17th centuries by William Hogarth, Van Dyck and others. Modern portraits by David Hockney. Modern still life. Some modern sculptures.

About 3PM we had lunch in the licensed restaurant for about £60. Carol was fascinated by the red cabbage served with her meal and looked for recipes for the rest of the trip.

After lunch we went through two special exhibits. One was of 400 of William Blake's works. The other was the Turner Prize entries. The 2000 artists included Glenn Brown, Michael Raedecker, Tomoko Takashi and Wolfgang Tillmans. Tillmans won the £20,000 Turner Prize.

The museum closed at 5. We exited and entered the cold, gray misty real world. Returning to the tube we found it closed. A taxi took us home.

Taxi Station

Shopping Tuesday. You may have observed there was little pattern to this visit. We wanted to see many of the museums since we expected the weather to be miserable. We had been to Westminster, and had no great desire to see the Buckingham Palace. I had seen London Bridge when it still spanned the Thames in London. Besides we were much older and a little less firm so we picked our visits with more care.

It was Tuesday morning when Carol found she could not plug in her hair drier. The requirement was for a polarized two-prong adaptor and none of the adaptors we had fit. Out I go into the cold to several shops to find an adaptor. Nothing was available. I purchased a new hair dryer for £10 and stopped by one of the bakeshops for breakfast rolls.

The laundry tumbled dry while we dressed and planned the day's agenda. To Mayfair, Piccadilly, Bond Street, Saville Row, Cork Street.

It was a cold, blustery walk to the tube and the wind was blowing a gale coming out of the tube station. The train took us to the Green Park station. The station was across the street from the Ritz hotel. We walked past the Ritz on Piccadilly for two blocks to the Royal Academy of Arts.

Immediately across the street from the Academy was the high-end department store called Fortnum and Mason. It had been founded in 1707 by one of Queen Anne's footmen. The first floor is a collection of fancy foods and two restaurants. The upper floors sell quality and fashionable clothing. We thought about having lunch there but there was a two-hour wait.

Across the street was the St Francis Hotel with an old world dining room. I had Bangers, Bubbles and Squeak and Carol had traditional Fish and Chips served with mashed peas. It was an interesting group for lunch. Like the set of a stuffy English movie there were men in suits and school ties and ladies in high fashion. It looked like most of the tables had at least one bottle of wine. Everyone ate European style with the fork in the left hand. Talk was subdued like it was all classified. Remarkable.

We window shopped down Duke Street and went into a gallery of 18th and 19th century paintings. They were beautiful works beginning at about £1,500. They were displayed on large sliding panels that maximized the number that could be managed in the space.

Since there was no particular plan of attack we went back to Piccadilly along St James past clothing stores Hackett, and Kent and Curwen. We past the Academy of Arts and turned on Albany Court Yard to Saville Row, across on Clifford to New Bond Street. There were several galleries and clothing stores like the Maas Gallery, Gieves and Hawkes, Vercace, Laura Ashley, Burberry. On New Bond Street we found the Fine Art Society, Aspery Gallery and the Bond Street Antiques Centre but had somehow missed Cork Street with its galleries. By asking I found I had crossed Cork Street without realizing it was a real street. Along the one block of Cork Street were Boukamel Contemporary Art, Mayor Gallery, Piccadilly Gallery, Redfern Art Gallery and Tyron and Swann. Nothing less than £100, not much less than £1,000, and many £20,000 to £100,000.

By the time we got back to Piccadilly it was almost 6PM, dark and cold. We walked the block back to the tube station and returned home.

The British Museum. It was Wednesday already. A whole week had passed almost. We got out early, at least for us, about 10 AM. So far it had been cold and overcast but no rain.

We got off a Green Park and transferred to go to Victoria Station to book something for Christmas and a general tour of London. Most businesses would be shut down on Christmas and even the tube and busses were on a holiday schedule.

There were a number of tours with a Christmas dinner. We decided on a trip to Greenwich and Canterbury Cathedral and got tickets for a London tour that allowed on/off as much as you like within 24 hours.

Back to the tube to go to the Russell Square station a block from the British Museum. In Russell Square I noticed the first public restroom I had seen. I still had not seen any water fountains. I did notice many streets had curb cuts possibly for the handicapped but the were all textured making it uncomfortable and possibly dangerous for the handicapped.

Near Russell Square was a cabstand. This was a small green building available to the cab drivers to rest and eat lunch. There were only a few left including one about a hundred yards from our flat near St John's Church Park.

British Museum

A homeless camp was tucked up under some bushes in the park. No one was home. We had seen one person camped in one of the tube stations and another sleeping on the sidewalk. Most of the parks had been private but were turned over to the public because of maintenance cost. In fact, Russell Square, named after Francis Russell, the fifth Duke of Bedford, had once been part of the Duke's estate and contains a statue of the Duke. A few private parks for members only still exist with locked gates.

We entered the British Museum through the north entrance off of Montague Place. This led directly into the mummy collection on the second floor of the north wing with mummies and burial objects from many cultures. Cultures included Egypt, the Middle East, the Orient and the tropical new world.

Down the east wing were collections from archeological sites in Britain. Displays dated from pre-Roman to 19th century industrial relics. Norse wooden objects, coins, jewelry, a chariot.

British Museum Greek Exhibit

We had lunch in the museum teashop. The menu included sandwiches, deserts and drinks. After lunch we went down stairs to visit the first floor exhibits and the gift shops.

The east side was rare books and documents and a single room of new world exhibits.

The 30 galleries on the west side contained numerous Greek and Roman statues and the Elgin marbles from the Acropolis.

We made a few purchases in the bookstore and gift shop and left as the museum was closing. The tube took us home about six.

We stopped in a local pub a block from the flat. The smoke was so thick we immediately left.

Local Pub

Back to Piccadilly and to the Wallace Collection. On Thursday we decided to have lunch at Fortnum and Mason so we left about 10 AM. It was drizzly and cold. We took the tube to Green Park. I noticed a sign posted in several locations in the station, "No Busking". Busking is what the street players do – juggling, singing and mime, etc.

We walked along one side of Old Bond Street to New Bond Street and back window-shopping. Cartier. Channel. Dunhill. Burberry. Sotheby's. One shop had a sign, "Staff Required" and another a sign reading, "Closing Down Sale".

Old and new Phone boxes

Back on Piccadilly we walked a block east to Fortnum and Mason and were seated with no waiting. After several minutes a waiter apparently got tired of waiting in the corner and came to take our order. I ordered fish and chips and a stout. Carol had a steak.

We took the Jubilee line back to Baker Street and a taxi to the Wallace Collection in the Hertford House on Manchester Square off of Oxford Street. This is the collection "pleasing paintings" of the fourth marquis of Hertford and housed in his London townhouse. He died in 1870. He lived most of his life in France and his collection includes 17th and 18th century French furniture, 18th century French clocks, Sevres porcelain, and gold boxes. Paintings include works by Boucher,

Canaletto, Fragonard, Gainesborough, Guardi, Hals, Rembrandt, Reynolds, Rubins, Titian, van Dyck, Velazquez and Watteau. There is also a collection of Oriental and European arms and armor amassed by Sir Richard Wallace the illegitimate son of the Marguis including some forgeries. Lady Wallace gave the collection to the public in 1897 with the provision that it would be a permanent collection and nothing would be added or removed.

It is a fascinating old house divided into 25 galleries furnished in antiques and priceless art. An elevator has been added in the foyer. Chairs are provided for resting and admiring the art. Imagine sitting in an 18th century chair.

When we left it was dark. We took a cab home and arrived in time for the news. There were less Christmas lights in London than many small towns in Texas.

Rain was expected. October had been the wettest October in the 240 years of record keeping. The year 2000 had the most rain in a hundred years. There had been severe flooding and this had caused rail problems responsible for several train wrecks.

Only 40% of the trains were running to Scotland and air traffic was backed up. They were expecting three million air passengers through London over the ten-day holiday period.

There was a scandal over a kid that had been killed by classmates.

Millennium Park was closing on New Years Eve. The park was a scandal being sold off for 25% of the construction cost. Attendance had been only 60% of the expected.

One of the assistant ministers for sports came out for terracing the soccer stadiums to allow standing. This had been outlawed in 1989 when 89 people were killed in accident in Leeds.

Mad cow disease was on the rise and there had been some cases of hoof-and-mouth disease in hogs.

A fan had announced he would buy the Spurs, a local soccer team.

Covent Garden and a Little of Soho. I was up about 7 and it was cold and foggy.

The morning news was more of the same - not very upbeat. Heating gas prices were tied to North Sea oil prices and the price was expected to rise about 25% with the removal of the price cap. Gasoline prices could reach £1 per liter (up from about 80p).

Several people had been indicted for "freshening" condemned poultry intended for pet food. Condemned beef was marked with stain but not poultry. No one had been injured but ....

Olympic training funds had been cut. All track training had been eliminated.

The European Union wanted to privatize the mail service but Britain disagreed.

Covent Garden

Today's outing was to Covent Garden. We took the tube to Green Park and transferred to the Piccadilly line to the Covent Garden station. Following the "Way Out" signs we found James Street and walked a short block to the Piazza and Central Market.

This area is north of the Strand, which originally was on the riverbank, and east of Piccadilly Circus. It began as an area where the monks of Westminster Abbey left their excess garden products for the poor. In the 1630s Inigo Jones laid the Piazza as the first square in London in the Florentine style based on the central plaza in Livorno, Italy. This was intended to be an up elegant housing development. He also designed and built St Paul's Church, completed in 1633. The church was built backward with the alter on the west end so that its grand entrance would face east into the Piazza. The Church officials objected and the interior was reoriented and the east entrance sealed. This east portico area has been used as a stage for outdoor productions and the church has become known as the actor's church. The church interior was burned in 1675 and rebuilt.

In 1670 Charles II granted the right to sell "roots and herbs, whatsoever" to the Earl of Bedford. In 1833 Charles Fowler designed and built a covered central market for wholesale fruit and vegetable sellers. Business blossomed and in 1872 the Victorian Flower Market was built. Jubilee Hall was constructed in 1903 to absorb some of the overflow trading from the adjacent streets.

The Theatre Royal was built in this area in 1663 as one of two legitimate theatres in London (hence the term). The present structure was designed and built by Benjamin Wyatt in 1812.

The Royal Opera House was built on the Piazza in 1732. It suffered fires in 1808 and 1856. The present building was designed and built by E.M. Barry in 1858. John Flaxman designed the portico frieze in 1809 for the previous building. The Royal Opra and Royal Ballet Companies share the building.

In 1974 the flower and vegetable markets were moved to a new £7.2M 64-acre site across the Thames at Nine Elms in Vauxhall 2.5 mile away.

We window-shopped and looked at the pubs and finally entered the Piazza. The glass roofed wrought-iron structure; a prototype of the covered train stations, it still contains the original forty stalls that have been converted to shops. The aisles were line with a double row of small vendors. Clothing. Jewelry. Crafts. T-shirts. Inexpensive art. We bought some pictures and then had lunch at the Punch and Judy Pub.

Outside on the lower lever were some buskers singing and interacting with the crowd. Near the east end was a one-man show getting the kids involved. On the east portico of St Paul's Church was a one-act play.

Two women dressed as Liza Doolittle were selling flowers. The piazza was the scene of Shaw's play *Pygmalion* and the musical version, *My Fair Lady*. Liza Doolittle and her friends sold flowers to the people attending the Royal Ballet.

Outside the east end of main building were a group of temporary stalls specializing in Christmas things. Across the Piazza was the Transportation Museum in the old flower market.

Covent Garden

We left the Piazza through Russel Street and turned north on Bow Street passing the Royal Opera House into the West End theatre district.

There are several clusters of theatres. The Adelphi and the Vaudeville are on the Strand just south of Covent Gardens. A couple blocks to the east are five along Aldwych and Drury Lane. Two the west along Charing Cross Road is a cluster of five theatres and another five are located along Shaftesbury Avenue. Three more are near the Seven Dials. We walked along Long Acre to Mercer and up to the Seven Dials where the Cambridge Theatre was presenting Andrew Lloyd Webber's *The Beautiful Game*. We purchased tickets for the night's show for £13.50 each.

It was late afternoon so we took the tube home to rest for a couple hours. I had asked the doorman at the theatre what proper dress would be. He said to wear something warm and casual so I did and so did most of the rest of the audience. We took the tube back down town to make the 7:45 curtain time and arrived early enough to have a cup of chocolate before the show.

The play was based on present day Ireland and "the troubles" between the Protestants and Catholics.

We got out about eleven. The pubs were closed or closing so we took a cab home. The driver asked how our new Prime Minister was doing referring to our new President. We talked about theater and weather and about the little green cabstands.

Harrods

Waiting for Charles. Saturday dawned cold and cloudy. The sky turned from the orange tint of halogen lights to a washed-out light gray. Pigeons played on the rooftop across the street. Starlings fed from the gutters and grass along the sidewalk.

Our son was due in about noon. We listened to Saturday morning TV and did the laundry. The heat went off at ten AM so we went out shopping. The supermarket had stretch-wrapped six-pack of Cokes for £2 instead of over £3 for loose cans.

Charles arrived about 2PM. He flew into Gatwick and took the train to Victoria Station and the tube to St John's Wood. He got unpacked and we went for a walk in the neighborhood and took what started out as an early supper at an Italian restaurant. The food was nothing special but their service was slow to make up for it. They seemed in no hurry for us to eat.

Charles was still on Texas time and watched TV until the early morning hours.

Sunday in Soho. It was Christmas Eve. We went to Soho and Trafalger Square in a cold blowing light rain.

Soho includes Trafalger Square, Leicester Square and Soho Square. It lies south of Oxford Street and west of Charing Cross Road to Reagent Street. This multicultural area is the home of many immigrant populations including Chinatown. People such as Charlie Chaplin, T.S. Elliott, Sir Arthur Conan Doyle, and Royalty have lived, worked and played in Soho.

Charles wanted to look at some used bookshops along Charing Cross Road. We found several stores but they were all closed for the holidays.

A wrong turn took us to Leicester Square. It was miserably cold so we did not look for the stature of Charlie Chaplin. We passed the Hippodrome, the world's largest disco. Now we were only two blocks from Gerrard St and Chinatown so we decided to find a Chinese restaurant. We made sure to point out McDonald's golden arches on Shaftesbury Avenue to Charles since it was his favorite restaurant in Hong Kong when he was about eight.

After a hearty dim sum meal Charles took off to visit Speakers Corner near Paddington Square. Carol and I wandered down Gerrard Street and back down Shaftesbury Avenue to Charing Cross and took the tube home.

The local butcher shop had hare, pheasant, partridge, goose, quail and turkey displayed in the show window. I guess they were properly hung.

Santa at Covent Garden

Christmas Day. We were up early. Since the tube was not running on Christmas day we called a cab at 7 AM to take us to the Marriott Marble Arch Hotel to catch the bus for our Christmas tour. We were going to see Greenwich and Canterbury Cathedral.

While we waited we had hot chocolate and Charles told about his trip to Speakers Corner. A communist. Send the foreigners home. End of the world. Space visitors. Pretty much the same as I saw thirty years before.

We were shuttled to Victoria Station to catch our proper bus. The bus got on the Mall, which turns into the Strand and crossed the Thames over the Waterloo Bridge into the South Bank. I got lost. The trip is only about five miles on the south bank. We came into Greenwich on the Greenwich High Road.

Victoria Station

St. Alfge Church sits on the corner of the High Road and Church Street. The church is named for the Archbishop of Canterbury who was killed on this spot by the Danes in 1012. The present church was designed by Hawksmoor and completed in 1714.

Cutty Sark

The first and only stop was to see the Cutty Sark. The Cutty Sark is the last remaining China Clipper. It was ordered by Captain Jock (Old White Hat) Willis and launched in 1869. It carried 30,000 square feet of sail and made several trips from China with tea including a record run of 107 days in 1871. It was superceded by steam power and spent several years hauling coal and converted to a wool-clipper. She was used as a training ship and was put in permanent dry dock at Cutty Sark Garden in 1954. It is open for tourists and had the world's largest collection of ships figureheads in her hold.

The Cutty Sark was named after Witch Nannie in Robert Burn's *Tam O'Shanter.* The figurehead is seen wearing a short woolen Shift called a "cutty sark" and is clutching the horse's tail.

There is domed structure that looks like a small observatory. This is the southern end of the only foot tunnel under the Thames. The 1200-foot tunnel exit on the north end is on the Isle of Dogs. It was built so workers could walk to work at the Millwall docks.

The bus passed down Romney Road passing the National Maritime Museum, the Queen's House and the Royal Naval College.

This area began in 1509 as a palace called Placentia. Placentia was started by Henry VIII but razed by Charles II. It was rebuilt by Christopher Wren as the Greenwich Hospital. This was a home for disabled and aged seamen. The structure became the Royal Naval College in 1873.

From the Queen's House the Thames can be seen through the Naval College. This palace was ordered by James I for his Queen, Anne of Denmark. Inigo Jones began work on it in 1616 but the Queen died in 1619 before it was completed. It became the property of Prince Charles who later became King Charles I. He wanted it finished for his Queen, Henrietta Maria. Jones began work on it again in 1629 and completed it in 1635.

The National Maritime Museum, the largest maritime museum in the world. It is relatively new having been built about 1806 as a boy's naval school. It was converted into a museum in 1934 and stocked with material from the Naval College.

The Royal Observatory sits on top of the hill in the midst of Greenwich Park. Charles II established it in 1675. Designed by Wren it was built in 1676 and was the site of the development of celestial navigation. With the accurate chronograph, Zero longitude was established and the Nautical Almanac was published in 1766.

Henry VI established Greenwich Park in 1433 as part of the grounds for his house by the Thames, Bella Court. This was replaced by the Tudor Palace in 1509.

On the way out of town was St Alfege Church. You can't miss it since the road goes around it. It is the spot where Alfege, Archbishop of Canterbury was murdered by Danish invaders in 1012. It is the third church on this site.

About an hour's drive took us past Leeds Castle to Canterbury. Leeds Castle was built on two small islands in A.D. 857. The original wooden structure was replaced by stone in 1119. Henry VIII converted it into a royal palace. I visited it many years ago but it was closed to visitors this day.

Canterbury was a medieval city on the Stour River. It has been the center of Christianity in Britain as the place where St Augustine arrived in A.D. 597. The first construction began about 1100. Henry II had Thomas Becket, Archbishop of Canterbury, killed there on December 29,

1170. Chaucer's *The Canterbury Tales* was written about a pilgrimage to Becket's shrine. Henry VIII destroyed the shrine in 1538.

Canterbury Cathedral

It was cold and cloudy as we walked through the old city over Roman pavements to the Cathedral. The architecture was a fairy-like design created out of cold gray stone. A service was going on so we could not go inside. We walked around the outside of the cathedral over cobblestones and under gray stone arches. Many members of royalty were buried in and around the church. Many of the graves were under the cobblestones we walked over. The guide was hurrying off with a few passengers leaving the rest strung out over a mile.

Christmas dinner was at an inn in a second floor dining room. Dinner consisted of turkey and dressing with trimmings. We were served as-pa-RAG-as soup. Two women who had been on Guam were our tablemates. The conservation was better than the food.

Dinner was finished about 3PM. We hurried through the countryside and arrived for a walking tour near Windsor Castle after dark in the rain.

Passengers were dropped off where they had boarded. Since we were not staying in a hotel we got a private tour from the Crystal Arch past the Beatles recording studio and within a block of home. We were home by 9PM.

Tuesday and a Big Bus Ride. Tuesday was about freezing and misty. We took the tube to Green Park and bought tickets on the Big Bus. This company had hop on/hops off for 24 hours and included a river tour. It was really cold riding on top of a double-decker and later on the deck of the tour boat.

The route went through the Soho theater district to Piccadilly Circus then down Haymarket past the Leicester Square, Planet Hollywood and the Trocadero. Trafalger Square was next with Nelson's statue and the Admiralty Arch. Down the Mall to St James's Park we passed Clarence House (the Queen Mother's London home) and Spencer House (built for the first Earl Spencer in 1766) and on to St James's Square. The bus turned back on Piccadilly at the Royal Academy of Arts the past the Ritz Hotel and Green Park to the Hard Rock Café and Hyde Park Corner.

Street Scene

The bus took us around Hyde Park. Hyde Park was the ancient Manor of Hyde and property of Westminster Abbey. Henry VIII at the Dissolution of the Monasteries seized it in 1536. It was Henry's hunting preserve but James I opened it to the public in the early 17th century.

We drove along Knight's Bridge Road past Harrods, the Victoria and Albert Museum and Albert Hall. Harrods is London's most famous department store dating from 1849. We went around Kensington Palace and Garden and back along Bayswater Road to Marble Arch and Speakers' Corner.

Kensington Palace was built in 1605. William III bought it in 1689 and hired Christopher Wren to make it into a royal palace. The grounds of the Palace became a public park in 1841.

John Nash designed the Marble Arch in 1827 as the main entrance to Buckingham Palace. It was too narrow for the larger carriages and was moved in 1851.

Speakers Corner was established in 1872 when a public law allowed anyone to gather an audience and address them on any topic. Interesting place on Sunday afternoon.

No. 10 Downing St

We changed busses at the Marble Arch and went through Mayfair past Grosvenor Square and Berkeley Square around Piccadilly Circus and Trafalgar Square. The bus went south on Whitehall past Banqueting House designed by Inigo Jones in 1622 and the Horse Guards. The Horse Guards was originally the tilt yard of Henry VIII and renovated by William Kent in 1755. We passed Downing Street where the Prime

Minister has lived since 1732 and passed the Cenotaph, which was designed by Edward Lutyen as a war memorial in 1920. Whitehall became Parliament Street passed the Treasury to Parliament Square. Here were Westminster Abbey and the Houses of Parliament and Big Ben.

The tour continued across the Lambeth Bridge to Lambeth Palace and the Imperial War Museum. York Road ran roughly north along the Thames past Waterloo station where the Chunnel trains load up and passed Millennium Park and the Waterloo and Embankment piers.

Thames R.

Crossing the Thames again on the Waterloo Bridge we proceeded to Aldwych and Covent Gardens then down the length of Fleet Street. We continued to St Paul's Cathedral and the City of London to King William Street to the new London Bridge. This became Tooley Street with the London Dungeon, Southwark Cathedral and the Globe Theatre restoration. The bus crossed the Thames again and we dismounted to walk around the Tower of London to the river tour landing.

We had lunch in a fast food shop in the mall leading to the landing on the Tower Pier. Fish and chips and a coke each totaled almost £30.

Boarding the cruise ship with almost a hundred other tourists we took a seat inside. I walked around shooting the Tower Bridge and other sights near the pier including the Royal Navy cruiser HMS Belfast that has served as a floating Naval museum since 1971.

I learned that the tide in the Thames at Tower Bridge fluctuated about 30 feet and that the Tower Bridge, built in 1894, still opens to let tall ships pass. The bridge does not open often since commercial traffic above the bridge was banned in the 1980s. It was once opened five times a day using the original Victorian steam powered winding machinery. This equipment was changed to electric power in 1976. When open, there is 135 feet clearance to the catwalk. The public can climb the 300 steps to the catwalk for a good view of the river and London.

The cruise finally cast off and I went out on deck to take pictures. The temperature was just above freezing but the cruising speed brought the wind chill to the low twenties.

As we preceded upstream the first building on the right (north side were the Custom House, the Old Billingsgate fish market, and St. Magnus the Martyr church. A customhouse has been on this site since 1272. The present building was erected in 1825. Billingsgate fish market with its distinctive fish weathervane had been on this site for over 1000 years. In 1982 the market was moved to the Isle of Dogs and the building turned into commercial property. St Magnus was the Earl of the Orkney Islands murdered in 1110. Christopher Wren designed the present church in 1671 at the foot of London Bridge. Inland a block behind St Magnus stands the monument to the Great London Fire of 1666 when most of the walled city of London was burned.

On the left bank stood the Hays Galleria, which had been a commercial wharf, the London City pier, and St Olave's House.

Passing under the new London Bridge we saw the Fishmonger's Guild Hall and the Swan Lane pier on the right and Southwark Cathedral behind some warehouses, a replica of Sir Francis Drake's *Golden Hind,* and the Clink Prison Museum on the left. The Fish Monger's Guild was established in 1272 and still inspects all the fish sold in London. The Clink, synonymous with jails and prisons, was the prison attached to the medieval palace of the Bishop of Winchester.

Passing under the Cannon Street Railway Bridge and the Southwark Bridge we were told all the warehouses had been sold and converted to office space and apartments.

On the left between the Southwark and Blackfriars Bridges were the Anchor Pub, the replica Globe theatre, the Tate Bankside Gallery and one end of the Millennium Bridge to St Paul's Cathedral. The Anchor Pub was founded in 1676. The replica of Shakespeare's Globe Theatre is open in the summer for plays. The Millennium Bridge was built as a footbridge but swayed and bounced so much it was closed. Estimates on the corrective work to make the bridge usable exceeded the original construction by twice. The Bankside Power Station had been abandoned and converted into the Tate Gallery featuring modern art.

Millenium Park

On the right were more converted warehouses, Blackfriars Railway Station and the dome of St Paul's Cathedral.

On the left between the Blackfriars and Waterloo Bridges in the Gabrial's Wharf craft center in converted warehouses and the OXO Tower whose windows were built to spell out the name of a popular meat extract. On the right were docked three ships including the Royal yatch, Britannia, the Temple and Inns of Court and Somerset House with the Courtauld fine art Gallery. Somerset House was built in the 1770's by William Chambers on the site of the palace of the Earl of Somerset. It was the first building designed to house offices. The Courtauld Gallery houses the collection of Impressionist and Post-Impressionist painting accumulated by the textile magnate Samuel Courtauld. The entire river is lined with the Victoria Embankment park.

Beyond the Waterloo Bridge to the Hungerford Railway Bridge the Savoy Hotel, Shell Mex House offices and Cleopatra's Needle stand on the right bank. The Viceroy of Egypt presented the Needle, originally erected in Heliopolis about 1500 B.C., to England in 1819. Across the river is the South Bank Center built for the Festival of Britain in 1951. It contains the Royal National Theatre, Queen Elizabeth Hall, Royal Festival Hall for the London Philharmonic and the Hayward Gallery. The Shell Building stands in the background.

On towards Westminster Bridge on the left are Jubilee Park and the giant Ferris wheel British Airways London Eye and the London Aquarium. The Aquarium originally housed the Greater London Council. There was nothing significant on the right side but the Westminster Pier where the trip ended.

We walked down the Victoria Embankment past Thorncroft's 1850 Statue of Boadicea who had resisted the Romans. We intended to continue the bus tour and stood under Big Ben waiting for the bus. It was below freezing with light rain and a stiff wind. After Big Ben had sounded off twice and no bus had arrived we caught a cab home.

Big Ben

Wednesday. Finish the Tour and a Little More. About nine we caught the tour bus at Baker Street down Regent Street and around to the Marble Arch. Charles stayed in that part of town shopping while Carol and I took the tube to Southwark to do the Tate South Bank Museum of Modern Art.

The Southwark tube station had been upgraded for the millennium with stainless walls and plastic shields along the track. Breaks in this shield controlled access to the trains. The station was more like a modern art gallery than the older stations. It is designed for easy maintenance but will it hold up to heavy use? I hope this is not the building wave of the future.

It was a couple blocks from the tube station to the museum. My stomach said it was lunchtime so we stopped for lunch at the Lord Nelson Pub. The pub was about a block from the Thames. This was probably in the right place to catch the going-home crowd from the docks 150 years ago. There was no no-smoking area and the barmaid and a customer were busy talking trying to ignore possible customers. They finally gave up and took our order. Carol had steak and chips and I had haddock and chips and ale.

We found the Tate and spent three hours absorbing modern art. Minimalists. Worhol. Picasso. The new footbridge across the Thames was treated like an exhibit with a big picture window. The bridge was unusable because of the vibrations and swaying. It crosses from near St Paul's to the South Bank.

New Tate Gallery

We had a coke and an ale at a sports pub near the tube station and headed home again. The walls were covered with boxing pictures and memorabilia. Several old men were talking about various fights hidden under a cloud of cigarette smoke.

Thames Bridge

Thursday. Snow and Harrods. About 6 AM I woke up cold. The boiler was going but the radiators were not doing much to warm up the flat. I looked out the window and saw snow.

The TV said it was the first snow in four years. Temperature was -6°C. This is 23°F and pretty chilly.

Charles and I got dressed and went out to the bakery. There were few people out and those who were bundled up. We exchanged a couple snowballs, picked up pastry for breakfast and returned home.

About 10 we started out for Harrods. Charles jumped ship at Baker Street to see Madame Tussauds Wax Museum and the Sherlock Holmes Museum. Carol and I continued on to Harrods.

We got off the tube at the Knightsbridge station and spent most of the day going through its 300 departments. Fancy foods and tea. Clothing. Art and antiques. Furniture and appliances. We looked and bought nothing.

Lunch was Oriental in one of their smaller eateries. About an hour later we headed home. It was about 5 under a cold, gray sky.

St John's Wood

Friday and We Split Up. It cleared up on Friday. It was still cold but no wind or rain. Charles went shopping old books and Westminster Abbey. Carol went to Church Street and Portobello Road for shoes and shops. I went to the Museums of Science and History then walked through Hyde Park and the Serpentine Lake and Gallery.

The Natural History Museum was wonderful. Dinosaurs. Shells and other invertebrates. Human biology. "Creepy Crawlies".

Birds. A large ecology gallery. An outstanding bookstore. Several of the curators I wanted to see were out for the holidays.

Science Museum

The Science Museum was well designed for its purpose. It was seven floors of displays. I started with Sir John Crapper's first commercial flush toilet. The old appliances and farm equipment looked much like those in the US. The science demonstrations were first class. The collections of medical history, meteorology, astronomy, and navigation were well done. The flight displays were the best I have seen.

I walked north to Hyde Park and visited the Serpentine Gallery. The modern exhibit was not very interesting.

I walked on through the park and around the Serpentine Lake. Several new waterfowl were resting on the lake. I found the tube station as the sun was disappearing in a cold white cloud mass and almost thawed out on the way home.

Charles was disappointed that most of the bookstores were closed for the holidays. Carol was happy with several nice scarves for gifts.

First Flush Toilets

Saturday and Kew Gardens. Charles and I got an early start to Kew Gardens while Carol returned to Harrods. We took the tube and train to Kew Station and walked the couple blocks to the Garden. We entered through Cumberland Gate.

Kew began in 1750 as the estate of Prince Fredrick and Princess Augusta. The Earl of Bute began the landscaping. King George III was the next owner and Sir Joseph Banks became the unofficial manager establishing plants brought back by Captains Cook and Bligh with such plants as rubber, quinine and tea. Sir William Hooker became director in 1841. He established the herbarium, the library and began construction on most of the buildings. The current collects include seven million plant and fungi specimens, 76,000 slides of wood sections, 10,000 botanical paintings and other plant art, wood products, medicinal plants, and an economic botany collection.

Kew Garden

The weather was just above freezing with snow covering the grounds so we began with hot chocolate and a walk through the bookstore. The last time I was at Kew was in June of 1976.

The Princess of Wales Conservatory and cactus house was closed as were several other facilities including the Temperate House, the Marianne North Gallery and the reference collections.

We walked around the Swan Lake listening to the bagpiper. The lake was frozen over much to the displeasure of the ducks. We entered the Palm House and spent about an hour looking at palms and other tropical plant that were familiar to us from the tropics.

The rose garden was pruned and the Cherry Walk was winterized. They were also covered with snow. Some one had built a snowman and there was evidence of a snowball fight. Several people were sitting on benches out of the wind in the thin cold sun.

The Evolution House was open. This was a display of the evolution of plants with all of the living plant groups represented. The display was well done.

Kewww Gardeen

We walked a few more of the snow-covered trails to the Japanese Gateway designed for the 1910 Japan-British Exposition, then to the 50 meter 10 stories Pagoda designed by Sir William Chambers and built in 1762.

We left by the Lion Gate and walked about a mile to the Village of Richmond where we stopped for lunch at a pub.

Along the street to the tube were several real estate offices and job brokers. Entry-level clerical jobs began at about £12,000. Entry-level management began at £17,000. A two bedroom, two bath house rented for £1,500 a month. A four bedroom, two-bath house with car park cost £1.2 million.

We caught the tube and arrived home in the dark. Supper was at a local French restaurant.

Sunday was New Years Eve. Dawn broke pink and orange for the first time since we arrived. It crept up behind the branches and chimneys across the way. This was followed by a light blue sky. It was cold but the wind had died.

We had breakfast of hot chocolate and sweet rolls. We did several tubs of laundry and discussed what to do in a country that was mostly closed.

Charles and I decided to take a walk along the Regents canal while Carol rested. We walked down snowy paths through St John's Wood churchyard and cemetery to Prince Albert Road. St John's church was not a working church and the cemetery, though active, was not well maintained with unreadable grave markers. Kids were throwing snowballs and an old man was walking his dog.

Regent's Park was a royal hunting preserve incorporating the village of Marylebone. As the population center of London moved west in the 18th century Robert Harley, Earl of Oxford, developed the area into an upper class suburb with terraces and Georgian homes designed by John Nash. Nash built the Regent's Canal to join the Grand Junction Canal near Paddington with the London docks at Limehouse. In 1874 a barge loaded with gunpowder blew up near the zoo. The canal fell into disuse due to competition by the railroad. It is strictly a recreational area at this time.

Reagent's Canal

We crossed Prince Albert Road to Park Road and took the steps down to the canal. A cold wind blew along the canal and ice cover the water in the shady areas. We passed the zoo and finally came to the lock at Camden Town. Several canal boats were tied up along with a floating restaurant.

We took the icy steps up to Regent's Park Road and walked into Camden. It was Sunday and New Year's Eve morning so I did not expect to see the crowd on the streets. Many were waiting for the bus or the tube. The main street, Gloucester Road, was lined with booths that sold everything from CDs to used clothing and shoes.

Several bookstores were open. We visited a new bookstore and one that sold used books. It was interesting talking to the owners but they had nothing we really wanted.

We crossed the canal and took the steps down to the lock. I don't known if it still worked but there was a difference in water level. We passed several more canal boats and took the steps up to Prince Albert Road. The zoo and Primrose Hill were on this route then several blocks of big Georgian style apartment buildings before we crossed St John's High Road. No people. Nothing was in bloom and there were no birds.

Canal lock

231

By the time we got back it was lunchtime. Carol wanted to go to Covent Garden for lunch and some more looking and shopping.

The tube exited about a block from the site into a misty afternoon just above freezing. We stopped at a bookstore mostly to warm up and bought nothing.

The street was full of pedestrians but not crowded. We headed straight for the Punch and Judy that was not crowed either. We ordered steak pies and cider topped off with a bite of cobbler and clotted cream.

The next hour was spent in looking at all the shops that were still open. Many of the shops and vendors had closed for the New Years celebration. A group of buskers was entertaining a group of children and a few adults.

We left through the stalls at the end of the building and found Santa handing out candy and taking pictures with children. We noticed most of the shops were closing. It was near sunset, below freezing with a breeze –driven mist. Definitely time to get inside. The pubs were getting full but we took the tube home.

We spent the evening watching TV with the English specials. The government was recommending people stay away from Trafalgar Square due to the weather but a lot of people showed up anyway.

New Years Day. Our vacation was drawing to a close. Tomorrow was go home day. The weather was cold with a light rain. I went to the bakery for rolls and we had them with hot chocolate.

We spent the morning rounding things up, doing the laundry and preliminary packing. We also called the cab for the ride to the airport.

About lunch time the rain quit. It was still cold but we decided to go to Chinatown for lunch and last minute shopping in Soho. The tube took us to the Leicester (pronounced Lister) Square station. Our street route took us past the Hippodrome and Notre Dame to Gerrard Street and Chinatown. We found a dim sum restaurant about a block from the Soho McDonald's.

It was nearly dark when we finished and the rain and temperature were both dropping. We walked the length of Gerrard Street and up Shaftesbury Avenue to the tube station.

Go Home Day. We were up early to get the packing finished. After breakfast we were washing dishes as the cab arrived.

The trip to Gatwick took almost two hours with traffic and the weather. The driver was chatty and we discussed housing, jobs, education, our trip, his job and family and his view of the government.

It seemed like only a few minutes till we boarded and were in our seats climbing out over Manchester towards Liverpool. Dublin and Donegal were hidden under the clouds. I dozed for a couple hours and woke over Labrador. Ottawa was covered with snow, as was most of the route to Houston.

We arrived home late in the afternoon and decided to wait until morning to pick up the cat. Our guest had left the house cleaner than we had. We will definitely try house swapping again sometime.

A home exchange was a new experience and what
would be a better place than merry old England.

Three Weeks In Berlin

19 July – 9 August, 2002

THREE WEEKS IN BERLIN, 19 July – 9 August, 2002

Almost a year ago we were contacted on the Internet about a possible home exchange in Berlin. This might be interesting since part of my family originally came from Germany about 150 years ago.

My wife, Carol, and I had done home swaps in the past so we considered it, our house in San Antonio for three weeks in an apartment in the Charlottenburg section of Berlin. This time we included car swaps along with the house after consulting with our insurance companies. Over the year about 30 e-mails were exchanged and arrangements were made. We settled on the period 19 July 02 to return on 9 August 02.

On the Internet we booked two e-tickets for economy class seats on American Airlines from San Antonio to Dallas to Zurich to Berlin. Departure time for AA1651 was noon Friday 19 July arriving about 10 AM Saturday morning in Berlin on Swiss Crossair flight AAA 6226.

We arrived at the airport Friday two hours early as recommended. We were checked in and headed to the gate in thirty minutes. I have one artificial hip and Carol has two. She got stopped for a pat down inspection but I did not. You never can tell about the check-in and security. Lunch in the terminal was a sorry chilidog and a Coke for $5.00.

The plane flew from San Antonio to Dallas where we changed planes, then to Chicago, up Lake Michigan to Sault Ste. Marie. We continued northeast over miles of Ontario forest to near Rupert House on James Bay. More forest with a few small towns rushed under the wings as we crossed Quebec to Cape Chidley on the south side of the Hudson's Straight.

The sun slowly faded to night and a quarter moon reflected off a quiet sea between ice flows as we crossed the Davis Strait. We found land south of Godthaab, Greenland. As we flew eastward across southern Greenland the ice cap glowed in the moonlight and reflected starlight. Ice floes sailed south beneath us as we crossed the Denmark Strait. More headed southeast riding the Gulf Stream south of Iceland.

In the early morning dark we turned to the southeast towards Ireland and London. Clouds hid everything to the English Channel. The sun rose at 30,000 feet as we passed north of Paris. Brown and green fields and fog filled river valleys were still in shadow. The towns were not lit like American towns.

Several hot air balloons shining in the morning sun greeted us as we approached Zurich. I can imagine the cool and quiet and the unobstructed view with only the occasional quiet roar of the butane burner and muted waking up sounds from the world below. The approach to Zurich took us down and over neat pastures, fields and tree plantations and past a castle sitting on a hilltop.

The plane was a Boeing 767 and much noisier the comparable Airbus and MD80. The American Airline was bragging about the extended seating room but the seats were less sturdy and some kids sitting behind me were wrestling in their seats and kept kicking the seat even after the stewardess explained to them that this was annoying.

It was early Saturday morning. The airfield was a blanket of wildflowers through which paraded several large black rooks. During the hour in the international area in Zurich we exchanged some dollars for euros before loading onto a purple bus for transportation to our new Swiss Crossair plane, an Avro RJ100. We flew north over scattered clouds, farms and scattered wooded valleys to Berlin's Tegel International Airport. Poppies and yellow Crucifers covered the airfield and one hooded crow watched as we taxied past. It was about 1000.

We passed through immigration quickly. I loaded our bags on a cart and we went out to find a taxi. I got the impression the taxi driver thought he was working beneath his status. It appeared that I interrupted his reading by asking if he was available. He opened the trunk from the drivers seat and sat there like he thought I was going to load my own bags. He reluctantly got out and helped. He looked at the address. He apparently did not know Berlin well and got out his map book, which he looked at several times during the trip. Since there was no parking available he stopped in the street and unloaded the bags in the street not even on the curb much less at the door. His fare was 25% higher than the return fare when we left. I'm happy to say most people were not like this.

I rang the buzzer for Mr. Smith. He came down and let us into the building and the apartment and even helped with the bags. Mr. Smith was from England but had lived in Berlin for 30 years. He was very helpful during our stay.

Mr. Smith suggested that if we wanted any groceries we should go quickly since the stores closed at 1400 on Saturday. Most stores were closed on Sunday and open from 1000 - 2000 week days. Bakeries could open for two hours on Sunday morning.

It was a two-block walk to the local market. Temperature was about 70°F and overcast. Sidewalks were about two meters wide made of porous paver blocks. There was about a meter of 6-8 cm square granite blocks along the building foundations and street edges apparently for easy access to buried utilities. Many sidewalks had a red lane designated as a bicycle lane.

Street trees were planted in wells near the street including London Plane trees and Gingkoes. The tree wells also supported ryegrass, foxtail, and other annual grasses, goosefoot, annual nettle, Sheppard's purse, dandelion, wild lettuce, wild pinks and other annual plants of disturbed areas. There was also a lot of dog poop.

The Alti market covered about 3000 sq feet with little selection. Maybe it was late Saturday before closing for the weekend. All products were displayed in the carton they were received in. We took their last liter of irradiated milk in an unrefridgerated cardboard carton, a loaf of bread, sandwich meat, and a six-pack of Coke Lite as they call diet drinks. Good thing we did not buy much since the stores do not provide bags. Apparently everyone has his or her own cloth grocery bags or cart. I put our stuff in an empty carton and we headed home.

About 1800 we went out for supper. About a block away we stopped at the Dalmatia. I had a naturschnitzel with a Jenner beer. Carol had Vienerschnitzel and Lite Coke. Some restaurant bills contained the tip while others did not. Some even had prices in marks and euros. We provided a tip and they responded with a shot of brandy.

The apartment was on the third floor. The elevator said it was on the second since the ground floors in Germany do not count. There were three bedrooms, two baths, kitchen, living room, dining room and a balcony. The building may have survived WWII with 12-foot ceilings with medallions and ceiling fans. There had been several upgrades since the 1950s. There were no closets except in the utility room but there were bookshelves and built-in drawers in the master bedroom and cabinets installed in the kitchen. The beds had feather bed covers. Public radio was available along with one channel of German TV. The windows were partially open with no screens and very few insects. Hardwood floors meant no shoes inside to keep from damaging the wood.

Sunday morning began to get light about 0500. We finally got up about 0800 and walked half a block to a local bakery for rolls and returned for breakfast.

About noon we drove to the Schloss Charlottenburg palace museum. We parked just as it began to sprinkle. We passed through a tall iron gate and across the ten-acre cobblestone courtyard as the storm progressed We took refuge in the gift shop for about 20 minutes while wind blew, lightning lit the sky, and heavy rain beat on the courtyard and the huge bronze baroque equestrian statue of Friedrich I. The rain slacked and we went to the entrance, bought a tour ticket and waited.

The tour was in German but we were given a four-page summary of the tour. This gets frustrating to hear the guide talk for ten minutes on a short English paragraph.

Sophie Charlotte built the Schloss in 1701. She was the wife of Friedrich I, the self-designated first king in Prussia (his father was king of Prussia). It began as a summer cottage and grew. The rooms are large, high and ornate. The palace was damaged during WWII but has been restored where they had good records or photographs. There are about sixty acres of gardens. Friedrich almost bankrupted the country with his spending.

The tour of the Schloss finished about 1630. It was still raining so we decided to tour the grounds on a later date and return home. We found a parking place two blocks away and walked home in a drizzle.

The rain stopped and we went to supper about 1900. I had fish with two beers, a Berliner and a Sion. Carol had rump roast and a Lite Coke. Each of my beers cost less than the Coke.

On Monday morning we set out to use the subway or U-Bahn. Between experiences on other systems, our 40-year old college German and a dictionary we got tickets, got them validated. The ticket is 2.10 EUR each and good for two hours all the modes of transportation - underground, surface rail (S-Bahn), bus or tram. At the rate of 4.2 EUR a day each we decided to buy 30 day passes for 56 EUR each.

One of the first things we did was to find a bank that changed money. Not all banks were authorized or did not want to bother changing money. Those that did charged 2 percent. The cambio at the Zoo station charged 3 percent.

We found our way to the Kurfurstendamm or Ku'damm. It is about 4km long and was old West Berlin's high end shopping area with hotels, restaurants, theatres, Versace, Rosenthal, Miesen, etc. We looked a lot checking the German fashion scene in the windows and comparing prices. I saw and bought unique glass tea pot and two cups and saucers.

One thing I noticed was that all the young ladies, even those with backpacks, were wearing the appropriate underwear and shaved their legs They were all wearing modish clothes and a number had tattoos. This was opposed to 45 years ago when hairy appendages were in.

We checked on a tour of Berlin. They asked 48 euros each so we declined. We also looked into day tours around Berlin. They were not available or too expensive.

Lunch was about 1500 in a nice Chinese restaurant.

That evening I called the three numbers listed for Lahser in the phone book. One was disconnected. One could not speak English. The third one spoke English well but knew little about the Lahser family. She was a Lahser and said her husband adopted the name.

The evening was cool so I turned on the heat. Nothing happened. The heat automatically went off when the temperature was above 17ºC (64ºF). It came on a little later when it got cooler.

Tuesday morning I did some laundry and put it in the dryer. An hour later it was still wet so I hung it on the drying rack. Much better. I am spoiled with our large capacity washer and dryer but I always liked air-dried clothing.

We were getting ready to go out for the day and I could not find my leather hat. We looked all over and asked the restaurant and bank we had been in the previous day but no luck. Darn. I had worn it several years and it was just getting broken in. Never did find it.

We took the U-Bahn to the big station near the zoo and change to the S-Bahn to the Freidrichstrasse station intending to see several of the landmarks like the Brandenburg gate and Check Point Charlie. We walked two blocks to Unter den Linden that is the main street in old Berlin. The name of the western end beyond the Brandenburg Gate was changed to Strasse des 17 Juni in memory of the massacre of workers in East Berlin in 1956 protesting the Communist program of more work and less pay.

We walked west a really long block towards the Brandenburger Tor or gate. The boulevard was lined with Linden trees and inhabited with fiberglass bears painted in by artists and a few portable snack shops that sold drinks and snack food.

The street numbers were strange going consecutively up one side of the street and continued in the opposite direction on the other side instead odd and even numbers but this arrangement was not consistent across town. Its not as bad as some Japanese streets where buildings were numbered in the order they were built.

The gate was visible from about half a mile. As we neared the gate we could see it was covered with a large tarp painted to look like the gate while the gate was under repair. I went on and took some pictures while Carol rested.

The Hotel Aldon sits near the gate in old East Berlin. It was built in 1907 and survived WWI and WWII. It had been temporary home for Greta Garbo and Marlene Dietrich and other important people. It was been rebuilt and reopened in 1997 as one of the leading hotels with rooms starting about $200 a night. President Bush stayed there a couple weeks previous to our visit. A brand new Starbucks was located across the street.

We walked back and stopped for a Coke Lite and a beer at an outside café and headed back to the S-Bahn.

The theatre district is near the train station. Walls and utility poles were covered with theatre bills. Some of the posters were stacked to a quarter inch thick.

Under the tracks are a couple blocks of antique shops and restaurants. We had lunch about 1400. I had spinach quiche with a Lowenbrau and a plum dumpling for dessert.

A new Australian ice cream outlet was being built across from the S-Bahn station. Wonder how this is different from regular ice cream.

On Wednesday we went back to the Freidrichstrasse area to shop antiques. A number of shops were huddled together for two blocks under the train tracks. Like in San Antonio many of the dealers ignored potential customers. I have never understood why you would get into the sales environment if you did not want to sell or did not like people. One dealer was too busy on bookwork to answer questions. A couple others were on the phone while potential customers wandered in and out. It would be terrible if they actually had to try to sell, to know their merchandise, to interact with people.

Several shops were helpful. One had an art deco alabaster statue signed by Caasmann and several paintings of interest. Another represented an artist group with some really nice work. One shop had some Hautzenrueter figures and a piece of Murano glass about a foot square and three inches thick with fish inside. Another shop had some African art as well as some art deco brass figures. One shop had replica art deco lamps.

We took the train to the Savignyplatz area with more antique shops. One shop was African art with neck rings, staffs, masks, and some religious fetishes. One fetish had a small blue bottle for holy water and was only the second of its type I have seen. She made annual shopping trips. Her prices were pretty good by US standards.

Another shop had art deco/art Nuevo pieces with fancy prices - coffee tables, wall hangings and lamps. They may have been original but there are so many copies available it's hard to tell originals.

A third shop has several pieces of Murano including an ugly signed vase. He also had other glass and two Hautzenrueter figures and pre-WWII signs and artifacts.

A fourth shop had premium furniture but was so crowded you could not get around. One item was a pitcher and 8 glasses circa 1900 of faceted crystal with gold trim, possibly Baccarat, for 500 Euros.

Back home we went out for supper and groceries. I had herring with sour cream, onions and dill pickles and a Schultheiss beer.

The supermarket was neighborhood size. It had two floors with an escalator for the shopping carts. We bought three bags full and hauled them three blocks. Guess I've been spoiled by driving several miles for a loaf of bread or a truckload and finding acres of parking.

Thursday morning we went to the Neue Nationalgalerie or New National Gallery. The gallery was a modern structure in the Teagardens and featured modern art at this time. The gallery was designed by Ludwig Mies van der Rohe and built between 1961 and 1968. The ground floor is glass and steel with the main painting galleries underground. Outdoor sculptures decorated the surrounding plaza and outdoor garden. There were some French impressionists but the major artists were 20th century German. Max Beckman, Edvard Munch, Picasso, Klee, Nay, Wol. There were new experimental exhibits using TV and multimedia.

We tried to find the Gemaldegalerie or Picture Gallery but could not locate it. I found that it was part of another museum complex and we had walked past.

We waited by the Philharmonie and caught the bus back to the zoo station. It was about 1400 so we had lunch at Joe's. I had bratwurst with kraut and mashed potatoes and a Diesel (beer and Coke).

The zoo and aquarium were handy. The zoo was is the oldest in Europe opening in 1844. It has the most species on display, about 1200, of any zoo in the world. The entrance is Elefantentor or elephant gate of an oriental arch mounted on two kneeling life-size elephants. We never did get around to seeing the zoo.

It was sprinkling so we went to the aquarium. The exhibits were outstanding with sparkling water treated with 21st century technology. Hard and soft corals and even jellyfish. Tropical freshwater and reef fish. Iguanas and alligators. They advertised an insect exhibit but I missed it.

The sidewalks leading back to the train station was crowded with racks of memorabilia and lots of young people hanging out. Shops of posters and tourist junk lined the walk. McDonalds, Kentucky Fried Chicken, and curry dogs were available for the hungry or bored.

Across the street were the Kaiser Wilhelm Gedachtniskirche with its war damaged bell tower and the Europa Center. We stopped by for a look.

Friday. Every morning it began to get light about 0430. The sun waited for a more reasonable hour to rise at about 0600. It was usually overcast getting good light about 0700. So far it had been sunny for an hour or so a day.

We caught the S-Bahn to Alexanderplatz. This was one of the centers of social life in old Berlin. It was named after Russian Czar Alexander I, who visited Berlin in 1805. At that time it was outside of Berlin and was used as parade ground an markets. In the 20th century it was the center of East Berlin and the German Democratic Republic (GDR) with the Rotes Rathaus (Red House) and Marx and Lenin Square.

One of the outstanding features is the Fernsehturm, a 1,100-foot TV tower with an observation deck and restaurant at the 610-foot level. The viewing radius is about 20 miles. It was designed by Henselmann and built by an architectural collective from 1965-69. The GDR used this for a TV tower and observation tower to keep an eye on West Berlin. We waited in line almost an hour for the 60 second ride to the observation deck. The weather was OK for viewing.

Back at ground level I made a wrong turn and we started off in the wrong direction. A street map at the bus stop showed I was 180 degrees off and we got back on course. Beyond the remaining walls of a Franciscan monastery built in 1249 and near the mint is the oldest pub in Europe, Zur Lenzten Instanz. It began in 1289 and has been in continuous operation. We finally found it and had lunch there. The pub had been visited by Napoleon.

On the way back to the bus we passed the Rotes Rathaus that had been the East Berlin city hall. It was named for the red bricks. It was built between 1861-69 and is in Neo-Renaissance style. It comes with a 74-meter clock tower. It is now Berlin's principle town hall where the Governing Mayor and city Senate meet.

On the backside of the plaza was flohmarkt (flea market) near the Neptunbrunnen (fountain). I bought two jackets and fanny packs and Carol bought a jacket. We crossed by the fountain on the west side of the TV tower. The Gothic Marienkirche (St Mary's church) is the second oldest church after the Nikolaikirche. It was built in 1270 and burned in 1380. It was covered with scaffolding for new restorations.

We stopped for a Coke and a beer and caught the train back to the Zoo. We were home by 1700.

The trains and busses were remarkably clean in spite of occasional riders who smoked or ate. The other riders looked at them but said nothing. I suppose one of the rare ticket checkers would have done something but we only saw one person checking tickets in the whole three weeks.

Saturday morning looked like a good day to go to Potsdam, Spandau or the Tiergarten. We chose Potsdam and never did get to the others. We caught the S-Bahn and rode the 15 miles to the Bahnhof Potsdam Stadt (station).

Potsdam has a lot to see and would make a good week's visit. There are boat rides on Templiner See and other lakes to visit. There is the Filmmuseum built in 1675 as an orangery and stable and the Museum Wasserpumpwerk. Nikolaikirche (St. Nicholas) is modeled after St Paul's Cathedral in London an several other historic churches. There are three gates: Brandenburger Tor built in 1770 modeled on the Roman triumphal arch; the Jagertor (Hunter's gate) in Tuscan style built in 1733; and, Nauener Tor in Gothic style also built in 1733. The "Tall Stables", partially restored, was the stable and exercise area for the "Tall Guards", all near seven feet tall that guarded Fredrick Wilhelm I called the "Soldier King".

We had lunch on the palace grounds at Sanssouci, residence of Fredrick the Great and walked over to the Schloss Sanssouci. This park consists of several palaces and other buildings on 260 hectares (about 600 acres) of manicured grounds and gardens.

Tickets were purchased for the tour, another tour in German with English subtitles. The tour would not leave for over two hours. We went out and looked over the Lustgarten (vineyard terraces) and fountain and noticed the Bildergallerie, specifically built as an art gallery for the royal painting collection in 1755-63. It is the oldest art gallery in Germany. We went through this collection of Flemish and Italian baroque along with several Rubens and van Dycks in huge ornate rococo frame. There were also some French art and statues. My main comment is that the windows should be shaded to protect the paintings and to get the glare off the pictures so you can see them.

We walked down to the fountain and Carol decided to rest. I took off alone for an hour. I walked through the Marley (Mule) Garten and Chinesisches Haus (a Chinese teahouse built 1754-57 with life-sized gilded statues), through the Rehgarten to the Neues Palais (built by Fredrick the Great 1763-69 after the Seven Years' War), By the Botanischer Garten to the Orangerie, past the windmill and back to the Lustgarten. The Marley Garten is a collection of 18th Century buildings that serve as staff quarters and offices near the mausoleum of Kaiser Fredrich III. There was a tour of the teahouse but I was charging onwards. The Botanical Gardens were out of season. I did see a Blackbird, an all black member of the Robin family. The Orangerie Palais was built in 1851-60 hold tropical plants over the winter. The Neuekammern was built as a mirror image to the art gallery as an orangerie in 1747 but renovated in 1771-75 as luxury apartments and a ballroom. The mill and the Schlangentor (Snake Arch) are located near the entrance to the Schloss.

We returned to the entrance to the Schloss in time for the tour. Our German hosts pushed and bullied their way in like there was some kind of contest. Once everyone was inside we all slipped heavy carpet slippers over our shoes to keep from scratching the highly polished floors. Good idea. Our English guide described an hour's tour in three pages. The Marble Hall had a gold inlaid ceiling and marble statues, the reception hall contained family portraits, and the vestibule had real Corinthian marble columns weighing 6000 kilos each. The library and study contained the royal flute and where Fredrick played flute concerts. Four bedrooms: Voltaire's room where Voltaire may never have stayed and three other unique rooms. All had what looked like 14-foot ceilings with elaborate decorations, individual floor treatments, paintings and statues, access to the outside, and sleeping compartments set into the back wall. There did not appear to be a dining room or separate sanitary facilities.

I bought a picture book of Potsdam and the palaces. We walked to the bus stop and headed back to Berlin. We stopped near the Zoo station for supper at Joes sitting outside under cottonwoods and with hanging pots of bougainvillea. I had goulash that tasted good but slept badly.

Each of the U-Bahn stations was individually decorated like the London tube stations. Ernst-Rueterplatz was done in blue tile. Deustche Opera was white tile. Bismarkstrasse station was white panels. Sophia-Charlotte Platz was white brick with large tile pictures. Savigntyplatz was open and had one wall covered with metal impressionist pictures. Our metro stations all look pretty much the same from Washington to San Francisco.

Sunday morning was overcast. We took the U-Bahn and S-Bahn to Tiergarten station to visit the Berliner Trodelmarkt (flea market) on Strasse des 17 Juni. It was a collection of semi-permanent stalls occupied by vendors on weekends. Prices were high and these vendors did not bargain. There were lots of items but many of them were damaged. There was a lot of Baltic amber for sale both mounted and raw. A couple stalls had military memorabilia and uniform parts. There were several stalls of African and oriental art and several stalls that sold paintings. I bought a chunk of the Berlin wall.

Monday morning we took the U-Bahn to Stadtmitte station to find the English Book store and visit Check Point Charlie. We got off the train and walked several blocks to the address of the bookstore and found it had moved. We walked two more blocks to Check Point Charlie museum.

We approached the museum from the East German side. A large picture of an American soldier and a sign saying we were entering the American zone sat atop a sandbagged glass enclosure that represented the checkpoint. This was not in the authentic historic location but was more convenient for traffic. All of the Berlin Wall was gone. The only remaining East German watch tower, an historic structure, had been demolished one night in 2001 to make way for a new building.

The museum was a private corporation. It was well done with numerous artifacts and interpretive displays. We spent a couple hours going through the displays and the children's art display and bought several books and post cards and the compulsory T-shirts on the way out. The only part of the Wall still standing and the museum called the Topography of Terror were a couple blocks away and we did not see them this trip.

Across the street we visited another book store and had lunch at the Check Point Charlie Café (lamb chops and a Beck dark beer cost only 17 Euros)

About an hour before sundown I was sitting out on our deck listening to the street sound and watching the clouds turn pink. Swifts were flitting through the sky. No bats were seen. The pink mare's tail clouds predicted a weather change.

Tuesday morning was cool and damp. We decided to go to Museumsinsel (Museum Island). This had been a Prussian military strong point in the middle of the Spree River. I got disoriented and we wound up at the planetarium. We caught a bus to the Schlossplatz.

The Neues Museum (natural history museum) was not open. We walked past the Lustgarten that had been used as a parade ground, and past the Berlin Cathedral to the Altenationalgalerie (Old National Gallery). This collection of paintings and sculpture was mostly 19th century works such as van Gogh, Manet, Monet, and Cézanne and many German artists.

Our next stop was the Pergamonmuseum (Pergamon Museum). We passed another museum under restoration and down a long covered wooden construction walk to the entrance stairs. Several vendors were selling Russian military hats and such. The museum was constructed between 1911 and 1930 and has been restored. The access is up wide steps and across a large plaza used for rock concerts and other entertainment. The plaza contains several statues and an outdoor snack bar. The building is a representation of the museum's prize possession, the Pergamon altar.

The main exhibit hall contains the Pergamon altar. The altar was constructed at what is now Bergama, Turkey, circa 180-160 BC. It was discovered in 1865 and excavated in 1878. The altar and the temple frieze were disassembled and shipped to Berlin where it was reassembled.

Other exhibits include a market gate from Mellitus and numerous Greek and Roman statues and artifacts.

We walked back to the train station stopping at an Italian restaurant for calzones and to look at antique shops. One last stop was at the new Australian ice cream shop for fantastic fresh ice cream.

We decided to go up to the Baltic on Wednesday. We went out for some groceries to take along. We stopped for supper and I had goulash with lots of fresh paprika that caused weird dreams and bad sleeping. The grocery shopping was easier this time since we took our own cloth shopping bags.

It dawned overcast Wednesday. I had the car loaded and a potential route laid out by 0745. We did not know where we were much of the time but I kept heading generally northwest. I finally stopped at a gas station to ask directions but was told by the clerk she did not know where they were in American. She called a boy of high school age that spoke English and we finally worked out where we were and how to get to the road north. He explained they did not drive and were not well acquainted with the roads outside of their neighborhood.

We finally found the four-lane divided highway 113 going north and drove a couple miles to Highway 96 heading for Griefswald.

Highway 96 had two lanes ten feet wide with no shoulder and trees planted next to the blacktop on both sides. We passed through patches of Birch and Fir trees and wheat and canola fields and small country towns. Practically no birds were seen except an occasional magpie. We passed from the state of Brandenburg to the state of Mecklenburg Vorpommern.

Griefswald was an industrial town. Nokia had a factory. The Max Plank Institute occupied a large industrial park. Lots of blocks of apartment buildings. We stopped for lunch at a Chinese buffet and headed for Wolgast.

Athough there are towns along the Baltic seeing the Baltic is like trying to see the Atlantic in Florida. The roads are inland. We drove through several villages on the coast with narrow streets with no stopping or parking signs and no place with even a view of the Baltic. Most of the villages had no public eating facilities and these that did had no parking for the pub or restaurant. We finally arrived at Wolgast without seeing the water.

From Wolgast we drove another 30 km on Usedom Island along wooded roads to Peenemünde. This was where my great uncle August had worked with Werner von Brund on the WWII rocket program. The facility power plant and some of the grounds had been turned into a museum. I talked to the director but there was no record of a Lahser in his files. The museum had static displays of the rockets and a number of Russian aircraft. Most of the old barracks had become apartments and the port was a tourist center with hotels and a tour boat. The village of Karlshagen, 7 km south of Peenemünde was where the staff had lived in case the Peenemünde was bombed.

We started back to Wolgast about 1600 intending to stay the night. There were a number of roads and foot trails leading to the beaches with toll parking along the road all filled up with a huge crowd of automobiles. It took over two hours to make what had taken 30 minutes on the way out. Cyclists on the bicycle path were passing everyone. We arrived at the lift bridge just as the bridge was opening which took another 20 minutes.

There were no rooms available so we headed towards Rugen Island through scattered woods, villages and grain fields. Both Greifswald and Stralsund were crowded and dusk was on us. We drove 80 miles south to Klatzow just north of Neubrandenburg where we found a nice pension (bed and breakfast).

On the drive to Klatzow after sunset I saw a small flocks of Spotless Starlings (*Sternus unicolor*), several Swifts, one Common or Mew Gull (*Larus canus*), a Hobby (*Falco subbuteo*), A Kestrel, Montegu's Harrier, several Rooks and Magpies stalking around cut fields and a Least Bittern heading for its rookery.

The Klatzowerberg Rastställe and Pension had several rooms and a nice restaurant and bar. The rate was 30 Euros an night with breakfast. My supper was a pork chop with red cabbage, a nice light Steiger ale and a dark Schwartzer beer.

The window was open for the night. There were no lights in sight. Several kids were playing in the pool until late.

Thursday morning came with a cow mooing and a train passing in the distance. The wheat had been cut and the large garden of fruit trees was full of fruit.

Several magpies and a group of female Spotless Starlings fed in the pre-sunrise dawn. A horse and colt and several sheep grazed quietly.

We had set 0900 for breakfast and it was ready when we arrived – a BIG breakfast. Bread and rolls, several kinds of jelly, a tub of butter, a boiled egg each, a plate of sliced ham and sausages, juice, tea, - enough for twice as many.

By 1000 we were loaded and on the road. We decided to go to the former Prussian port of Stettin currently called Szczecin, Poland, on the Oder River. This was the port from which my great grandfather was supposed to have sailed to America around 1840.

The weather was overcast in the 70s as we drove south through Neubrandenburg to highway L33. We passed through several villages and fields of wind generators to highway B104. Wind was plentiful. I noticed several tower designs and the generators shoed marks of several manufacturers.

Both roads were narrow two-lane with no shoulder and trees or ditches along the road. The gently rolling hills were oriented north-and-south indicating a long glacial history. Additional proof was occasional prairie potholes (but no waterfowl) and a few large granite boulders indicating relic moraines.

Some of the homes were modern complete with lawn and flower gardens. Some of the villages had what looked like dorms. The few downtown areas were unexciting with no parking or inviting shopping areas.

We were surprised to find fields of corn. It may still be considered animal food and unfit for humans. Anyway, the corn was about ready to pick and tractors pulling large trailers loaded with corn and hay held up traffic for miles. We passed another 20 villages at 5-10 km intervals all the way to the Polish border. I liked the name of one village, Carlslust. Sounds may wild but it only translates to Carl's or Charles' garden.

Crossing the border was unexciting. They looked at our passports and waved us through.

A couple miles inside Poland was located a large flea market. Permanent stalls covered almost 10 acres with parking for maybe 500 cars and busses. We wandered the aisles for half an hour finding cheap new clothing, sporting goods, shoes, farm products and toys but nothing we really wanted.

We drove another 30 km into downtown Szczecin and began looking for a hotel. The first one we stopped at was equivalent to a Motel 6 for 130 euros a night. If did not look worthy of the price so we continued further into town where we found the Raddison and the Orbis. Both were 90 euros a night and both were five star rated. We checked in the Orbis.

This is a European hotel chain apparently built in conjunction with their casino. We got a nice room on the third floor with CNN on TV. The parking garage was at the Raddison. It charged 5 euros and the attendants were dressed in coat and tie.

We asked for directions to any antique shops or art galleries. We were directed to a shop about four blocks from the hotel. Carol decided she needed to have her hair done so I checked out the gift shops and sat at the bar and had a local beer, Okocim. I also made reservations for a guided tour the next morning.

We walked over just before quitting time and found a small shop with 19th and 20th centaury paintings, a few art porcelains and tools and a few pieces of furniture. We bought several hand colored prints including one from Berlin. The evening rush was on as we walked back to the hotel.

Supper was in the hotel restaurant. Carol had pork steak and I had fish stew with another Okocim and a shot of a local licorice aperitif. We skipped the hotel's casino.

I was awake about 0400 Friday morning. The city was dark with only a few streetlights and an occasional lighted window. Landscape lighting and security lights in office buildings were missing. As the sky began to look like dawn the few gulls in the air out numbered the people on the streets.

About 0600 I went for a walk down to the Oder to walk where my great grandfather may have walked. I walked south on Matejki Street past a small red and white trailer-looking fruit and coffee stand that was just opening. Three blocks along was the Brama Krolewska, a Baroque gateway that was part of the old Prussian fortifications. It now houses a café. I crossed the Polsklego with its trolley stop and its flower shops and coffee shops not yet open. I could see a ships mast mounted in the median. This was a maritime memorial from the m/s "Kapitan Maciejewcz" and constructed on the site of the former city theatre destroyed in WWII. Just east of this was Gothic 15th century St. Peter's and Paul's Church. Across from the church was a row of 15th century Gothic houses built to house the faculty of St. Mary's Convent.

I crossed the street and continued south towards the antique store we had visited. It was located across from St Mary's school built on the site of St. Mary's Convent. There were two other antique stores with notes they were closed for the holidays. Across the street was the location of the Palace of the Prussian Regimental Commander and the birthplace of Sofia Augusta Frederika von Anhalt in 1729. She became the Empress Catherine the Great of Russia.

Another block further sat the Bazylika or St. James's Archicathedral, a 14th century Gothic church. It was destroyed in WWII but has been rebuilt. We went inside later to look at the church and Diocese museum.

There were memorials to a German priest in Auschwitz who volunteered to die to save several Poles with families and young Poles that were massacred killed by the Russians. Behind the church is the 15th century Gothic Curate's house. Across the plaza is Plaza Orla Bialego or horse market with an 18th century Baroque Statue of the Goddess Flora and the Eagle Fountain erected in 1732.

I crossed the footbridge across Karo Wyszynskiego Street to the old barracks built in 1818 near the "Schneckentor" or city gate and the old city wall and back across the street to see the Manzel Fountain designed in 1898. It had a bronze statue of Sedina, the guardian of the City that was melted down in WWII. Across Nowa Street sits the Neo-Gothic Ratusz Nowy or New Town Hall built in 1875-79. I walked through the park with its large Linden trees to the Post Office No. 2 was built in 1872 and has always been a post office.

Crossing Kolumba Street I walked along the Oder for a couple blocks to the Dworzec Glowny PKP or railway station originally built in 1843 then north along Mala Boulevard past the Brama Portowa or Harbor House Gate. This Baroque city gate was built between 1724-40.

It was near 0700 and people were beginning to populate the street. The streets were clean. No homeless. No doorways with empty bottles and urine odor. At least I saw none. At Plac Zolnierza I turned into Wyzwolenia Street and stopped for pastries and hot chocolate. At Plac Bodla I turned towards the hotel east on Pilsudskiego to Matejki.

CNN news was on in the room as we ate pastries and juice. We rounded up most of the stuff in anticipation of a 1300 checkout and went down to meet out guide at 0900.

Our guide was a woman of about 40 years who spoke fluent English. She had been raised in the US but had been in Poland for about 20 years. I went to get the car and returned to pick them up. The guide navigated well. Our first stop was near the antique shop we had visited. The shop was closed, as were the adjacent shops. We walked over to the cathedral and took the interior tour. We visited several other antique shops and art galleries and returned to the hotel at noon.

We packed up and checked out. The hotel gave us directions for getting on the road to Berlin. We naturally got lost but I headed south by west and finally found the main highway and followed the signs to the border.

The country was open once we left town. Gray skies and occasional showers. On Highway 2 there was nothing but farmland until we arrived in Kolbaskowo and the border. We intended to stop for lunch but there was no place. We easily found the access to E28 or Autobahn 11 and headed south towards Berlin. A few signs for small towns. Fields of grain. A few patches of woods, as we got closer to Berlin. We tried one of the villages and found nothing open except a gas station.

From all that I had heard I expected the Autobahn to be different from what we found. This part of the Autobahn resembled the old interstate highway system back in the 1950s. It was a divided highway of cement slabs sometimes covered in asphalt. About a third of the 100+ miles was one-lane traffic due to road repairs. Speed limit was 120km or about 80. There was little difference in speed since both lanes were full cars, trucks and campers all flying along.

About 1600 I thought we were headed the wrong way and found we were on the E55 headed west around the north side of Berlin. I saw a sign for the Tegel airport and we were home by 1700.

We unloaded the car and went to a Bavarian restaurant. I had rabbit and a beer and a shot of brandy.

On Saturday morning we decided to make a hotel reservation at the Novotel Berlin Airport since our flight was at 0700. I called and got the reservation. We eventually cancelled this and ordered a cab for a 0400 pickup.

It was raining at sunup. It was cool 72ºF and breezy. People were walking around wearing coats and sweaters in the street and carrying umbrellas.

Berlin Rain

A cool wet morning in August
In Berlin

Rain falling slowly straight down
A gray day
In August
In Berlin

Jackets and coats
In August
In the rain
In Berlin
Carl 3Aug02

The rain stopped but it was cool and overcast as we wandered through the flomarkt again. Still no bargains. We took the train to Fredricstrasse station and the antique shops. We went through the shops once more and bought the Caasmann statue circa 1900. It is an Art Nuevo 42 cm alabaster on a marble stand signed by the artist. Caasmann was a designer for Rosenthall in the early 20th century.

A new Australian Ice Cream shop had just opened across from the train station. Their mango ice cream was outstanding.

We took the statue home and went back out to the Kurfurstendamm for more looking. On the way back we found an African art shop and a nice pottery. The pottery style was much like Harding Black in San Antonio. We bought several pieces and the airline managed to crush a cup and bowl and break some pieces of the Berlin Wall.

Carol wanted to have supper at the observation deck on the Funkturm (radio tower). This tower called the "Langer Lulatsch (Beanpole) was opened in 1926 and survived WWII. Instead of calling we walked several blocks to the general area of the tower and the Kongresshalle ICC part of the trade fair ground. We could not find access to the radio tower and museum. On the way back we took another possible route and found the entrance with a sign indicating it was closed for repairs.

We stopped at the bus station to see if they would change dollars for Euros. No such luck.

About another block sat the Alsatian restaurant about a block from home. Schnitzel and beer!

Sunday morning began with bad sleeping due to onions and paprika. Must be getting old. We puttered around and went to the Zoo station to change money and have lunch. The vendors for a 9 km walking tour were getting ready to go so I signed on and Carol went shopping.

We gathered in front of McDonalds and walked past the zoo. The guide took us into Tiergarten and through the woods. Trails were full of walkers, joggers and bikers. Ponds were into the ground water showing a shallow water table. A bridge took us over the Landwehranal and into Lichtensteinallee. Numerous large picnic grounds were filled with groups playing soccer and cooking.

Berlin Trees

Berlin was originally called the bog.
It is now a city of parks and trees
with the Rivers Spree and Havel
carrying off the ground water.

In 1944 the Third Reich
would not let the people leave Berlin
to keep up appearances.

In the record cold winter of 1945
the Tiergarten and City were stripped of wood for heat.
Conquering foresters replanted Berlin
With fast-growing alien species

This infrastructure is 50 years old
The trees are overage
but not being replaced.
It is disappointing to see
only a few species of trees
and those not native.
carl03Aug02

We arrived at the traffic circle at the Siegessäule or Victory Column. A system of tunnels led under the Grosser Stern to the 67 m monument. It was originally built on Konigsplatz in 1873 as a memorial to Prussia's war victories and the founding on the first Reich in 1871. Hitler moved it to its present location in 1938 as coming one step closer to France. The friezes around the base disappeared after WWII but were returned by

France in 1989 from their resting place in the Louver. The monument was in the British sector after the war but the French wanted to demolish it. Britain, who had no great love for France, said "No", that it was a historical monument.

We descended the tunnel stairs and came out on Spreeweg then turned into Kastenien Allee. This tree-lined street led to Haus der Kulturen der Welt an John Foster Dulles Allee. The House of International Culture is also called Kongresshalle or Congress Hall and nicknamed the "Schwangere Auster" (Pregnant Oyster). It is a unique structure with an 18 m suspended arched roof of reinforced concrete. It does kind of look like an open seashell. It was built and given to Germany by the US in 1957 and is used for conventions, plays, and other large cultural presentations. It has a large pond with a huge bronze statue and a memorial tower.

We continued east on Scheidenhannstrasse to the Reichstag. The Reichstag was erected between 1884 and 1894 by Kaiser Wilhelm II. It is a large gray building in the Italian High Renaissance style. On 9 November 1918, Philipp Scheidemann proclaimed the German republic from one of the windows. On 27 February, 1933, the Reichstag was gutted by fire and Hitler began his rise to power. The building was not restored and was finally demolished. Restoration began in 1970 and the building was used by the West German parliament. After reunification the building was enlarged and completed in 1999 when the new Reichstag was dedicated and used as the home of the new government. The new building has a glass dome over the plenary hall with a spiral staircase that is a big tourist attraction.

We passed the Reichstag and went to the Brandenburger Tor or Brandenburg gate. This was one of the gates between East and West Germany. Strasse de 17 Juni ends and Unter dem Linden begins. Carl Gotthard Langhans built it in 1788-91 based on propylaea on the Acropolis with six Doric columns topped by a quadriga, the four-horse chariot of the goddess Victory. The quadriga was originally designed by Johann Gottfried Schadow as the goddess of peace Eirene. After Napoleon defeated Prussia he took the statue to Paris. It came back to Berlin when Germany defeated France in WWI when it became Victory.

The gate was covered by tarps and scaffolding for repair. We walked through the gat into Pariser Platz with the Hotel Aldon and other new buildings. We passed a display of fiberglass bears to the site of Hitler's bunker. The Third Reich headquarters building had been made of red granite but the Russians totally destroyed it without knowing the Hitler had a three story bunker buried beneath it.

We came south on Mauerstrasse to the only Nazi building still in use. This was the former Air Force headquarters. Behind the building the street had been the no-man's-land on the East side of the Berlin Wall. The only remaining part of the wall still standing is here.

Below the Wall in what had been basements located in the West has been built a museum called the Topography of Terror. We did not have time to visit it during the walk and I did not make it back before we left Berlin.

The Berlin Wall

The wall did not extend to the moon
Nor last a hundred years
It was only ten feet high
With a sewer pipe and barbed wire on top
After only 28 long years

And before the third generation wall as built
It failed
And fell
And was disposed of as rubble
Along with the GDR.

Carl 03Aug02

The next stop was Check Point Charlie. This was discussed and we went up Freirichstrasse a block to a 15-minute break at Schlotzskys with free restrooms. Besides their sandwiches and fountain drinks they had pastry and bottled drinks.

We left on the last part of the walk heading to the Gendarmenmarkt. on Beherenstrasse a block south of Unter dem Linden. This is an 18th century square containing the Schauspeilhaus or theatre built by Schinkel in 1818. It was destroyed but rebuilt and reopended in 1984. On either end of the square are mirror churches. The Französische Kirche (French Church) and the Deutscher Kirche (German Church) or also call Dom

(Cathedral). Both were built in 1701 and both have domed towers built by Gontard.

We crossed to the Kommode (Universitatsbibliotek). This open plaza, Bebelplatz, was the site of three book burnings, the most recent prior to WWII. It is across the street from Humboldt University whose professors took part in the burning. This is an open square with a glass window in the center that looks down into a room with empty bookshelves. This site had been slated to become a parking area but public protests prevented this. One lone protestor still protests something – just anything – daily.

We continue east on Unter dem Linden across the bridge to Museuminel (Museum Island) past the natural history museum and the national cathedral. We passed the abandoned former headquarters of the GDR. We crossed the Spree again into Nikolaiviertel with statues to Marks and Lenin. Here the walk ended. I was happy to quit since I had developed a couple blisters.

Across from the park was the Rotes Rathaus, the big red sandstone old city hall. Past this were Alexanderplatz, the fountains, TV tower, and the train station. I caught the train and was home by 1900.

Monday dawned cool and rainy. About 1000 we caught the train for Potsdamerplatz and the largest shopping mall in Berlin. It is three floors and covers about a block. It contains a lot mostly US and European franchises like Footlocker. We returned home about 1500 in a slow cool rain.

Tuesday was overcast but no rain. About 1000 we went to see the Picasso Museum located near the Charlottenburg Palace. We took the U-Bahn to the Sophie-Charlotte-Platz station and walked about three blocks along a tree-lined street of apartment complexes. We arrived at the museum across the street from the Egyptian museum and spent two hours looking at over 100 Picasso paintings, sketches, and statues and many paintings and other works by Klee, Bucher, Braque, Cézanne, and Matisse. This is the private collection of Heinz Berggruen, an art dealer and collector.

We went next door to the Bröhan-Museum of industrial arts. The displays were of furniture, glass, pottery, textiles and art in styles of Art Deco, Art Nouveau and Functionalism (1889-1939). Furniture by Hector Guimard, Jacques Emile Ruhlmann, and van de Velde. Pottery and porcelain by KPM and Meissen and from Copenhagen, Stockholm and other studios and factories. Paintings by Karl Hagemeister, Willy Jaeckel,

Leistikow. Silver and pewter. Glass by Tiffany, Baccarat, Böhmen, Moser, and Sohne. Really impressive.

We walked back and stopped for lunch and sat outside under a grape arbor. I had squid and a beer mixed with lemonade and another mixed with cranberry. I will stick to straight beer.

We got back to our U-Bahn station and decided to look at a gallery that had been closed every time we had passed. The owner was an old man (81) thinning his private collection. He had worked as a stockbroker in New York before returning to Berlin.

Wednesday was overcast but dry. We explored the Zoo station area. We visited the Kaiser-Wilhelm-Gedächtniskirche. This was a private church as can bee seen from the statues and portraits of knights and armor instead of saints. The church was replaced with a new modern structure but the original bell tower was left as a memorial.

We went up the Tauentzienstrasse to the Breitscheidplatz and the Europa Center with the Mercedes emblem on top. The sculpture "Berlin" stands in the median of the boulevard. This building was mainly office space for like the Berlin Tourist Information Office and the Berliner Multivision offices. There are three floors of shops, twenty restaurants, and a nightclub. This was a major attraction when it opened in 1965. One restaurant, Tiffany's Terrassencafe, has a water garden of large metal water lilies and flowing water. One feature is the "Clock of Flowing Time".

In the Breitscheidplatz sits the sculpture called the Weltkugel brunnen (World Globe Fountain). This had been dubbed "Wasserklops" (Water Meatball).

About a bloc further is the shopping center called the Ka-De-We for Kaufhaus des Westens. This is a great crowded store with both cheap and first class items. It has an entire floor of food, snack bars and a large formal restaurant. We could not get into the restaurant but we had hot chocolate and cake.

We left the Ka-De-We and went to the subway station in Wittenbergplatz where Kurfürstendamm begins. We returned to Joe's Restaurant for lunch about 1400. I had Eisbein (pig's knuckle) and a Diesel (Coke and beer). We did not go to the Sex Museum, which was one of the most visited museums in Germany and we did not go to the zoo.

Thursday was a nice day. There was still much to see like the parks at Spandau and the Olympic Stadium. We decided to go to the new Jewish Museum. We took the U-Bahn to Stadtmitte then to the Hallesches Tor station. It is a block off Friedrichstrasse on Lindenstrasse.

The museum has collections and archives with research and teaching facilities and includes the Rafael Roth Learning Center and the Leo Baeck Institute. The design was by Daniel Libeskind as an open Star of David. It is constructed of stainless steel with 1005 windows of different sizes and shapes. Entrance is through the Kollegienhaus, which contains the gift shop and a kosher lunchroom. The museum is partially underground down a long ramp or by elevator. Branching halls go up and down with exhibits. The main hall is the Axis of Continuity. The Axis of Exile contains displays of personal stories of refugees and their escapes. It leads upwards towards the surface and the Garden of Exile with a maze of elevated planters containing willow oak trees. The Axis of the Holocaust contains personal displays of holocaust victims and ends in the Holocaust Tower, a bare, unheated tower several stories up to a single narrow slit of light and outside sounds. There is a chamber of displays and computers.

We returned home in mid afternoon to pack and clean up. Everything fit except the statue, which I carried all the way to San Antonio.

Friday came early. We were up at 0300 and were transferring the bags down stairs when Mr. Smith and the taxi both arrived promptly at 0400. We left the keys and the remainder of our transportation passes with Mr. Smith and headed for the airport.

Another bit of miscommunication – the airline said to be there two hours early (0500) but airport did not even open until 0600. When they finally opened we checked in and went through security in about 15 minutes.

The flight to Zurich jumped off the ground into the clouds and stayed there until we hit the ground. The shuttle bus took us back to the terminal in a drizzle. We found our plane and settled down for a really long day of flying.

I woke up south of Iceland and could see little white ice flows speckling the blue of the Gulf Stream. Numerous large bergs crowded the Greenland coast north of the coastal village of Timmiarmuit.

We crossed a melting Greenland ice cap. The track approached the west coast of Greenland south of the big marshes north east of Nuuk near where the Davis Strait empties the Baffin Bay into the Labrador Sea.

I could see several contrails to the north where other planes had flown. I had not realized the atmosphere would be saturated or that there was that much traffic up north but all the flights to or from Europe fly this "Great Circle" route.

Numerous ice flows were visible in the Labrador Sea until we crossed over Resolution Island. There was less ice as we flew west through Hudson Strait. A collection of buildings was visible on the south of Baffin Island possibly Iqaluit.

We crossed Fox Channel and south of Southampton Island and turned south along the western edge of Hudson Bay crossing into Canada near the Winisk, Ontario. We flew over mainly woods to Thunder Bay the across Wisconsin to Dallas. We change planes in Dallas and were home in San Antonio before dark.

Another great home exchange completed. Where to next!

Postscript. On returning home and after writing up my notes and processing my pictures I wrote a letter to the mayor of Berlin discussing the need for an urban forestry plan and tree replacement program to increase biodiversity and to replace many of the trees reaching senility. I never received a reply.

Birds and Mammals of Berlin (18 July – 9 Aug 02)

Ciconiiformes – Herons and allies
Ixobrychus minutus   **Little Bittern**   Baltic

Falconiformes – Birds of Prey
Circus pygargus   Montagu's Harrier   Baltic
Falco subbuteo   *Hobby*   **Baltic**
Falco tinnunculus   Kestrel   Baltic

Lariformes – Gulls and Terns
Larus canus   Common Gull   Baltic coast

Columbiformes – Pigeons and Doves
Columba palumbus   Wood Pigeon   Potsdam

Apodiformes - Swifts
Apus apus   Swift   Berlin, Baltic, Scezecin

Passerines - Passerines
Corvus corone cornix   Hooded Crow   *Tegel, Tiergarten,*
                                                    Potsdam

                              Baltic

Corvus frugilegus   *Rook*   *Tegel, Baltic*
Passer domesticus   *House sparrow*   *Berlin*
Passer mantanus   Tree sparrow   Tiergarten
Pica pica   *Magpie*   *Tiergarten, Klatzow*
Sternus vulgarus   *Starling (f)*   *Baltic*
Turdus merula   *Blackbird*   *Potsdaml*

Mammals
Otter   **Roadkill**

Porcupine   Roadkill

Vegetation of Berlin (18 July – 9 Aug 02)

During WWII much of the native vegetation was destroyed. Trees that made it through the war were cut for firewood during the severe winter of 1944-45. Many trees were planted resulting in a single size class and limited species. Many of the plants are introduced and prefer disturbed grounds. The species seen are listed below.

Pinaceae (Pine Family)
Pinus sylvestris   Scots Pine   Baltic

Ginkoaceae
Ginko biloba   Ginko   street tree

Gramineae (Grasses)
     Annual Ryegrass   tree wells
     Foxtail   tree well

Juglandaceae (Walnut Family)
Juglans regia   Walnut   Tiergarten

Fagacece (Beech Family)
Betula pendulata   Silver Birch   Baltic
Quercus rubra   Red oak   Tiergarten

Ulmaceae (Elm Family)
Ulmus minor   Small-leaved Elm   Street tree

Urticaceae (Nettle Family)
Urtica dioica   nettle   Fence line

Polygonaceae (Dock Family)
Reynoutria japonica   Japanese Knotweed Fence line

R. sacnalinensis	**Giant Knotweed**	**Fence line**
Rumex acetosa	Common Sorrel	Fence Line

Chenopodaceae (Goosefoot Family)

Chenopodium bonus-henricus	Good King Henry	Tree wells
C. rubrum	Red Goosefoot	Fence line

Caryophyllaceae (Pink Family)

Dianthus plumaris	Wild Pink	Tree wells

Papaveraceae (Poppy Family)

Papaver rhoedus	Common Poppy	**Zurich, Tegel**

Brassicaceae/Cruciferae (Mustard Family)

Brassica rappa	tree wells	
Capsella bursa-pastrois	Sheppard's Purse	Tree wells

Platanaceae (Plane Family)

Platanus hybrida	London Plane tree	Street tree

Rosaceae (Rose Family)

Crategus monogyna	Hawthorn	Street tree

Leguminose (Bean Family)

Trifolium repen	White Clover	tree wells

Simaroubaceae (Quiassia Family)

Ailanthus altissima	**Tree of Heaven**	**Street tree**

Aceraceae (Maple Family)

Acer opolus	Italian Maple	Street tree

Tiliaceae (Lime Family)

Tilia cordata	**Lime Tree**	**Street tree**
Oleaceae (Olive Family)		
Fraxinus excelsior	Ash	Tiergarten
Scrophulariaceae (Figwort Family)		
Verbascum thapus	Great Mullein	Roadside
Labiate (Mint Family)		
Glechoma hederacea	Ground Ivy	Lawns
Bignoniaceae		
Catalpa speciosa	Northern Catalpa	backyard
Plantaginaceae		
Plantago major	Dooryard Plantain	roadside
Compositae (Daisy Family)		
Achillea millefolium	Yarrow	Road side
Mycelis muralis	Wall Lettuce	Tree wells
Taraxacum vulgaris	Dandelion	Tree wells

A Quick Little Christmas Trip

19-30 November 2009

Carl Lahser

A Quick Little Christmas Trip

19-30 November 2009

Carl Lahser

Viking River Cruises offered a good price on their "Holiday in the Rhineland" cruise - half price. First we would fly to Amsterdam Schiphol Airport and spend a couple days in Amsterdam. Then we would sail up stream to Cologne, Rüdesheim, Heidelberg, Mannheim, Mainz, Koblenz, and Bonn and back to Cologne. Returning we would take a bus to Frankfurt and fly back. Carol said it sounded like fun and we could afford it and I had never been to this part of Europe so guess what? - We went. Carol called her friend at a travel agency to work the arrangements. The agency found that we could get better connections cheaper and could stay a couple extra days in Amsterdam for the difference.

It's going to be the beginning of winter so I did not expect many birds or much easily recognizable vegetation. The list at the end of this tale should be relatively short.

Now to find background on the places we could possibly visit with a few Google inquiries:

Amsterdam. Amsterdam's population is currently about 750,000. Amsterdam began as a trading village, Amstelledammein, in 1275. It developed during the 14th and 15th centuries. Its Golden Age began in1585 and ended in 1672. The city grew in size and importance but was attacked by both the French and English in 1672. The city established the Republic and became a financial center. In 1795 the Republic was overthrown and Napoleon occupied the country in 1808. In 1813 the French left. There followed a period of financial recovery due in part to the Industrial Revolution and a period called the New Golden Age. 1920-1940 was a period of economic recession. There was rapid construction of low quality low cost housing and many of the canals were filled to make way for roads.

What is there to see? Besides the famous Red Light Districts and Coffee Houses, there are several museums (the Rijksmuseum, Van Gogh Museum, and Stedelijk Museum), the Old and New Churches and the Houten Huis (Wooden House) at the Begijnhof where firewood wad unloaded and stacked dating to the 12th century. There is also the town hall in the Dam Square (now the Royal Palace), the Westerkerk, Zuiderkerk, as well as a large number of canal houses among which De Dolfijn (Dolphin), De Gecroonde Raep (Crowned Turnip), the Bartolotti Huis, the Huis met de Hoofden (House with the Heads), the Poppenhuis, Kloveniersburgwal 95 (commissioned by the Poppen family), the Trippenhuis (built for the Trip family), the Van Raey-huizen, Keizersgracht 672-674, and Sweedenrijk, Herengracht 462 from the 17th century. During the 19th century recession many houses were vacant and some even collapsed for lack of maintenance. Fortunately - some facades and interiors dating back to the Empire period survive today. 1813-1940 was called the Age of Recovery and Expansion. This was also the period of large-scale damage to the historical city center and some more canals were filled in to make way for new traffic roads to be built.

Individual important sites include:

The Oude Kirk in the middle of the Red Light District

Dam Square with the Amsterdam Historical Museum and the Royal Palace

The Het Houten Huis (Begijnhof) built around 1420

The canals and the <u>Magere Brug</u> **or** "skinny bridge"

Canal or "dancing "houses

Jordaan, a renovated commercial area of trendy housing

The Hortus Botanicus or Botanical Garden established in 1632

Rembrandtplein (square)

What's good to eat?

Dutch cheeses like Edam and Gouda.

The *stroopwafel* (syrup waffle) is a thin sandwich of two buttery waffle layers stuck together with a sweet, gooey molasses.

Dutch pancakes, called *pannekoeken*, similar in texture and taste to French crepes.

Poffertjes. Smaller, puffed pancakes traditionally served with butter and powdered sugar.

Vlaamse or patat frites are our French fries.

Seafood including mussels and sole.

What to drink and where? Try the beer bike? A beer tour?

Belgium draft beers are ales (*De Koninck, Palm*), witbier (*Hoegaarden, Dentergems*) and Abbey Blonde (*Leffe, Grimbergen*) or Dubbel (ditto).

Bottled beers include *Westmalle Dubbel* and *Tripel, Duvel* and all three colors of *Chimay*.

There are three small microbreweries, seasonal breweries and even a couple of contract brewers in Amsterdam. Neither Heineken nor Amstell is still brewed in town although Heineken has opened a museum in their old brewery.

For harder stuff, A. van Wees and Bols distilleries makes spirits made to flavor or enhance food like chocolate and ice cream, genevas or flavored alcohols similar to gin, and distillates like Oranjebitter.

Cologne. Cologne's current population is a little over one million people. It was established in 39 BC as a Roman military outpost. The next important date was 50 AD when Agrippina the Younger, wife of the Emperor Claudius, who was born in Cologne, asked for her home village to be elevated to the status of a city or *colonia*. In 260 AD, it became the capitol of Gallic Empire. In 455, the Salian Franks captured Cologne and made it their capital city. The Catholics controlled Cologne from the 4th century until 1821. France occupied the city in 1794 and held it until 1814. It was under Prussian control from 1814 until the end of WWI. The German Nazi government took over what was a historically Catholic and Communist area. The city was bombed extensively during WWII. Reconstruction was officially completed in the 1990s.

Cologne's Jews have a complicated history dating from 321 AD. The first pogrom was in 1349 when Jews were blamed for the Black Death. They were again evicted from the city in 1442 and allowed to return in 1798. At the beginning of WWII, on *Kristallnacht* (Crystal Night or the Night of Broken Glass) on 1-10 November, 1938, Cologne's synagogues were set on fire.

Things to see:

Botanical Garden, first landscaped in 1863, was completely destroyed in WWII and has been rebuilt.

Romisch-Germanisches Museum. Founded in 1946, former Roman and German departement of the Wallraf-Richartz-Museum. European and Rhenish early history, Roman city history and arts and crafts of the European mass migration times.

Cologne cathedral with its two spires 157 m. in height. It took 632 years for construction of the largest German cathedral to be completed. After the laying of the foundations in the year 1248 and making rapid progress initially, construction work gradually came to a standstill. It was only with 19ᵗʰ century romantic enthusiasm for the Middle Ages and the commitment of the Prussian Court that construction work resumed in 1842.

Krieler Dömchen. The smallest and oldest remaining Cologne church erected around the year 900 on the Suitbert-Heimbach-Platz.

City Gates. With the Severinstor, the Eigelsteintor and the Hahnentor, only three of the total of twelve city gates from the mediaeval city fortifications (1180 - 1220) have been preserved.

City Hall (Hansasaal). The city hall was built in 1330, with the Renaissance arcade (16ᵗʰ century) and tower (15ᵗʰ century) being added later. The building complex suffered extensive damage during the Second World War and underwent reconstruction until 1972.

Museum Schnütgen – Medieval Arts. Named after Alexander Schnütgen, who collected lots of medieval art right after 1802, when Napoleon closed the monasteries and churches.

Wallraf-Richartz Museum. Rated as one of the best in Europe for art.

Strolling along the Rhine. Stretching for 35 kilometers on each side, both banks of the Rhine are the preserve of walkers, cyclists and sportsmen and women.

Rüdesheim am Rhein. This is a wine making town of about 10,000 people. It lies at the foot of the Niederwald on the Rhine's right (east) bank on the southern approach to the Loreley (Lorelei). This is in a UNESCO World Heritage Site.

The area was already settled early on, first by the Celts, then after the turn of the Christian era by Ubii and later by Mattiaci. In the first century, the Romans pushed into the area. They were followed by the Alamanni, and along with the Migration Period (*Völkerwanderung*) came the Franks. Rüdesheim was first recorded in 1074 for winegrowing, forestry, and shipping.

Things to see:

There are several museums and a distillery.

The *Drosselgasse* (an historic street).

Pfarrkirche St. Jakob ("Saint James's Parish Church") from the 15ᵗʰ century

Burg Ehrenfels (ruined castle)

Brömserburg, the oldest castle in the <u>Rhine Gorge</u> <u>World Heritage Site</u>

We may get there in time for *Tage des Federweißen* (year's last wine festival) late October to early November and will be there for *Weihnachtsmarkt der Nationen* ("Christmas Market of the Nations") 120 stalls, from late November until Christmas.

Heidelberg. Heidelberg has a population of about 150,000 people with 80% involved in services and tourism. It is located on the Necker River about 20 miles from Mannheim where the Necker joins the Rhine.

The history is long and complicated beginning in the 4th century BC as a Celtic settlement. The Romans settled here in 40 AD and remained until 260 AD when Germanic tribes took over. The village of Bergheim was settled in the 5th century and currently is located within Heidelberg.

What to see:

Heidelberg has a number of small museums and the oldest university in Germany (**Ruprecht-Karls-Universität Heidelberg**).

The Red Ox and the student prison

The Heidelberg Castle and Old Town.

The Old Bridge and the gate house.

Auf dem Heiligenberg is about a one-hour walk from the Old Town area of Heidelberg.

The Thingstatte, a Nazi-built open-air amphitheatre.

Mannheim lies at the confluence of the Rhine and Neckar Rivers. Rare among German cities is its layout, a grid pattern (or "quadrates") similar to those found in North America. The grid was originally plotted in 1606 originating at the Friedrichsburg fortress, that later became the site of Mannheim Palace. Today, it partly houses the University of Mannheim.

Mainz (Mayence). Mainz is located on the west bank of the river Rhine, opposite the confluence of the <u>Main</u> River with the Rhine River. The 2008 population was 196,784, an additional 18,619 people maintain a primary residence elsewhere but have a <u>second home</u> in Mainz and it is also a part of the Rhein Metro area consisting of 5.8 million people. Mainz is easily reached from <u>Frankfurt International Airport</u> in 25 minutes by commuter railway.

History dates back to 13 BC when a Roman fort was built on the northern borders of the Empire. The name comes from the Latin Menus or river. After a turbulent history under the Romans, Alamanni forces under Rando sacked the city in 368. In last days of 406, the Siling and Asding Vandals, the Suebi, the Alans, and other Germanic tribes took advantage of the rare freezing of the Rhine to cross the river at Mainz and overwhelm the Roman defences. Atilla destroyed Mainz in 451. Complicated politics included Catholic and Romans, the adventures of Charlemagne and the Christianization of Germany. During the French Revolution, the French took Mainz in 1792. The French surrendered to the Prussians in 1793. In 1797, Napoleon took Mainz and left in 1814. In 1816, the German Confederation took over until 1866 and part of the German Empire in 1871. After WWI and through 1930 Mainz was again French.

What to see:

Wood market, a tower from the 14th century.

The Gutenberg Museum.

The Mainz Old Town.

The Botanischer Garten der Johannes Gutenberg-Universität Mainz, a botanical garden maintained by the university.

Koblenz. Koblenz (also *Coblenz* in pre-1926 German spellings; French *Coblence*) is a city situated on both banks of the Rhine at its confluence with the Moselle, where the *Deutsches Eck* (German Corner) and its monument (Emperor William I on horseback) are situated. (As Koblenz (Latin *(ad) Confluentes*, "confluence" or "(at the) merging (rivers)", Covelenz, Cobelenz; local dialect "Kowelenz.) In 1933 Hitler took it back. Heavy Allied bombing destroyed much of the city and General Patton took the city on 22 March 1945. The city came under the French from 1945-49 when it again became a German city.

Things to see include:

the Roman-Germanic central museum (*Römisch-Germanisches Zentralmuseum*).

The Antique Maritime Museum (*Museum für Antike Schifffahrt*) with 4th century Roman craft.

Roman remains, including Jupiter's column, Drusus' mausoleum, the ruins of the theatre and the aqueduct.

Mainz Cathedral of St. Martin (*Mainzer Dom*) from the 10th century. The Iron Tower (*Eisenturm)*, tower at the former iron market), a tower from the 13th century.

The Wood Tower (*Holzturm*, tower at the former site where cut firewood was unloaded and stacked

Around 1000 BC, early fortifications were erected on the Festung Ehrenbreitstein hill on the opposite side of the Moselle. In 55 BC Roman troops commanded by Julius Caesar reached the Rhine and built a bridge between Koblenz and Andernach. About 9 BC, the *"Castellum apud Confluentes"*, was one of the military posts established by Drusus. The town celebrated its 2000th anniversary in 1992. It was part of Charlemagne's Empire, the Germanic Empire, the Holy Roman Empire and the League of Rhenish Cities. The Teutonic Knights founded the Bailiwick of Koblenz in or around 1231. It prospered until the Thirty Years War. It became French in 1632 then Swedish and then French again in 1638 and finally retaken by the Germans. It was invaded by France in 1688. After the French Revolution, it received numerous French refugees. In 1794, it was captured by the French and by the Prussians in 1814 but given to the Prussians in the peace treaty. After WWI, it became French again but changed the spelling of its name to the Germanic for spite in 1926. It was extensively bombed in WWII.

Things to see:

Strong forts crowning the hills encircling the town on the west, and of the citadel of Ehrenbreitstein on the opposite bank of the Rhine.

The Moselle is spanned by a Gothic freestone bridge of 14 arches, erected in 1344, and also by a railway bridge. The city, down to 1890, consisted of the Altstadt (old city) and the Neustadt (new city) or Klemenstadt. Of these, the Altstadt is closely built and has only a few good streets and squares, while the Neustadt possesses numerous broad streets and frontage to the Rhine.

The Basilica St. Kastor or *Kastorkirche*, dedicated to Castor of Karden, with four towers built in 836.

The city is close to the Bronze Age earthworks at Goloring, a possible Urnfield calendar constructed some 3000 years ago.

Bonn. From the late 1940s until 1990 Bonn was the capital of Cold War West Germany. It is a city of 315,000 on the Rhine River just south of Cologne. Since reunification, Bonn has retained a political role as

"Federal City" and has established itself as an important international hub even after the Capitol was moved back to Berlin. Its university is one of the largest in Germany.

Bonn has more than one important Romanesque church:

The Bonn Münster from about 235 AD

The Doppelkirche Schwarzrheindorf from 1115)

A regional museum full of fascinating religious treasures.

It is also home to a popular non-religious attraction:

The Beethovenhaus, where Ludwig was born in 1770.

Many post-WWII administrative buildings

Let's see. Tickets. Passport. Checked Amsterdam weather. Clothes. References. Stop the mail and newspaper. Almost ready to go.

Day 0. 18 Nov 09. We are all packed and ready to go. We have a friend coming over to house sit for the trip. The Weather Underground said Amsterdam weather will be 40's to 50's for the week with high clouds and little rain. Weather forecast for the week is much the same for the Rhine Valley. Carol had a cough but it would probably go away.

Day 1. 19 Nov 09. We flew from San Antonio to Houston on one of Continental's little jets and had a three hour wait in Houston for a 787 to Amsterdam. Our track was over Memphis, Cleveland, down the St Lawrence crossing PEI and Newfoundland, across the Atlantic to Dublin, Ireland, then just SE of Manchester and north of London where a loop to the north took us into Schiphol Airport SW of Amsterdam.

The plane was cold at about 70°F. We had a pillow and a blanket but it was too uncomfortable to sleep.

Immigration and customs was nothing since The Netherlands was a part of the European Union.

Day 2. 20 Nov 09. The morning was clear and in the lower 40's. A front was expected form the SW with lots of rain. Not quite the forecast I saw yesterday.

We took a van to the hotel. The driver must not like tourists since he took sharp corners and hit speed bumps like he was in a demolition derby. I told Carol to save his tip for the chiropractor.

We checked in and by the time we unpacked it was time for lunch. Dutch pea soup and an Amstell beer for 12€ (1€=1.30$). Carol had a hamburger and fries and a coke for 16€. Time to crash for a couple hours.

I was awake about sundown – about 4:30. Carol was coughing so I went out alone to get some laundry soap and disposable razors. There were a couple grocery shops and restaurants. Other shops in the area had souvenirs and all kinds of sex toys and shops that sold marijuana or cannabis in colas, chocolate, gum, lollipops and other concoctions. There were hundreds of people on streets that were already decorated for Christmas. I bought some cold waffles covered with frosting. No *stroopwafe* anywhere. No *schnitzel* either. During the trip I tried several beers including Amstell and Grolsch and noticed these were 0.33 liter (about 10 ounces) instead of 12 like US beer. There were non-alcoholic, low alcohol, and enhanced beers. Soft drinks were smaller also.

Pot Shop

Back at the room out of the drizzle the TV said the subtropical jet stream coming from the southwest over the Atlantic would bring drizzle for the next few days. The Lakes District of England had record flooding from this system. Other news included Amsterdam proposing a driving tax to reduce fuel use and air pollution. In Cologne there were student riots about the universities reducing graduation requirements.

Day 3. 21 Nov 09. We went to the hotel dining room for their breakfast buffet. Twenty € each for all you can eat.

It was chilly and blowing and Carol's cough was worse. The hotel got her a doctor that made house calls. He said it was a respiratory infection and gave her an antibiotic and a prescription for a cough suppressant all for 150 Euros hopefully covered by trip insurance.

Meanwhile I took a walk. It was cool and gray but there was no wind or rain. The hotel doorman said it was a beautiful day for Amsterdam. Next week it would start to snow and quit in April.

Carol wanted some handkerchiefs so out I went. Down by the train station and passed St. Nicholas Church. Along the canals to Dam Plaza where Amsterdam began. Houses were tilted and often projected out over the street. This was partially because of settling and partly because the property was taxed on the street level dimensions. Several houses had clematis or grape vines as potted plants.

Between the narrow streets and the bicycle paths there was not much left for people to walk on.

In Dam Plaza the Royal Palace and New Church were being repaired. There were a dozen mimes and several carriages attracting tourists in the plaza. One of the streets radiating off the Plaza, Kalverstraat, was a shopping street with no traffic. I stopped is several men's store but no one had handkerchiefs. I finally found a shop that had what I wanted at 8€ each. I observed that many of the clerks did not like tourists, little subtle things like ignoring customers or handing you something and letting go of it before you could grab it.

Dom Plaza

I went to the flower market and was disappointed. It was like a dozen plant nursery stalls all in a row with potted plants and lots of tulip bulbs that I could not take home. I went on to the New Market, Rembrandt Plaza where the subway was under construction and then to Waterloo Plaza with more construction. The Tripp House and the Rembrandt House were closed for the day.

I walked through the middle of the red light district and back to the hotel. The red light district is about five blocks along two canals centered on the Old Church. There were restaurants and shops selling sex toys and pot, a couple of theatres offering "soft porn, hard porn and live sex shows 24/7", and finally about half a dozen 4X8 foot windows with young ladies wearing more than a Victoria's Secret catalog model. There was also the cannabis museum and the seed store that sold everything needed to grow pot. Interesting. I was curious about the economics of these enterprises but could not find any information. I got back to the hotel about 1600 as the sky darkened.

Red Light District

After the doctor Carol had gone out and done some shopping. She returned about 1700.

We went out for supper at a seafood place called the Koptic. I had mussels in tomato sauce and salmon on penne pasta. Carol had a fillet.

We walked a couple blocks in the cold and mist looking in store windows and at the street decorations. Businesses were not decorated for Christmas yet if ever.

Day 4. 22 Nov 2009. We were up about 0700 and went to the buffet for breakfast. This was the day to go to the boat so we packed up and put the bags in storage.

About 0930 we started for the Van Gogh museum. An electric train stopped about a block from the hotel. We got on. There was no one selling tickets by the time we reached our destination so we hopped off.

The museum opened at 1000 and the senior tick was 10€ each. I really did not know much about Van Gogh so his life and works were interesting. I had seen a few of his works but was not familiar with his oriental period or his black and white sketches. He had a mental problem that could be easily treated today but the treatment might have ended his painting. He did not cut off his ear, only park of one ear lobe.

There was a display of Alfred Georges Stevens. He began in society portraits and advanced into social commentary. Very good paintings.

We walked a couple blocks in the drizzle to a coffee shop that actually served coffee. We both had a sandwich and hot chocolate and then took a taxi back to the hotel.

We could not check on to the ship, the *Viking Helvetia,* until 1500 so we waited until about 1400 to take a taxi to the ship. They took our bags and we went to the lounge to wait for the rooms.

I noticed the 2 euro coins had a variety of pictures on the reverse of the coins like Gibraltar and vineyards.

I took a walking tour of the ship through all three decks, the lounge, the dining room, the library and topside from bow to stern. Our room was available at 1500. We unpacked and crashed until the tour briefing was announced at 1830.

Supper was served at 1900 (7 PM). The ship had a real chef. Appearance of the serving exceeded the quantity and resulted in only gaining two pounds during the trip.

Day 5. 23 Nov 09. We were up about 0630. There was a light breakfast from 0600 to 0700 and regular breakfast buffet from 0700 – 0900 American style food. A canal boat tour began at 0830.

While getting off the boat I saw several Mallard Ducks, a Great Crested Grebe, and several mute swans in the river. Crack flowers (flowers growing in pavement cracks) included Sea Kale and Feverfew.

We split into several groups and each group had an assigned frequency with a receiver for each person and a transmitter for the group guide. The range was about a quarter mile. Very efficient.

The busses took us to the cruise line passenger terminal where we boarded out boat. The route took us over the tunnel and under the train tracks and past NEMO the city museum with a Dutch packet moored along side. We passed the library and the train station then up canals passing the Ann Frank House and the Rembrandt house and under the Magere Brug and around the town back to the harbor.

City of Bicycles

Back at the ship we had lunch and crashed. We were scheduled to see the Ann Frank House tomorrow at 0830. We were up about 18:30 PM for the day's briefing and supper. This was a Mexican dinner that a Texan would never recognize. After a shot of blue Bombay gin I watched CNN for a while and crashed.

Day 6. 24 Nov 09. We were up for breakfast about 0730 and off to see the Ann Frank House by 0815. I had not read Ann Frank's diary so much of the information was new. We were back at the ship about 1100.

There were several house boats moored in the canal. There are two kinds of house boats – real boats and houses built on a floating concrete slab. A house boat is expensive. The boat runs 500K to 1.5 million Euros plus the annual mooring fee, plus property tax because you live there, plus a boat tax, plus having to pull the boat for cleaning and maintenance and inspection every other year. Sewage in released into the canals and the canals are flushed with a slug of water from the Zuider Zee early every morning.

Amsterdam Canal

The guide said the canals were about ten feet deep with three feet of clear water; three feet of turbid water and 3-4 feet of silt and bicycles since a lot of bicycles are stolen ("borrowed) each year. There are more people than bikes since many people come from the suburbs. There are several large bicycle parking areas. One held about 5000 bikes and one floating garage could store about 3000.

There were some little hybrid cars called "Green Cars" although they are actually red. They rent cheap to commuters who come in by ferry.

Comparing the Amsterdam in the introduction to what we actually saw Amsterdam appears to have changed over the past few years and it would take more time than we had to see many of the sights.

At 1245 the *Viking Helvetia* weighed anchor and set sail up river for Cologne. Lunch was at 1300 as we watched farms, forest and villages pass by and passed under numerous modern bridges. Utrecht. Duisburg.

Magpies were flitting between trees. Common gulls patrolled the river. Crows were crossing the river. Swifts were hunting the river's edge. Several Shoveller and Mallards ducks were resting in backwaters.

Farms pastured sheep and cattle. There were no crops or vineyards along this part of the river

Day 7. 25 Nov 09. Overnight sail passed more small towns and a couple castles and Düsseldorf in the Neanderthal Valley then on to Cologne arriving about 1300.

Coots were paddling along shore and Cormorants sat on rocks and sand bars. Carrion Crows were perched in some trees.

On board the ship there was: an exercise session; a cooking discussion; and a half hour of tourist German. The sun set about 1630 and we charged on through the night passing minimally lighted villages. A highway and a railway were built along both banks with a lot of traffic.

Crews of many of the tugs pushing barges lived on board their tug and even took their cars and boats with them.

About 1200 we docked at the Frankenwerft along the Rheine. We disembarked at 1300 for a walking tour with the earphones. Walking along the Rhine the guide said they had annual flooding and that there were six-foot pop-up walls to handle bigger floods of over 35 feet for the thousand year flood. Last year the water rose over 40 feet for the 10,000 year flood.

We passed a brewery and walked through one of the Christmas markets on the way to the Cathedral. The structure is sandstone and cannot be cleaned of the black mold and soot. The construction took 632 years being built in increments as funding became available. After the Cathedral we went through the Roman Germanic Museum with an outstanding collection of Roman glass and many artifacts from the Roman occupation including the tomb of Poblicius a retired Roman soldier that made a fortune in glass.

The Rhine and vineyards

Cologne Christmas Market

On the way back I stopped at two breweries to sample their beer. Both were to bitter with hops for my taste.

Back on board it was German food night. Pea soup. Beef salad. Tough venison. This was different.

W pulled out about 2300 for Rüdesheim.

Day 8, 26 Nov 09. We made a night run passing Bonn, Remagen, and Koblenz reaching the middle Rhine about sun up.

We were up for breakfast about 0730. We passed Schloss Stolzenfels and Berg Lahmeck and noticed the first vineyards on the south side of the river between Spay and Boppard. The rows were planted perpendicular to the river instead of forming terraces like I expected. Many of the vineyards looked like the workers would fall out of the fields they were so steep.

We passed several other castles including Berg Maus and Berg Katz (the mouse and cat castles). Above Boppard the vineyards were mostly on the north side with several castles. We passed the Lorelei and the Seven Virgins rocks where the vineyards began occurring on both sides of the river. About 80 KM from Cologne we passed Berg Reichenstein, Berg Rhemstein and the ruins of the Ehrenfels castle and arrived at Rüdesheim.

Cat and Mouse Castle

We docked in Rüdesheim about 1400. The tours began with a street train ride to the top of Old Town. We wandered through the Christmas Market and many shops for over an hour along the hilly twisting streets. It began to get dark and cold and took about 20 minutes to walk back to the ship in a misty breeze.

I tried a cup of Glühwein. This is a mulled red wine with sugar and spices. The drink was 2€ plus1.5€ if you wanted to keep the cup.

Back at the ship we had Thanksgiving dinner. Leek soup. A pretty plate with a little turkey breast, green beans and mashed potatoes. Ice cream. Reminded me of a Thanksgiving dinner in Mexico with roast turkey, boracho beans and tortillas.

Day 9. 27 Nov 09. We left about sun up for the 15KM trip to Mannheim and Heidelberg on the Necker River. We passed Wiesbaden with the Schloss Biebrich and Mainz. Other cities including Worms that had about a 6000 year history and important religious significance including where Martin Luther had refused to recant in 1521. It is also home of the Gothic Liebfrauen Church and Vineyards where Liebfraumilch originated.

We docked about 1000 at Speyer across the Rhein and several miles outside Mannheim/Heidelberg. A bus shuttled us through some of the Heidelberg University and dropped us in Mannheim for a tour and visit to the Christmas market.

Heidelberg

We visited Heidelberg Castle in a cool overcast. The castle overlooks the city. The exterior was restored. Only some of the interior had been restored (the interior was not open to tourists but available for parties). The wine cellar was open. I had what was claimed to be the largest cask in Europe. The moat was still there but much of the moat and terraces had been converted to gardens. Heidelberg is the oldest university in Germany and is scattered about Mannheim.

The architecture was not particularly impressive. Mannheim was built where the Nekcar River empties into the Rhein. It is unique in Germany in having streets laid out on a grid instead in meandering. We were there during the lunch break from 1230 to 1400 when everything was closed. I took a walk across the river on the historic Old Bridge and through the gate house. The historic Red Ox bar and the student prison were not available. The Philosopher's walk and the Nazi-built Thingstätte were not readily available across the river.

The bank and post office were closed for another twenty minutes so the exchange rate at the tourist shop was $1.60 instead of $1.30.

The bus took us back about 1530.

Day 10. 28 Nov 09. We pulled out at 0500 for a three hour trip down river to Mainz. We had time for breakfast before arriving at 0815. The walking tour left at 0900.

The tour went through Rheingold square with several large art pieces. The city hall was built modern style and is near useless but cannot be replaced because this is a heritage site. We passed through the Christmas market that would not open before we left and toured the cathedral. This was the largest church in Germany built by leaders who wanted the largest church so the kings could be crowned there. It was built in increments when money was available. It was burned once and WWII burned its roof off and broke all the windows. The foundation began to spread and buttress walls were built to hold it up. It was built in a swamp on piles which were rotting so about 200 years back the piles were dug out and the foundation replaced. Down the center aisle were sarcophagus covers hung on the pillars. Ranking people had been buried in crypts under the church but they were all removed to a grave yard and the covers saved. On the outside of the church was evidence that the masons had not been paid at different times from the color of the stone and the detail of the carving.

We had about half an hour to get back to the ship so the Gutenberg printing museum had to be skipped along with the Roman sites and the Iron Tower and the Wooden Tower and the botanical garden.

We weighed anchor about 1100 for a short run to Koblenz and docked at Koblenz about 1700 near the German Corner (Deutsches Eck). The walking tour took place in the dark to see the Berlin wall monument and the statue of William I. The point is where the Mosel enters the Rhein. From there we walked to the Münzplatz in center of old town to the Christmas market. There were a number of old houses surrounding the square. Carol and I stopped for a chocolate for her and a glühwein for me then shuffled back to the ship. All the cities had stone streets that were hazardous in the drizzle and dark. We missed the Basilica of St Kastor and the Bronze Age site near Goloring.

Deutsches Eck

Day 11. 28 Nov 09. The ship cranked up at 0530 for a run to Konigswinter across the river from Bonn. We boarded busses about 0830 to tour the area and visit the Beethoven House. First leg was a ride to see Petersburg palace. This had been a high security resort for VIPs during the Cold War era. The road is winding through a forest to a mountain top.

Back at the bottom we had a tour of Konigswinter and then across the bridge we toured Bad Godesberg there many government officials lived then through the former Cold War administrative area and downtown Bonn. We stopped to visit the Beethoven House. After leaving we were on the central market with no Christmas market. This would be an interesting visit with more time. Nothing was open on Sunday but a couple restaurants were opening after 1200.

Bonn

Trash collection appears to be automated. The containers and many walls were covered with graffiti. I finally got a close look at several flowers and took pictures for later ID.

About noon we headed back for the ship. We left for Cologne about 1230 arriving at 1500. The docking area was lined with pollarded Plane trees hosting crows and pigeons.

Carol said she needed some over the counter medicine. The ship said everything was closed but there was an emergency pharmacy open somewhere but they were not sure where. Maybe in the train station? We went to the station and found many of the businesses open but the pharmacy was closed. We asked several taxi drivers but they did not know which pharmacy was open.

Back on board the ship the attendant called around like they should have done before and found the open one. They sent Carol off in a taxi with instruction to the driver. The open pharmacy had a small window in the back door and quickly filled her requirement. The taxi had waited for her and had her back to the ship in about an hour.

We went to the Captain's farewell cocktail party followed by the farewell dinner and ceremony. Supper was cappuccino of mushroom soup followed by beef tenderloin with truffle crust or fillet of sole with morel sauce all followed by baked Alaska.

Day 12. 29 Nov 09. It seemed like Carol spent most of the night packing and repacking but by 0530 the bags were in the hall for pick up. We went to breakfast and waited for our bus to leave at 0730. We identified our bags for delivery to the bus and went out to the busses.

It was a two-hour ride to the Frankfurt airport flying down the autobahn. Fields of green and leafless forests. The trees had a reddish tinge like they were ready to bud out here at the start of winter.

We arrived at the airport and finally located the check-in area. At the gate we sat for about two hours before loading.

Frankfurt

Loading the plane was a real goat rope. Passengers were loaded on a bus which drove a couple miles to the plane. Everyone got off the bus and headed for one of the two boarding ramps with no regard to seating. We found our seats and waited another hour before we were off the ground.

The flight path home was Frankfurt to Amsterdam then north over the North Sea to Kirkwald, Scotland. Over the Atlantic against the jet stream to Greenland. Over the southern tip of Greenland and the Labrador Sea to Hebron, Labrador. SW to Detroit and south to Houston.

It took another hour to get through customs and immigration and get rechecked to get our plane to San Antonio. Sure wish there were direct flights out of SA to anywhere.

We walked in the door at home about 2300.

In general this was a good trip. Accommodations and food were very good. Tours presented an only a brief overview and highlights.

There were few bird watchers or plant people among the passengers and none were evident in the crew.

One other thing missing was shopping time and the lack of art in the Rhine Valley. History yes but art no.

The weather was typical for the season – cool and drizzly. Since this was an El Niño year the fall was long and warm.

One of the locals said it would begin to snow in a couple weeks and not stop until April. Brrr. Fergit it.

Biologicals

PLANTS

Platanaceae	London Plane	Platanus hybrida
Loranthaceae	Mistletoe	Viscum album
Ranunculaceae	Traveller's Joy	Clematis vitalba
Urticaceae	Pellitory of the Wall	Parietaria judaica
Fumariaceae	Yellow Corydalis	Corydalis lutea
Cruciferae	Sea Kale	Crambe maritima
Campanulaceae	Bearded Bellflower	Campanula barbata
Compositae	Feverfew	Tanacetum parthenium
Compositae	Ox-tongue Hawkweed	Picris hieracioides

Birds

Grebes	Great Crested Grebe	Podiceps cristatus
Cormorants	Cormorant	Phalacrocorax carbo
Herons	Great Blue Heron	Ardea Herodias
Swans	Mute Swan	Cygnus olor
Ducks	Mallard	Anas platyrhynchos
	Shoveler	Anas clypeata
Coot	Coot	Fulica atra
Gulls	Common Gull	Larus canus
Doves	Collared Dove	Streptopelia decaocto
Swift	Swift	Apus apus
Magpie	Magpie	Pica pica
Crows	Carrion Crow	Corvus corone
	Jackdaw	Corvus monedula

Zurückbekommen Liebenswürdig Rhineland